"Sci-fi author Brandon Sanderson wrote, 'The purpose of a storyteller is not to tell you how to think, but to give you questions to think upon.' That is exactly what each of the wonderful storytellers who contributed to this important book do. As a former Fulbright Scholar (Peru 1979–80), it was especially gratifying to read so many inspirational stories from fellow Fulbrighters. Curtis J. Bonk and Meina Zhu co-edited this volume with the overall goal of making a positive impact on teachers and learners. There is no doubt that it will do just that."

—**Thomas C. Reeves**, Professor Emeritus of Learning, Design, and Technology at The University of Georgia, USA

"I wish I had had this book years ago. By bringing together the experience and guidance of award-winning teachers and educational technology specialists from all over the world, this book yields a cache of knowledge-with-wisdom and helps make our journey of teaching and learning more enjoyable and successful. *Transformative Teaching Around the World* is a must-read for both enthusiasts and skeptics of innovative teaching with technologies regardless of their cultural and contextual differences."

—**Insung Jung**, Professor in the Education & Psychology Program at International Christian University, Japan

"What is impact? Measuring impact in education is never easy, as it takes time to capture the impact and articulate a causal relationship. Stories are often used to demonstrate personal lived experiences of change as evidence of impact, and this book presents such stories in plenty. They relate experiences of innovation, grit, and resilience across national boundaries and provide food for thought and reflection. This book is a testament to the popularity of its source—*R546: Instructional Strategies for Thinking, Collaboration and Motivation*, a university course taught by Professor Curtis J. Bonk that has attracted teacher education students from Africa, Asia-Pacific, Europe, as well as North and South America—and the number of minds it has ignited to promote innovative teaching practices. Once in a blue moon, teachers can demonstrate such huge impact of their teachings. By collating their stories, the editors have taken a further step forward to spread the impact beyond those who benefitted from their classes."

—**Sanjaya Mishra**, Education Specialist of eLearning at Commonwealth of Learning

"As a former Fulbright-Hays Group Projects Abroad Program recipient who traveled internationally with pre- and in-service teachers from the U.S., I can attest to the importance and timeliness of this enlightening book. These stories of other like-minded educators overcoming various challenges while continually moving forward are truly inspiring. Curtis J. Bonk, a preeminent and visionary author on global education and emergent technologies for learning, and his colleague Meina Zhu have done an extraordinary job sharing genuine transformative teaching examples that can add value for other educators considering similar endeavors. Rarely does an academic book so accurately and compellingly tell the story of what's involved in the process of transformative teaching and learning within a global context."

—**Heejung An**, Professor in the College of Education at William Paterson University of New Jersey, USA, and editor of *Handbook of Research on Efficacy and Implementation of Study Abroad Programs for P-12 Teachers*

"This book reaffirms that individuals with ideas and passion can change perceptions and practices. Timely and relevant, it provides global educational and historical perspectives through personal stories and shared experiences across a range of countries and educational situations. With a focus on the application of technology to learning and teaching, it is pertinent reading for both pre-service and in-service teachers. There is something very powerful about storytelling, and I applaud how the reflection questions for each story prompt the reader to think more deeply and share their own personal stories. Innovation starts with one idea, and this book provides hundreds of ideas (not to mention contact information for the contributors) such as augmented reality-based curriculum, online collaboration, cultural adaptations of technology use, active and personalised learning objectives, to list but a few. This book leverages the power of storytelling, going above and beyond mere instructional design, to share gems of inspiration that we can all learn from. In today's educational climate, it is a powerful contribution to and catalyst for improving learning and teaching globally."

—**Julie Lindsay**, Senior Education Technology Advisor at the University of Southern Queensland, Australia, Director of Learning Confluence Pty Ltd, and Founder and CEO of Flat Connections

"The world's most successful schools encourage students to set goals that are meaningful to them, draw on their own passions and interests, focus on knowledge domains (not subjects and courses), and develop the skills to become lifelong learners. *Transformative Teaching Around the World: Stories of Cultural Impact, Technology Integration, and Innovative Pedagogy* shares the experiences of Fulbright teachers from twenty-two countries who transformed their classrooms to do exactly this. The teachers from every discipline and across every type of learning environment—from schools and virtual classrooms and gaming worlds to prisons, farms, and cityscapes—describe the leaps they took in their professional lives to establish learning environments that sparkle with motivation and innovation. This book is a rich addition both to the literature about school transformation and to the editors' previous work documenting practices that teachers can use in learner-centered and technology-enriched classrooms. *Transformative Teaching Around the World* is valuable not only for teachers but also for school leaders and policymakers who must lead the charge for policy change to make these examples the norm in schools in the U.S. and globally."

—**Susan Patrick**, CEO of the Aurora Institute

"Few events in our lifetimes are as transformative as doctoral studies—getting married and having baby come close. For most, it will be a significant watershed moment, a turning point for new beginnings and perhaps new lives. Such is the impact of that kind of sustained effort which Curtis Bonk and Meina Zhu have so successfully captured in this book with the lived experiences of a selection of their graduate students. These are stories of the trials and tribulations, joys and triumphs—not only of their graduate study experiences, but also of how they themselves are transforming the lives of others throughout the world. Such is the impact of these indefatigable and indomitable educators on their students. Their enthusiasm for what they do is infectious. This is a book you will want to read slowly and savor. Enjoy!"

—**Som Naidu**, Executive Editor of *Distance Education*
and Principal Associate at Technology, Education and
Design Associates

"*Transformative Teaching Around the World* is a compendium of compelling stories told by innovative practitioners from across the globe. These are firsthand accounts of the motivational, creative, and joyful practices that characterize the technologies, collaborations, and cultural exchanges of twenty-first-century education excellence. Bonk and Zhu have curated a very comprehensive sampling of short field narratives of educators speaking in their own voices. A reaffirming and worthwhile read."

—**Tom Reynolds**, Professor in the Sanford College of Education
at National University, USA

"*Transformative Teaching Around the World*, edited by Curtis J. Bonk and Meina Zhu, was born from a fortuitous and far-sighted program in which dozens of talented teachers from around the world spent four months at Indiana University's School of Education as Fulbright Distinguished Teachers. They learned from the courses they took, the faculty and students with whom they connected, and the school visits they made. They took back more student-centered and innovative approaches to teaching and learning. Now, in this book, they reflect their learnings back to us. They emphasize the importance of tailoring teaching to each individual, addressing social and emotional learning, and employing technologies as diverse as Zoom, social media, and augmented reality. And they describe the benefits of creating collaborative exchanges among educators from different countries and cultures. This book comes at a pivotal time when the world is facing unprecedented crises. Climate change, COVID-19, and political extremism demand that the next generation of students advance their societies in ways that their predecessors have not. These authors—and this Fulbright program—offer hope for the future and should lead us to support more of them."

—**Milton Chen**, Senior Fellow at the George Lucas Educational Foundation

"*Transformative Teaching Around the World* reads like a recommendation from the United Nations. In reality, this excellent book is the endeavor of two faculty members, Professors Curtis J. Bonk and Meina Zhu, in collaboration with many Fulbright-winning teachers. Successful educational practices in one country often cannot be replicated in other countries, and teachers must often creatively adapt instructional theories for their own environments. *Transformative Teaching Around the World* includes forty-one exciting stories that exemplify this form of creative adaption. More than ever, in this new era of education, learning depends on learners' own self-directed learning competencies. This book reveals how instructors and students can change their roles in today's changing learning environments. I trust that the wisdom from these stories will support how you think of your own educational practices and creative possibilities. Read this book!"

—**Okhwa Lee**, Professor in the Department of Education at Chungbuk National University, Republic of Korea

"The value of any book on technology and innovation in K–12 and higher education is in its application of personal storytelling into the real and complex world of a classroom. Curtis J. Bonk and Meina Zhu have assembled powerful and truly useful stories by experts from around the world—innovative classroom teachers themselves, who share what has worked in their educational practices. This is an excellent resource to which teachers can come back time and again for practical examples to enhance their teaching and learning."

—**Edwin H. Gragert**, Co-Founder of Global Woods Consulting and Interim Executive Director of iEARN-USA

"Instead of going to the theorists for a portrait of education at its best, Curtis J. Bonk and Meina Zhu have made a radical choice: they've gone to the teachers. This exceptional collection of classroom stories brings together the voices of forty-one outstanding educators from twenty-two countries, many of whom have been honored with Fulbright teacher scholarships or other educational recognitions. Whether reflecting on their own educational journeys, exploring teaching with technology, sharing their innovations, global educational adventures, and active learning strategies, or reflecting on the ongoing lessons of the COVID-19 pandemic, these contributors offer the authenticity and honesty that can only come from lived experience. Each story offers a window into the challenges of teaching and learning in a distinct educational and cultural context, and each one ends with reflection questions designed to spark growth for the reader as well.

Bonk and Zhu have gathered an important array of narratives, and any educator's thinking and pedagogical practices will be expanded by reading them."

—**Jennifer D. Klein**, CEO of Principled Learning Strategies and author of The Global Education Guidebook: Humanizing K-12 Classrooms Worldwide Through Equitable Partnerships

"*Transformative Teaching Around the World* explores how innovative and courageous teachers can be regardless of the challenges they face in the classroom, but especially in response to a worldwide pandemic. Each classroom described in the book has its own unique story, but they come together as a series of transformative teaching narratives that both pre-service and in-service teachers can learn from and be inspired by. I was amazed at the level of diversity that these stories represented."

—**Joan Kang Shin**, Associate Professor of Education and Academic Coordinator of the Teaching Culturally & Linguistically Diverse & Exceptional Learners program at George Mason University, USA

"*Transformative Teaching Around the World* is a refreshing and critical new look at education. Curt and Meina offer a perspective into the changing world of education, both in how *we* impact it and in how *it* impacts us. A must-read!"

—**Marshall Goldsmith**, author of Triggers, Mojo, and What Got You Here Won't Get You There

"Bonk and Zhu have assembled a collection of essays by world class individuals from twenty-two countries who have gone beyond the limits of what they thought was possible for their students. Their passion for teaching and learning fills these pages, and they convey their struggles and creativity as they pursue innovative teaching practices. Each essay concludes with a set of challenging and thought-provoking questions that would stimulate both the collaborations within teaching and learning communities and the imaginations of university students who aspire to teach. Bonk and Zhu have captured the vast diversity of teaching in the real world. Their narratives are insightful and powerful."

—**Jack A. Cummings**, Professor Emeritus of School Psychology at Indiana University, USA

"This book is Bonk at his brilliant best, and, with Zhu as a notable co-editor, it is supercharged for success. Embrace our new era of the online world, yet note that a handy volume still plays its part."

—**Brian J. Ford**, Fellow of Cardiff University, UK, President Emeritus of the Cambridge Society for the Application of Research, and award-winning research biologist, broadcaster, lecturer, and author of dozens of books including *Nonscience Returns, Too Big to Walk,* and *Secret Weapons*

TRANSFORMATIVE TEACHING AROUND THE WORLD

Transformative Teaching Around the World compiles inspiring stories from Fulbright-awarded teachers whose instructional practices have impacted schools and communities globally. Whether thriving or struggling in their classrooms, instructing in person or online, or pushing for changes at high or low costs and risk levels, teachers devote intense energy and careful decision-making to their students and fellow staff. This book showcases an expansive variety of educational practices fostered across international contexts by real teachers: active and empowering learning strategies, critical thinking and creative problem-solving, cultural responsiveness and sustainability, humanistic integration of technology, and more. Pre- and in-service teachers, teacher educators, online/blended instructors, and other stakeholders will find a wealth of grounded, motivating approaches for transforming the lives of learners and their communities.

Curtis J. Bonk is Professor of Instructional Systems Technology in the School of Education and Adjunct in the School of Informatics at Indiana University, U.S.A.

Meina Zhu is Assistant Professor of Learning Design and Technology in the College of Education at Wayne State University, U.S.A.

TRANSFORMATIVE TEACHING AROUND THE WORLD

Stories of Cultural Impact, Technology Integration, and Innovative Pedagogy

Edited by
Curtis J. Bonk and Meina Zhu

Routledge
Taylor & Francis Group

NEW YORK AND LONDON

Cover image: © Getty Images

First published 2022
by Routledge
605 Third Avenue, New York, NY 10158

and by Routledge
2 Park Square, Milton Park, Abingdon, Oxon, OX14 4RN

Routledge is an imprint of the Taylor & Francis Group, an informa business

Library of Congress Cataloging-in-Publication Data
Names: Bonk, Curtis Jay, editor. | Zhu, Meina, editor.
Title: Transformative teaching around the world : stories of cultural
    impact, technology integration, and innovative pedagogy / edited by
    Curtis J. Bonk and Meina Zhu.
Description: New York, NY : Routledge, 2022. | Includes
    bibliographical references and index.
Identifiers: LCCN 2021044565 (print) | LCCN 2021044566 (ebook) |
    ISBN 9781032101460 (hardback) | ISBN 9781032073798 (paperback) |
    ISBN 9781003213840 (ebook)
Subjects: LCSH: Education and globalization. | International education. |
    Fulbright scholars. | Comparative education.
Classification: LCC LC191 .T675 2022 (print) | LCC LC191 (ebook) |
    DDC 370.116—dc23/eng/20211006
LC record available at https://lccn.loc.gov/2021044565
LC ebook record available at https://lccn.loc.gov/2021044566

ISBN: 978-1-032-10146-0 (hbk)
ISBN: 978-1-032-07379-8 (pbk)
ISBN: 978-1-003-21384-0 (ebk)

DOI: 10.4324/9781003213840

Typeset in Bembo
by Apex CoVantage, LLC

Access the Support Material: www.routledge.com/9781032073798

To my advisor Gary A. Davis who taught me that "Creativity is Forever" and to Robert (Bob) and Donna Rae Clasen who helped me discover myriad ways that "Teachers Tackle Thinking" and to all the other thoughtful, kind, and creative professors with whom I took classes at the University of Wisconsin so long ago.

Curtis J. Bonk, Indiana University

To my professors, friends, and family who encouraged me and supported me each day.

Meina Zhu, Wayne State University

CONTENTS

FOREWORD

The Power of Story

Gerardo M. González is Dean and Professor Emeritus of the Indiana University (IU) School of Education. From 2000 to 2015, he directed administrative and budgetary activities for the School on the Bloomington and Indianapolis campuses and provided academic oversight to education programs on the six regional campuses of IU. During his deanship, *U.S. News & World Report* ranked the IU

School of Education among America's top education schools for 15 consecutive years. Upon his retirement from the deanship, Memorex listed him as one of the 30 most influential deans of education in America and IU President Michael A. McRobbie awarded him the President's Medal in recognition of sustained excellence, achievement, and leadership.

Introduction

My name is Gerardo M. González. I am a storyteller. In my memoir, *A Cuban Refugee's Journey to the American Dream: The Power of Education* (González, 2018), I tell the story of an 11-year-old boy from a small town in Las Villas, Cuba, coming to the United States as a refugee following the Cuban Revolution. After many struggles as an English learner in American schools, that boy managed to persevere and go on to be the first in his family to graduate from college. Not only did he graduate from college, but also he went on to earn a PhD and become Dean of the School of Education at Indiana University (IU), one of the world's premier research universities.

Of course, I am that boy. My lived experience is testament to the power of education. I also believe in the power of story. In my memoir I wrote, "Facts and figures have their place, but nothing conveys a message like a story" (p. 94).

Thus, it is an honor to offer this foreword to Drs. Curtis J. Bonk and Meina Zhu's remarkable treatise of stories from teachers and scholars engaged in transformative, learner-centered, and technology-enriched pedagogical practices throughout the world. Professors Bonk and Zhu, as well as all the chapter authors in this book, have connections to Indiana University—and more specifically, to Professor Bonk's seminal course R546, "Instructional Strategies for Thinking, Collaboration and Motivation." The Instructional Systems Technology Department, where R546 resides, has an international reputation for excellence in instructional design and for producing leaders in the field.

Indiana University as a whole is renowned for being one of the most international and wired institutions of higher education in the world. Not surprisingly, when I became dean of the IU School of Education in 2000, in collaboration with faculty, staff, students, and other stakeholders, I led a strategic planning process in the School that among other things produced a clear and focused mission statement: "to improve teaching, learning, and human development in a global, diverse, rapidly changing, and increasingly technological society." A central goal under that mission was to provide leadership in the use of technology to enhance teaching and learning. We invested greatly in translating the new mission and strategic goals into action. Today, I am proud to say that the work described by the editors and chapter authors in this volume represents a salient example of the success that our efforts to articulate a clear mission and measure the impact of our goals continues to have across the globe.

The stories of innovative, impactful pedagogical practices told in these pages are inspiring. Experts tell us that technology innovations often occur long before people are willing and able to use them. Nevertheless, here we hear the voices of a truly diverse and accomplished group of educators from every corner of the globe who are at the vanguard of transforming the change process through the integration of new technologies in education.

When the faculty of the IU School of Education approved our strategic mission and goals, we knew there would be challenges in bringing them to fruition and seeing their lasting impact. None of us, however, could have envisioned that in 2020 COVID-19 would envelop the world in a pandemic unlike anything seen in over a century. COVID-19 has affected everything heretofore familiar—the way we socialize, work, bank, communicate, travel, shop, teach, learn, and perform many other seemingly routine tasks—but the pandemic also underscored a time-honored constant: that is, dealing with humankind's most perplexing problems requires innovation and creativity.

That is what this book is about: inspiring innovation and creativity in the educational change process. For all its perils, the pandemic has pushed everything, especially education, faster into the future. There is no going back. More than ever, the world now needs creative leaders and innovators who can demonstrate effective learner-centered, technology-enriched educational practices and can teach us about their application in different learning environments by example. It needs more storytellers like the editors and authors in this book who can motivate us to create and innovate. It needs readers like you willing to explore ways to improve teaching, learning and human development in an increasingly technologically driven, diverse, and rapidly changing global community.

The stories in this book will encourage you to learn about and adapt innovative teaching practices to your own environment, reflect on those practices, and share what you learn with others. Every story of transformative change and innovation begins with courageous individuals or groups of people willing to try new things and learn from their mistakes.

My sincere compliments to the editors and authors of this book for offering readers a road map to begin that creative process. As the famous Chinese philosopher Laozi once said, "A thousand-mile journey begins with the first step." May this be your first step to grow and beget new transformative practices in education—to make impact.

PREFACE

Before Making Impact

Curtis J. Bonk is Professor in the School of Education at Indiana University (IU) teaching psychology and technology courses and Adjunct in the School of Informatics at IU. He is a former software entrepreneur, certified public accountant, corporate controller, and educational psychologist who presently is an educational technologist, award-winning writer, highly published researcher, statewide and national awardee in innovative teaching with technology, and internationally acclaimed presenter. Curt is the author of nearly 400 publications and has given close to 2,000 talks around the world. He can be contacted at cjbonk@indiana.edu and his homepage is http://curtbonk.com/.

Meina Zhu is Assistant Professor in the Learning Design and Technology in the College of Education at Wayne State University. She received her PhD degree in Instructional Systems Technology at Indiana University Bloomington. She pushes boundaries with her work on self-directed learning and open education. In 2020, Meina received an early career award from AERA. She can be reached at meinazhuiu@gmail.com or meinazhu@wayne.edu.

A Little History

Educators in all sectors are struggling with wave after wave of educational change. Many recognize the need for shifting their teaching philosophy to a more learner-centered or hands-on approach. This trend is especially evident in this third decade of the 21st century; the age of STEM, competency-based education, personalized instruction, adaptive learning, game-based learning, problem-based learning, digital learning, Wikipedia, AI, and MOOCs. Today, learners can be more self-directed. However, learners often lack sufficient time and resources. In response, this book provides a road map for those stuck in the murky swamp of paradigm change and educational reform.

You might wonder why we titled this preface "Before Making Impact." Well, because we hope that is essentially what it is. Hopefully, you are reading this preface before venturing too far into this book and begin to be personally impacted by the ideas expressed within it. In effect, we hope that this chapter is the precursor to the myriad ways in which you will be making an impact in teaching, training, and other opportunities for instruction in the coming years.

Stated another way, this preface is situated before you venture too far into this book and begin making impact with the ideas in it. If you're reading sequentially, all you have read thus far are the foreword and the endorsements. So now, perhaps you can sit with a quiet mind that has not yet wandered into the various stories that could bias you in terms of your teaching plans and ideas. Contemplate the possibilities. Think about the personal changes you might want to make. You have not done anything yet. There are an endless array of ideas to consider, test, embrace, rethink, and try again with some minor or more modest tweaks. Go ahead. There is much for you to impact.

It is time to tell a story. Actually, this book, *Transformative Teaching Around the World: Stories of Cultural Impact, Technology Integration, and Innovative Pedagogy*, offers dozens of stories of the change process in education. These are exhilarating, educationally powerful, purposeful, impactful, and transformative changes. They might take root at the learner level or arise virally in the classroom, the school, the community, or the entire country.

As such, this is a book about educational transformation toward more active and engaging learning that is occurring across the globe. We initially titled the book "Making Impact" as that is always our goal; hence, the title of this book's preface. Each of the main chapters of this book showcases how educators worldwide are finding success with their innovative pedagogical ideas.

When you explore the various chapters and reflect on the themes and patterns, we think you will acknowledge that the world is in the midst of an educational transformation that has accelerated during the COVID-19 pandemic. Aspects of that transformation are being fueled by more free and open educational practices (Bonk, 2009) as well as by an increasing societal focus on fostering creativity and entrepreneurship. During the past few decades, there have been trends toward learner and instructor autonomy and empowerment that have dramatically increased during the pandemic.

Since the last few decades of the twentieth century, there also has been a pervasive push to foster higher order thinking skills related to critical thinking (Clasen & Bonk, 1988) as well as creative thinking (Davis, 2004). As a result, it is a rarity to walk into a bookstore today and not see a book near the entrance featuring creativity and innovation (e.g., Catmull & Wallace, 2014; Isaacson, 2014; Robinson & Aronica, 2015; Wagner, 2012). It is also rare to be in a higher education setting and not hear complaints about the lack of critical thinking skills on the part of students. As we all know, too many people have difficulty distinguishing fake news from facts.

As you will see, the contributors to this book have been in the midst of the COVID-19 pandemic and have had to make a sudden pivot to virtual learning environments. It is vital to grasp where teachers are making an impact in this new teaching and learning age. Enter the stories contained in this book. The various anecdotes can serve as a springboard to other educators to find areas in which they too can make such an impact. Adding fuel to these stories, all the educators sharing them were in one particular class (i.e., R546) at Indiana University (IU) in Bloomington, Indiana, that was nicknamed "the Saturday class." It is a course on alternative instructional strategies for critical and creative thinking, cooperative and collaborative learning, motivation, and technology integration. This course has been offered at IU for three decades, and as such is the longest running elective in the IU School of Education offered by the same instructor.

A number of highly talented, creative, and dedicated educators have taken part in that class over the three decades in which it has been offered. As Chapter 2 from Jacob Butler points out, during the past decade, a number of teachers who participated in the Fulbright Distinguished Awards in Teaching (DAT) Program at IU were enrolled in the Saturday class. Given the diversity of the teachers in the DAT Program and the diversity of the students in the School of Education at IU, it often felt like a miniature United Nations meeting when in this class. Consequently, readers of this book will hear stories from outstanding teachers in 22 countries: Mexico, India, Morocco, China (mainland China and Taiwan), Bhutan, Papua New Guinea, Thailand, Cyprus, Singapore, Finland, Botswana, New Zealand, Yemen, Saudi Arabia, Yemen, Rwanda, Costa Rica, Kazakhstan, Israel, Uzbekistan, Korea, and the United States. When instructional innovations for thinking, collaboration, and motivation can find applicability across such a vast range of regions, there is true hope for educational change.

As you turn the pages of this book, you will learn about both educators' struggles and successes. You will discover their bouts with academic decision-making pain. At the same time, these chapters are filled with intense educational energy and rich sagacity. You should find these stories to be an educational food platter of hopes and dreams. Don't be afraid to fill up when needed or nibble on a few fruits and veggies if that is all you need. Whatever ones you consume, they should inspire you to take action and make your impact felt; from the preservice teacher in his first education class still wondering if teaching is the right path or not to the first-year induction teacher struggling with the countless unanticipated demands from students and parents to the mid-career educator pausing to think about what to do with the rest of her life and on to those wanting to make a substantive impact when nearing the end of their professional careers. Each will find something of substance that we hope is scrumptious and that you will want to yelp about. But this book is more than that.

The vast majority of the contributors to this book are the award-winning Fulbright teachers in the DAT program who undoubtedly are well respected in their communities for their creative pedagogical styles and innovative leadership. As indicated, all were once enrolled in the same R546 class on "Instructional Strategies for Thinking, Collaboration, and Motivation." With them emerges a unique ethos in education. Not just a "can do" mentality but also a "must do" and "will definitely do" approach. And, as you will see, they did!

Ideas embedded in this book should percolate and proliferate across the globe. Some of these pedagogical activities and experiences will be low risk, low cost, and low time, whereas others may tend toward the higher levels of the risk, cost, and time continua. When combined, the possibilities for transformative change across regions of the world expand in untold ways. Our specific goals and intentions are detailed next.

Impactful Goals

- Help readers appreciate the range of ways to impact learning in the 21st century;
- Reflect on the ways an educational idea might be implemented in different countries or regions of the world;
- Obtain a better grasp of the local and global impact of new ideas, methods, and approaches in education through the rich storytelling in each chapter;
- Highlight pressing issues and controversies in countries and communities where there presently is passionate debate;
- Gain insights into ways teachers are adopting and transforming various instructional strategies and ideas to their local context;
- Personally relate to one or more stories expressed in the chapters;
- Appreciate teacher and student inspiration in regard to the implementation of innovative instructional ideas;
- Grasp how teachers proactively react to challenging educational issues and problems;
- Connect emotionally to the stories, experiences, pilot testing situations, and so forth, of educators attempting a creative or novel approach to instruction;
- Integrate various educational reform efforts.

The Plan

As alluded to earlier, this book is a series of short stories of more than two dozen award-winning Fulbright teachers and several other teacher educators who have changed their schools or communities with their creative pedagogical approaches and ideas. Each of these teachers has a highly unique or novel story to tell that is still unfolding.

As distinct as these projects and initiatives are, these anecdotes coalesce into an integrated corpus of educational change and hope. It is our hope to inspire. It is our intention to offer a useful glimpse of the future of education. And it is our dream to have a book that is not only recommended reading but also required reading in teacher education, college teaching, corporate training, and beyond. Perhaps it will find its way into a multicultural education course or one on teaching methods. Maybe it will be a key resource when taking time out from one's present work situation to reflect on one's higher purpose or next calling.

A key advantage of this book derives from the array of pedagogical approaches that are employed in the chapters. Second, as these chapters coalesce, it should be apparent that the methods, principles, and ideas work across regions of the world. Third, this is a book of inspirations, aspirations, experimentations, and innovations. During your reading, you will come face-to-face with an endless stream of passions and emotions. The chapters showcase the fine line between success and failure that all teachers face each term, if not on a daily basis. As such, it may be a handy teacher recruitment tool and therapeutic for teachers who have doubts about their selection of teaching as a profession.

The Audience

Readers of this book will learn how to develop learning environments that stimulate critical thinking and creativity, and that promote cooperative learning and motivation. Along the way, they will also learn vital technology integration strategies and ways to spur digital literacy. To highlight method similarities and differences and to link theory to practice in each area, many scientifically researched strategies and programs are featured in the chapters of this book. Embedded in these activities will be much experimentation and risk-taking. When done, while readers will likely have learned dozens of instructional strategies, they will, more importantly, be continuously reflecting on their overall teaching philosophy.

As such, we hope that the book starts a dialogue about the change process in education and what it is like to be an innovative instructor in any educational environment or educational sector; in particular, PreK-12 education. This book should be of interest to educators and learning professionals as well as politicians, IT managers, and other educational stakeholders. Such stakeholders need to begin to grasp, from an educational standpoint, the seismic pedagogical shifts in education from the teacher- and content-centered past to the learner-centered present and future now underway.

This book will be of value to preservice teachers as well as newly minted in-service teachers who are searching for inspiration, ideas, and innovative pedagogy. It may also be a guide to those seeking transformative educational practices that are perhaps more possible post-pandemic due to increased flexibility and openness to change. Practicing teachers searching for professional development opportunities for engaging learners should find much sage advice in each of the eight sections of this book. Along these same lines, the contents of this book may find some value among PreK-12 principals and other administrators hoping to integrate various educational reform efforts. At the same time, this book may find a niche among graduate students wanting to feel better prepared to teach, train, or learn something new. Graduate students across disciplines realize that college teaching, especially in online and blended learning environments, has been getting much attention during the past decade. Still another intended audience for this book are parents seeking to find instances of enlightened pedagogical practices and ideas.

Looking across the educational spectrum, this edited volume should provide valuable information to school and college administrators, PreK-12 educators, instructional designers, curriculum designers, trainers, undergraduate and graduate students who are majoring in education, and scholars attempting to capture the educational change process. We also hope it can prove illuminating for countless millions around the globe who are highly curious about educational change and are hoping for brighter days.

In effect, the audience could be anyone who stumbles upon the book and opens it. Deans of teacher education and colleges of education might use the book at faculty retreats. Given the scope of the stories, educators might use the book in special topic courses and seminars. We are also hopeful that this book appeals to PreK-12 administrators struggling with how to inspire innovative educational models or higher standards of achievement. At the same time, higher education professors wanting to enhance their instruction with innovative teaching might open up a few chapters for ideas, examples, and inspirations. Even corporate trainers wanting to embed practical strategies into their training workshops and classes may glean some valuable lessons and strategies.

All these individuals can conceivably benefit from the ideas, activities, and various passionate pleas embedded in this book. The book can provide a wake-up call for some instructors and administrators that it is now time to stop talking and debating the need for 21st-century learning skills and, instead, challenge themselves to find ways to foster extensive critical and creative thinking, powerful motivational activities, deep collaborative teaming, and innovative technology integration. Each story or chapter will provide a genuine and honest account of local educational issues, opportunities, and challenges that can serve to inspire others to move, at least temporarily, to the high end of the risk and innovation continuum.

Opening Spaces

In his 2007 book, *The Courage to Teach: Exploring the Inner Landscape of a Teacher's Life*, Parker J. Palmer stated:

> Like most professionals, I was taught to occupy space, not open it: after all, we are the ones who know, so we have an obligation to tell others all about it . . . Our resistance to opening rather than filling the space is compounded by the fact that if we decide to change the way we practice our craft, it takes time to make the transition—and while we are in transit, we are not

very good at what we are doing. En route to new pedagogy, there will be days when we serve our students poorly, days when our guilt only deepens.
(p. 135)

This book, too, will be one of the opening spaces that empower students and offer them a sense of agency or control over their own learning lives. It will offer a vast array of stories of educators in transition, filled with the myriad doubts, dilemmas, and challenges that Palmer is admitting to. Many of the contributors to this book have been deeply embedded in the change process and are attempting to overcome one or more significant reservations. As such, you will find numerous examples of self-doubt. In addition, a few chapters allude to an inner dialogue that the authors are having; an internal conversation with oneself that can serve as a tension reducer for those reading and reflecting on one or more chapters of this book.

Special Touches, Special People

Without a doubt, there are likely dozens of such books which have been published since the start of the millennium. What makes this book different? First, the majority of the authors are Fulbright scholar-teacher awardees. You can safely assume, therefore, that they are accomplished educators who have spent much of their adult lives at the edges or outer boundaries of teaching and learning transformation. You can also assume that they are recognized in their local communities as leaders of change. As evidence, they were selected by program officials to represent their countries from countless Fulbright applicants. Just being selected is a minor miracle. You can read more about this particular Fulbright program in Chapter 2 by Jacob Butler.

Second, all the contributors have a common experience of having attended a graduate course at IU, namely, R546. As such, all have been trained in critical and creative thinking theory and techniques as well as instructional strategies for cooperative and collaborative learning, motivation, and technology integration. Perhaps more importantly, when in that course, they were all made to reflect on their teaching philosophies.

Third, all the Fulbright recipients in this book have returned to their respective countries and had a chance to pilot one or more learning strategies discussed and employed in R546, as well as experimenting with unique variations, combinations, extensions, and innovations specific to their local contexts. Simply stated, they are taking pedagogical action within a specific context.

Fourth, these 41 book chapter authors and educators all form a loose network or community through common experiences as graduate students or visiting scholars at IU who all attended the R546 class. You will find that the cultural diversity and wide-ranging areas of expertise of the various contributors combine to offer an assembly of highly unique and engaging stories.

Finally, as noted, all the chapter contributors have IU affiliations, including a few current international graduate students, several more recent alumni, a handful of former visiting scholars from China and Korea, and dozens of former Fulbright awardee teacher scholars. What you may not realize is that the highly illuminating foreword was written by former IU School of Education Dean Gerardo M. González (dean from 2000–2015). We are deeply thankful for and most privileged to have his masterful perspective reflected in the opening pages of this book. Given that all the contributors of this edited book have past or present IU School of Education affiliations, the volume appropriately closes with insightful thoughts and reflections from current IU School of Education Dean Anastasia S. Morrone. If you are in the habit of tallying deans, that makes two of them magnificently assisting us in opening and ending this book.

By now, it should be clear that not only was R546 a special class but so too were all the individuals in it. Perhaps this book on "Transformative Teaching Around the World" will serve as magical guideposts for your own R546 experience allowing you to make an impact in multiple educational spaces here in the 21st century.

Instead of relying solely on magic, we offer several questions to ponder both here and in the final chapter to help you operationalize some of the content of this book. For instance, will the impacts you make affect students cognitively by promoting higher order thinking skills and dispositions? At the same time, will your powerful ideas and activities energize learners emotionally with a robust sense of community and caring in the classroom? And just what is a classroom in a post-pandemic world anyway? Perhaps the impacts you foster will begin to transform reliance on deep-rooted standardized curricula and outdated assessments toward making all learning a curious adventure filled with self-directed inquiry, meaningful projects, and learner ownership over one's own learning. And perhaps the impacts you make will charge you up and change you forever. Let's hope.

1

TIME FOR MAKING IMPACT

Curtis J. Bonk and Meina Zhu

Curtis J. Bonk is Professor in the Instructional Systems Technology Department in the School of Education and Adjunct in the School of Informatics at Indiana University. He teaches and researches at the intersection of educational psychology and educational technology. Curt can be contacted at cjbonk@indiana.edu. His homepage is http://curtbonk.com/.

DOI: 10.4324/9781003213840-1

Meina Zhu is Assistant Professor of Learning Design and Technology in the College of Education at Wayne State University. Meina can be reached at meinazhuiu@gmail.com or meinazhu@wayne.edu.

Learning Transformations

Since the early 1980s, countless reports have detailed the shift toward an information-based economy and the need for a more technologically sophisticated workforce. Life in 2022 is much different from 1982. The skills and experiences required to succeed today are vastly different from four decades ago. A modern-day workforce clearly demands skills such as creativity, flexibility in thought, the ability to make decisions based upon incomplete information, complex pattern recognition abilities, and synthesis skills. Those who cannot keep up with the perpetual changes in skill demands and competencies often find themselves redundant and replaced by robots or intelligent agent technology (Arantani, 2020; Kelly, 2020; Semuels, 2020).

Such changes are occurring faster than most individuals and organizations can adapt. They are also accelerating the massive transformations in teaching and learning environments seen today across all sectors of education. Make no doubt, learning is changing. And it is changing for every member of this planet, young to old, self-directed to teacher-reliant, budding chemist to violinist. Whether you have limited means at your disposal to acquire a high-quality education or are financially quite well off, your learning resource and educational delivery options are radically changing. For many, learning today is often more game-like, hands-on, immersive, and visual in nature than it was a decade ago (Bonk, 2016b).

That is only a start. Learners also find that their learning avenues are more informal, online, blended, massive, and mobile too. These same learners are simultaneously being encouraged to learn new things by their peers through social media and various global collaborations and exchanges. At the same time as these online social influencers take hold, learning today is increasingly personalized and self-directed wherein a quality educational experience is highly reliant on learners taking responsibility for much of their own learning, whether one attends a local high school, virtual school, community college, or has successfully found entrance to Harvard or Indiana University.

These are just a few of the ways in which learning is changing today; there are dozens more (Bonk, 2016b), and there likely will be just as many more in the coming decades. If just one of those learning trends, let's say mobile or blended learning, had impacted life here in the 21st century, it would likely have been proclaimed a learning revolution unlike no other. However, with the dozens of major technology trends occurring simultaneously all around us, we must stop and think about how best to prepare learners for a rich and successful learning life on this planet.

Finding Education 4.0

In response to the emerging global marketplace, there has been a renewed interest in innovation and creativity. It does not matter if one is in a public school, a higher education setting, or in a military or corporate training environment. The shift in perspective from the reception of learning from some type of expert toward an emphasis on learner choice and options is the same. Every educator is seeking the Holy Grail and hoping to become more inventive and productive than the next person or organization. Some are labeling this new age "Education 3.0." In fact, countries such as Thailand are creating national policies and models for Education 3.0 ecosystems and communities (Songkram, Chootongchai, Khlaisang, & Prakob, 2021). Others speak more boldly about "Education 4.0" (Salmon, 2019).

You might ask how to find or identify an Education 3.0 environment. The markers of this time are tinkering, making things, invention and innovation, human-to-human and idea-to-idea connectedness, seeking and finding meaning, collaborative knowledge construction, the open exchange of ideas, and the utilization of and contribution to free and open educational resources (see Bonk, 2016a, Keats & Schmidt, 2007). Additional components of the emerging Education 3.0 world or new generation in teaching and learning are freedom to explore ideas and make mistakes, flexibility and choice in assignments, play, convenience, expanded resources, meaningful and authentic learning, imagination, global collaboration, engagement, passion and purpose, perpetual support and feedback, and empowerment and autonomy. Add to that a resource rich instructional space and a caring and committed instructor who displays collegiality, passion, spontaneity, and optimism and you find yourself in a learning transformation.

There are more elements to this transformation, of course, but these will do for now. You will see many of them explicitly and implicitly stated and becoming substantiated, cultivated, and even duplicated in the upcoming chapters. You might try growing your instructional gardens with a few of them.

But perhaps we are being conservative. We may be entering Education 3.0 today, but is Education 4.0 around the corner? If so, what does it look like? Gilly Salmon (2019) in the United Kingdom offers a peek. She argued that the development of the Web has paralleled the way we think about the progressive shifts to more advanced educational levels or generations. As she points out, the Web has significantly evolved during the past few decades.

Salmon suggests that the Web was transformed from the Web 1.0 version when it found a vital role as a giant conduit for the transmission of information and ideas to the often celebrated and, at the same time, bantered label of the Web 2.0 for social exchange and collaboration. Salmon also argues that we are now in the Web 3.0 or the "Semantic Web" that pervades our lives with never-ending movement to and from our digital lives that rely heavily on learner mobility. For instance, as young members of Gen Z move back and forth between their physical and digital lives, they are said to be phigital learners (Stansbury, 2017). Salmon argues that soon we will find ourselves in the Web 4.0 where there is a symbiotic relationship between artificial intelligence and human intelligence. She relates these generations of Web technology to educational shifts from 1.0 to 4.0.

Consequently, we challenge you to begin to craft a vision for your own Education 4.0 space when reading the various chapters of this book; just what does Education 4.0 represent for you and your educational community? Each reader might find his or her own sense of meaning or philosophy of this next generation of teaching and learning in the pages of this book.

In Education 4.0, people will no longer tolerate a curriculum that emphasizes the rote memorization of facts over problem-solving and creativity. Instead, innovative instructors and trainers engage learners with more authentic and active learning experiences. Even with such renewed interest and resources, most teachers still lack the time and resources to adequately deal with the proliferation of instructional practices and associated ideas regarding educational change. The ideas in this book can change all that for you.

This opening chapter should help you begin to understand overlapping trends in education related to creative thinking, critical thinking, motivation, and cooperative and collaborative learning, as well as how to design an active learning pedagogical system using technology-enhanced learning. Throughout this book, you will be exposed to ways to use technology to increase student thinking skills and teamwork. In starting on this path, specific techniques and ideas will be described as well as implementation steps. At times, advice will be offered for getting started using some of these alternative instructional strategies. A set of reflection questions at the end of each chapter should help you ponder the pedagogical opportunities and challenges in front of you.

Finding the Holy Grail

We, humans, are goal-driven creatures. Among the key goals of educators is making an impact on learners of any age level and learning in all its various stripes, formal or informal, passive or hands-on, mobile or stationary, self-directed or expert scaffolded, personalized or standardized, online or classroom-based, or perhaps some hybrid or blended combination. The next 42 chapters of this book touch on a diverse array of learning formats or situations. They will allude to instructional techniques employed to foster robust learning from Costa Rica to Morocco to Cyprus to Yemen to Uzbekistan to India to Thailand to China to Korea to Mexico and on to myriad other exciting destinations.

Each of these award-winning educators has been on a quest to find a magic lamp that can be rubbed for assorted powers to engage learners. They are searching for the Holy Grail of learning and instruction. We don't think we are spoiling the secret when we admit that no one found that particular Grail; at least not yet. All of these educators embarked on this teaching and learning journey long before they enrolled in the R546 course of "Instructional Strategies for Thinking, Collaboration, and Motivation" during the past decade. Theirs is a hunt that will not likely ever end; yet, with their determination, passion, innovation, and inspiration, it will likely produce delicious fruits at many stops along the way.

The chapters are relatively brief stories of how these 40+ educators have made an impact in their local communities; preferably using one or more of the instructional strategies learned in the Saturday class at Indiana University. The book contains eight sections: (1) Personal Transformations, (2) Innovative Education, (3) Teaching With Technology, (4) Pandemic Practices, (5) English Education and Collaboration, (6) Active Learning Strategies, (7) Global Education, and (8) Overcoming Challenges. We recommend sampling from all and focusing your energy on sections that are the most delightful to your palette. We will reappear when appropriate to introduce each of the eight sections of the book and again at the end.

As you read the chapters in these eight sections, you may notice that the Holy Grail of learning and instruction might be right in front of your eyes. It often exists in the humble strategies instructors utilize in their classes. Many of the instructional strategies highlighted in the upcoming 41 chapters include the use of flipped classrooms, project-based learning, brainstorming and reverse brainstorming, technology-enhanced concept mapping, and experiential learning. A few other chapters involve role play, cross-cultural exchanges, multimedia storytelling projects, crafting storybooks, and poem anthologies. These same methods are among the hundreds of strategies discussed in R546. Strategies such as super summaries, anchored instruction, public tutorials, real-time cases, an online séance, the starter-wrapper technique, collaborative video editing, oral history interviews, and so on permeate this particular book but are not explicitly mentioned.

The reason why so little in the present book is devoted to specific instructional techniques is that the first author (Bonk) has already produced two theory-to-practice books with models or frameworks for online teaching. Each of these books contains more than 100 activities for online instruction, most of which can be also used in face-to-face instruction or blended environments (Bonk & Khoo, 2014; Bonk & Zhang, 2008). One of those books (Bonk & Khoo, 2014) is free to download in both English and Chinese (http://tec-variety.com/). And a third such book is on the way (Pawan, Daley, Kou, & Bonk, 2022).

Accordingly, the present book will not be a rehash of previous work or a guide in such strategies and approaches. And there will not be a step-by-step instructional techniques guide. Instead, there will be a series of stories with embedded use of dozens of powerful instructional approaches designed to enhance learner creativity, critical thinking, cooperative and collaborative learning, and overall motivation, many of which will entail the use of different technology tools and resources. As such, this is not meant to be another "how-to" type of book. Of course, the Grail has never had a how-to guide to find it.

Finding the Principles

While not explicated, you can perhaps find the learning and instruction principles that underly the stories in this book. Simply put, when opening this amalgamation of stories, one will immediately find innovation and uniqueness as well as an integrated pattern of progressive educational practices. When reading this series of short narratives, there will likely be a set of instructional principles that emerges that can serve as models, frameworks, or templates for others. We do not explicate these principles, but, rather, want you to discover them in the chapters that you find interesting and inspiring to read. Simply put, we do not want to ruin the epiphanies that are to come.

But we do recommend that you take out a pen or marker when you start reading. These short anecdotes of hope and transformation contain perhaps ten, perhaps 20, or perhaps even more instructional principles and learning guidelines to foster critical and creative thinking, motivation, collaborative learning, and innumerable aspects of technology integration. In effect, these chapters should shed light not only on how to prepare learners to become skillful critical thinkers but also on how to prepare teachers to become effective reflective practitioners. When that happens, educators will have a better chance of preparing students for the jobs of tomorrow while finding instructional success today.

Finding the Entry Ramp

It is now time for you to venture into the 42 wondrous stories and think about how you can start to make an impact. We have laid out the goals and intended audiences of this book. Now it is time to read some of it so that you too can make a difference. Yes, you can make an impact that is most likely local, but for many of you, it will be global. Write to us when you do. We would love to hear your story.

Of course, we will return to introduce each major section of this book and then appear again near the end of this book with some questions for you to contemplate before, during, and after making impact. See you then. In the meantime, start searching for an entry ramp where you can make a meaningful, substantive, and sustainable impact on learners and learning. Now get going, for it is time you made an impact.

SECTION 1
Personal Transformations

The first section of this book is filled with deep reflections on the transformative changes taking place all around us. If you are a teacher in any educational sector or discipline struggling with life challenges or in the midst of rethinking your overall teaching philosophy, you are not alone. Fortunately, there are several chapters in this section which might be of value. Of all the sections in this book, we open with the one on personal transformations that will likely outlast the latest fad, technology trend, or pandemic. It is likely that you will find a chapter or two in Section 1 on personal transformations that you repeatedly return to.

In Chapter 2, the introductory chapter of this section, Jacob Butler provides background information on the role of international education in facilitating professional development and cross-cultural exchange. Specific emphasis is placed on the Fulbright Distinguished Awards in Teaching (DAT) Program, an exchange program hosted by Indiana University Bloomington from 2014 to 2017. Many of this book's contributing authors are alumni of this exchange program. This introduction outlines the multifaceted impact of cultural and professional exchange on educators from around the world. Read this chapter and reflect on the program design components that you might replicate and borrow from for your own cross-cultural exchanges and global education initiatives.

The following chapter is the first of 41 consecutive chapter reflections in the form of personal stories. In Chapter 3 from Alba Rosario Marrón Canseco in Mexico, readers are made to reflect on issues of power, sharing, and service in education. This chapter is filled with energy, passion, creativity, and caring related to her work with disadvantaged youth. As its root, the chapter asks how do you find your true calling? Is it in the classroom where you are face-to-face with your students? Alba asks what is more important—teaching grammar and definitions or understanding the people in your classroom?

DOI: 10.4324/9781003213840-2

Before she left the world of teaching, Alba admits that she constantly battled with this question in her mind. Like most classrooms worldwide, the pressure to evaluate as much as possible was the first priority. Importantly, Alba also reflects on the students who cannot be evaluated simply as a number. In this chapter, she also talks about how time and mistakes helped her to find some sense of balance between mandatory assessments and personalization or at least to develop techniques that are both efficient and sensible. When that balance is found, teaching skills can be elevated to address the myriad obstacles faced daily by an English teacher in a non-English-speaking country.

Chapter 4 from Keitumetse Thobani in Botswana offers a similar reflection on the challenges of teaching; however, her chapter is more concerned with how learning has changed during the past decade and will continue to change in the coming one. In effect, this chapter shines a light on the realization that the 21st-century learner is different and evolving. Consequently, there is a need for tasks and activities that involve learner collaboration and cooperation, critical thinking, creative expression, and empowerment or motivation in the 21st-century classroom. Keitumetse describes the exploration of the impact of the new pedagogies and the resulting teacher-learner motivation while practicing them in this world of endless possibilities.

It is in Chapter 5 that the book explores "questions that matter." In her stated epistle to the learner, Pratiksha Chopra from India has a heartfelt communication penned for the learner within each of us. The formulation of the epistle is driven by the need for quality control in one's thinking and reasoning in this content-fueled world. Throughout her chapter, Pratiksha makes us believe in the power of metacognitive thinking and metaphors by asking pertinent questions from which she hopes readers will seek meaningful answers.

The following chapter is also from India. In it, we exit the epistle to the learner and find some "sun on the snow" that can hopefully lead to better things for learners and teachers alike. In Chapter 6, Remya Parameswar Iyer presents a mosaic of evolving forms and dissolving patterns centered on her life as a practicing teacher. Her journey, from an aspiring doctoral fellow in the United States to a teacher in the Northeast region of India, is inspiring. A paradigm shift in her perception made Remya grow beyond teaching and evolve into a facilitator and co-learner enabling students to receive experiential and joyful learning. Remya guides students to apply their classroom learnings in negotiating real-life challenges. Being agile and adaptable, she converted the challenges related to COVID-19 into assorted opportunities for technology-enhanced blended learning. Her "Mindfulness" and "Tapping Happiness in Daily Life" sessions have enabled children to cope with the assorted pandemic-induced stressors and high levels of anxiety. Remya derives daily motivation from the joy of enhancing children's well-being, thereby contributing to the wellness of the planet.

In Chapter 7, the final chapter of Section 1, Nourit Ben David Erez discusses her earlier struggles to find ways to motivate and help students with learning disabilities (differences) to be active learners. This was what drove her to apply for the Fulbright DAT program in 2016. At that time, she began experimenting with pedagogical tools that might enhance teacher creativity and learner autonomy and empowerment. Accordingly, Nourit developed the "Web-Based English as a Foreign Language Course for Students with Learning Disabilities" project that relied on hybrid forms of learning. As she correctly points out, during the pandemic, most educators have become quite familiar with hybrid learning. Upon returning to Israel, Nourit realized that such hybrid learning was viewed by her superiors as science fiction, not as a viable teaching method. She took it upon herself to use and promote her hybrid learning ideas by disseminating them through her teaching and counseling. Of course, during the pandemic, these methods and techniques quickly became a must.

It is time to read the chapters of Section 1 that interest you and witness the personal transformation that these educators have experienced. When you do, you will see how they are each making an impact in education.

2

PROFESSIONAL GROWTH AND CROSS-CULTURAL EXCHANGE

A Glimpse Into a Fulbright Program's Lifelong Impact on Global Educators

Jacob Butler

Jacob Butler serves as a senior coordinator for the Center for International Education at Northern Arizona University in Flagstaff, Arizona. Jacob previously served as Fulbright Project Director for the Center for International Education,

DOI: 10.4324/9781003213840-3

Development, & Research at the Indiana University School of Education. He has an undergraduate degree in secondary education as well as a graduate certificate in higher education and student affairs from Indiana University Bloomington. Jacob also has an MA degree in African studies from University of Illinois Urbana-Champaign. Prior to his work in international higher education, Jacob received a Fulbright award and served as a visiting faculty member at the University of the Free State in Bloemfontein, South Africa. Jacob has also served as a classroom teacher in secondary schools in Tanzania, Kenya, and the United States. He can be contacted at jacob.butler@nau.edu.

Background

The Indiana University (IU) School of Education served as the lone host institution for the Fulbright Distinguished Awards in Teaching Program from 2014 to 2017. This program, sponsored by the U.S. Department of State, Bureau of Educational and Cultural Affairs, was an intensive professional development and cultural exchange program for primary- and secondary-level teachers. In total, during those four years, 67 international teachers, representing 11 countries and territories, spent four months living and learning in Bloomington, Indiana, United States.

As part of the program, each international teacher was involved in a number of professionally relevant activities, including the following:

- Enrollment in two graduate level classes at Indiana University Bloomington;
- Weekly individual school visits to local schools with an American host teacher;
- Whole-group school visits to local schools with unique approaches, diverse student populations, and alternative organizational methods;
- Monthly check-ins with an IU School of Education faculty mentor to discuss observations, professional growth, cross-cultural differences in teaching, and guidance on an educational topic or issue of inquiry;
- Completion of a practitioner-based inquiry project into an educational topic or issue of their choosing.

The impact of the Fulbright program is multilayered and must be looked at through multiple lenses. You will get a glimpse into the lifelong cultural and professional impact of the exchange program experience on participants when you read the chapters of this book that are written by Fulbright program alumni. When you do, you might pause for a few minutes and reflect on how your cultural background and any professional experiences outside your comfort zone have influenced your classroom teaching. What role do cross-cultural experiences play in fostering growth among students, teachers, and administrators? What teaching methods have you used to encourage your students to consider other cultural perspectives? Where might global educational activities and opportunities arise with advances in learning technology in the coming decade? There is much that can be gleaned from the eight sections of this book to help you build powerful and profound life-changing experiences for your students no matter their ages, backgrounds, or interests.

Cross-Cultural Exchange

In regard to the Fulbright program participants, the individual growth of the international teachers as cultural ambassadors, professional educators, and change agents was profound. Not only did many participants visit the United States for the first time, but also, for some, this program was the first experience outside their home country. Having the opportunity to experience life in the United States as both a professional and a cultural outsider was high impact for all.

In addition to deep interpersonal growth that came as a result of living in the United States, participants experienced cultural dissonance and growth within the program by interacting with their international teaching peers in their cohort. In a context where everyone was outside of their comfort zone, the program facilitated incredible friendships and cultural exchanges across different world nationalities, languages, religions, and perspectives. Those deep bonds were built through classroom discussion, visits to places such as the local Bloomington farmer's market, assorted IU events, and group trips to Chicago, Illinois, and the Muhammad Ali Center in Louisville, Kentucky. Cross-cultural celebrations with shared music, food, and traditions became a common occurrence during the weekends as well as when celebrating holidays and birthdays.

Individual Professional Impact

Without doubt, having the opportunity to step away from the classroom for four months to focus on professional development, growth, and cross-cultural awareness had a tremendous impact on all the international teachers in the program. During the program, all 67 Fulbright teacher participants investigated an inquiry project into an educational topic of their own choosing. Typically, these projects held deep personal meaning for each of these teachers as they were informed by real-life challenges they had faced in their respective professional careers. In turn, it was easy to feel a sense of passion and commitment since the work they were undertaking would make a tremendous impact in their home communities upon their return. As a result of being deeply interested in the topic, international teachers went to great lengths to further their understanding of myriad complex topics in education.

Some examples of project topics were second language learning, promoting global competence and cross-cultural awareness, incorporating the arts into STEM, involvement in local environmental sustainability efforts, authentic science and mathematics instruction through project-based forms of learning, and other content area specializations. Unique projects that were completed by these Fulbright teachers focused on Deaf Education in Botswana, Supporting Blind and Visually Impaired Students in Morocco, Preventing Teen Pregnancy and Supporting Teen Mothers in Botswana, Using Theater for Social Justice in India, and Empowering Students Through Film Studies in Israel. As you read the various chapters and sections of this book, you are bound to come across dozens of other innovations in pedagogy and stories of cultural impact.

Community Impact

Each international teacher made weekly all-day visits to local schools throughout their program. During these visits, these teachers observed classes, participated in school field trips, and co-taught lessons. Over the course of the program, 49 American teachers served as hosts to the international teachers in the Fulbright teacher program. In addition, along the way, the number of American students who were exposed to these fabulous teachers from diverse locations around the world was in the hundreds. In these classes, the international teachers gave cultural presentations about their home countries and cultures, helping to broaden the perspectives of American students and facilitate global awareness.

Additionally, while auditing IU classes, the Fulbright teachers brought diverse global perspectives, innovative ideas, and rich and recent teaching experiences to graduate-level courses and seminars. Such perspectives and ideas helped to further enhance and, at times, transform discussions on teaching best practices, innovative uses of technology, and various issues, challenges, and possibilities related to educational access, equity, and inclusion across the world.

Return Home

As a result of their own profound experiences abroad, these award-winning teachers returned home with a broader cultural lens in which to see the world as well as a greater understanding of the importance of incorporating diverse perspectives into the curriculum. Furthermore, participants had an expanded professional network of colleagues around the world whom they could call upon for collaboration, support, feedback, and to exchange ideas.

Upon return to their home communities, program participants re-entered their classrooms with new professional skills and knowledge about how to incorporate technology in instruction, facilitate critical thinking skills, and foster motivation amongst their students. Additionally, the teachers who were already highly accomplished in their professional field had developed a renewed sense of purpose to positively impact those around them through their leadership, mentorship, and cultural ambassadorship. Undoubtedly, that impact continues today in classrooms around the world, as shown in the ensuing chapters of this book. As you read various chapters, reflect on how you, too, could make an impact in your classes and communities. You might reach out to one or more of the Fulbright teachers and inform them of your innovative pedagogical ideas and activities, thereby expanding the global dialogue and possibilities for others. So many exciting things are now possible!

Reflection Questions

1. In general, how has the global pandemic permanently impacted cross-cultural exchange through the use of new learning technologies, both positively and negatively? Specifically, how have these changes impacted opportunities for you to get involved in global and intercultural education?
2. In what ways can you more effectively integrate diverse perspectives into your workplace or classroom in the future?
3. How do cross-cultural exchange programs sponsored by governments and philanthropic organizations positively impact global dialogue, innovation, and exchange of ideas across cultures? In your own school community, what types of innovative policies might help encourage more students and staff to pursue professional opportunities which help facilitate cultural exchange, professional growth, and exposure to diverse perspectives?
4. How can you facilitate cross-cultural competence among students who are unable to travel abroad? What role does technology play in opening up cultural windows to the world for your students?
5. What role have cross-cultural experiences in your own life impacted the way you see and interact with your students, your colleagues, and the community you live in?

3

ENERGY FOUND ME; ENERGY KEPT ME

Thoughts on Power, Sharing, and Service

Alba Rosario Marrón Canseco

Alba Rosario Marrón Canseco has worked since 1994 as a teacher for teen-agers. She is also an educational designer, writer, and training coordinator for teachers in Mexicali, Baja California, Mexico. As an outreach coordinator, she

DOI: 10.4324/9781003213840-4

focused on educational environmental programs and writing agreements with universities that benefitted teachers and students including promoting students' visits to local industries. Alba attended Indiana University in 2015 as part of the Fulbright Distinguished Awards in Teaching Program. She later presented at 12 conferences about her award experience, travelling solo in 12 countries and discussing the globalized student. In 2019 and 2020, she wrote four books about business management and accounting. She is editing her two new books about short stories and poems. She can be reached at albamc67@gmail.com.

Introduction

Education found me. I found my passion in teaching. The energy that I feel when I look at my students and I start talking is something I have not felt doing in any other activity. I have worked as an accountant and later as chief in charge of designing instruction for thousands of teachers. Now I am a business entrepreneur. None of those occupations compares to the intense emotional and cognitive state in sharing what I know and the awareness that in doing it, many students' lives will change for the better. I once read that three things move people: power, sharing, and service. Teaching fulfills all three. You have power in the classroom. You are sharing your knowledge and, in the process, you are perpetually serving others. Sometimes this can result in a clash of powers, but most of the time, there is a sense of caring along with its notable accomplice, empathy.

I often experience mixed emotions for my students, a heartedness toward them because they are so young and naïve, and life will undoubtedly teach them many hard lessons. When I started teaching at an underprivileged high school in a border town in Mexico, my husband was worried about the insecurity of the neighborhood. Never, not even once, have my students stolen something from me or offended me. A majority of them were from homes relying on a single mother's income, and some had no parents around. During the years, I heard terrible stories about tragedies. Sadly, some came from shattered homes or had no water or electricity; in spite of such difficult circumstances, you would not believe how much they admired their mothers or grandparents with whom they lived.

When reviewing assignments in that intimate close space, sometimes I could see head lice or their heads smelled bad, as some could not wash their hair. Nevertheless, what I received from them for a quarter century was respect and love. And it was reciprocal as they knew I respected and cared for them. They could sense it, and they responded fully to it.

Two moments in my classroom changed my whole perspective, even as a human. The first occurred on a rainy day. The school's neighborhood did not have paved streets, so when it rained, it was difficult to drive there. I was very strict in teaching my 50-minute class, not ending it even one minute less. My class was quite restless that day and a student asked to leave early, and I vehemently stated, "*No! My class is not over!*" Soon he replied with a sad, anguished voice, "*Hmmm. What do you know? You do have a car! You are going to arrive safely at your house.*" At that moment, their reality slapped me hard. How selfish I was to see only my reality.

The second was circa 1997. I was describing to my students that Mexico was an incredible country. I had a student who came to class whenever he wanted. I could sense he had no idea about what I taught. He once defied me in an intense way, demanding that I explain to him why he had to learn English if he was Mexican. I attempted to explain as best I could. To this day, I cannot forget his sadness when I said, "*Mexico is so beautiful,*" and his reply was "*Hmmm, rich people say that.*" How terrible must his life have been that all he could see was such a sorrowful present. Like thousands of students in my 25 years as an educator, he quit school during the first semester, and I never saw him again.

How did I create my teaching style? The first decision was related to education and training. The more I studied, the more I understood how extremely complex the teaching-student-learning-evaluating-performance phenomenon was. I felt obliged to learn as much as I could and studied for 20 years. I signed up for talks, lectures, workshops, coaching, and neuro-linguistic programming (NLP) seminars. I enrolled for one year in a language teaching degree. I paid attention closely and tried to learn everything I could. I studied many textbooks by myself. I recall them as very valuable, as they helped me to understand difficult topics. I received certifications in English and teaching competencies. They were useful as well.

The second decision revolved around learning technology. My teaching style was significantly impacted by learning to use a computer early on. In fact, in my first summer as a teacher, I bought a very expensive computer and started learning about it. I was one of the first teachers in my school to use the internet. One student, who was poor but very smart, created my first email message. Since then, I have been using technology in my classes.

I searched for websites related to learning English, used real English texts, songs, and so forth. I relied on computer labs the most, but only when administration allowed me, as I was always fighting for space. I designed a blog and used it as a didactic tool where my students could read their own writings. Another powerful teaching technique was to ask students to watch videos about environmental issues, human values, and similar social issues. These videos are posted on my blog. Students had to watch one and write a 500-word essay. Every semester, I always cried with amazement when reading their reflections and aspirations. Their motivation and words were immensely valuable in the human context.

As the years progressed, I developed a methodology that I felt could foster their learning growth more substantially. However, my time in the classroom was reduced, so I had to maximize my opportunities. The following techniques helped in that regard.

1. *Controlled Learning Environment.* I asked for a lot of work from my 45 students (average per group, seven groups per semester): to do exercises, writings,

readings and to research at home, and so forth. Students knew I read everything and would grade it all. I called roll assigning numbers so students could familiarize with them, though I would know most of their names. It saved me eight minutes each class. Using numbers also helped me grade faster.

2. *Time to Work.* The first thing I did when I walked into the classroom was to assign an exercise in our book, some were written by me, or make them write five repetitive sentences with the grammar tense I was teaching them. It is extremely important to start working with a quiet group, it allows you to feel the emotions in the group and, in addition, gives time to grade homework. To have a controlled environment of the group is vital. Students felt they were in a secure place to learn.

3. *The Sound of Music.* I used music in classes. Of course, students loved it. It soon became a motivation to stay in my classes. I looked for songs that exemplify grammar tenses (i.e., past, present, modals, etc.) and then the students and I analyzed lyrics and grammar use. Sometimes students chose the songs.

4. *I Care Who You Are.* During the first class, I asked every student how he or she wanted to be called: by first or second name. The important thing was to show I cared. I explained in detail the rules of my evaluation and that I adhered to them, no matter what. I stated clearly that students would pass and learn only because I demanded a lot, and it was their responsibility to learn by themselves. Asking for more was the rule, and to be consistent. Another core principle was that I did not stand mean people. Hurting others in my class was not allowed.

5. *Self-Esteem.* When I took a workshop in self-esteem, I learned how hard it was for students to speak aloud in English if their self-esteem was low. So even when I made everybody participate in some way, I tried not to force them.

6. *Mindfulness Conscience.* In every class, my communication would always carry a positive tone or meaning. Every sentence I wrote was aligned with real life. Every sentence and grammar explanation was written with a valuable meaning. *If I work hard, I will get into college; If I work hard, I will have a better future,* and so forth.

When we learned about adjectives, I asked my students to write 50 positive adjectives or traits that described themselves. Negative adjectives were not allowed. Students were to find meaning in every sentence: if we were learning superlative form, sentences asked, who is the most important person in your life? Who is the most honest? What is the most important value in your life? What is better: to be rich or to be smart?

I applied techniques learnt in NLP seminars. I am a kinesthetic learner, so it was easy for me to move all around the classroom. I started using some Total Physical Response techniques: when I arrived in the classroom, if I sensed that students were full of energy or if it was just the opposite, I would say,

"Stand up! You are going to say aloud and do exactly what I do." I started doing stretching exercises and using prepositions aloud paired with my body: arms, hands, shoulders, head showing the prepositions: up, down, left, right, back, to the front. I taught students to do breathing exercises, and I explained how important breathing correctly was and how it could help in emergency situations. It was marvelous. The entire group got into this magic calm feeling, and I then presented a difficult grammar explanation.

Every semester when teaching modals, I highlight important issues such as hygiene, drugs, image, self-esteem, values, and so forth. In the *must* modal, I taught about using hygiene facts such as (1) *Razors and toothbrushes must not be shared*; (2) *You must not use drugs because you could lose your freedom and health*; and (3) *You must not worry a lot about your body size and suffer for your image.* I attempted to motivate girls to study and work independently: *a single woman can travel and spend her money.*

7. *Inspirational Pedagogy.* I did not discuss my personal life, but I spoke a lot about my job experiences or mistakes to avoid. When teaching business English or accounting, reflecting on my own experiences was a key part of the class. I considered it a teacher's obligation to prepare students for life and employment, and my stories and anecdotes might help them in avoiding mistakes.

Once, when teaching English, I was mad because students were not handing in their homework assignments. I knew that they could not pass without working. Unfortunately, they flunked mercilessly. It really was a vicious cycle: they did not do the homework and had poor performance. As a result, their tests were almost blank, thereby making it impossible to approve.

It was even worse with the afternoon groups. They were fated to flunk and then quit school. As a result, I shed tears many times in the classroom. It was extremely frustrating to see them wasting their opportunity to get into a college or disappearing as a failure of the educational system. I made attempts to help them understand that being in the school may be their final opportunity for a better future. Regrettably, former students have later told me in the street, "Teacher, why did I not listen to you?"

So, one day I was lecturing them with a harsh tone, speaking about the cost of diapers, formula milk, and pediatrician fees (my own kids were babies at the time). I mentioned just how hard it was for their parents to send them to school. Eventually, I asked them if they were not ashamed of their commitment to education given their parents' efforts, and yet, they were wasting their opportunities.

When I finished my exasperated words, one older student spoke up: *"Teacher, nobody has ever told us this. Teachers come, teach their class and leave."* I could not believe it. At every teacher workshop, we read about powerful learning activities and authentic learning experiences and how education could transform realities. I really believed what we all were doing was the same—adding my own grain of sand into their lives.

Furthermore, I always said to them that English was an important tool that could make them richer. Once a student asked me, "*And why are you here with us?*" "*Because I really like to be here!*" I answered despite my astonishment for confronting my life decision to teach.

I spoke about my travelling, because I wanted them to pursue goals and to believe in bright futures, full of trips and dream jobs. I told them that I grew up in a poor neighborhood with no advantages. I also talked about former students who were doing great things. I begged them to work hard and try to get into college.

8. *Significative Learning and PBL.* When teaching business English, the students would choose an international company and conduct research about it during the entire semester. They would present information about its vision, history, founders, products, location, and so forth. In the process, they were learning about the real world. They were also taught how to introduce themselves in a business situation: how to shake hands and look into the eyes when saying their name. *If you do not say your name aloud, nobody will care for it. Say it out loud and clear!*

After my Fulbright Award experience with fellow Fulbrighters from around the world, I asked my students to do their own research about different countries. They were to provide statistics such as population, currency, cost of living, and transportation, including airfare and booking hotel rooms. It was a really eye-opening experience to listen to the data presented, watch videos on different cities, and ponder living there. Each student presented for ten minutes, teaching the class about marvelous cities, huge companies, and well-known products.

I also asked students to research their own family information: to find out about the origin of their grandparents as well as the indigenous tribes from their states and their own history and why and how their grandparents came to our city. I often saw how they felt proud of their history. I would exclaim, "*If you do not know your history, it will be lost!*"

The most important thing was to teach students to learn by themselves, to strive, and to believe that the world is open and they can reach their goals and desires, no matter what they have been told or even if people laughed at their dreams.

Teaching them made me a better human being. I am very grateful for the moments wherein I laughed and also cried in the classroom. We, teachers, have the privilege to work with humans that are full of hope and joy. They have this incredible faith in the future. I could not have been the human I am now without having grown up as a teacher paired with them in this never-ending learning life cycle.

Reflection Questions

1. How can you measure how successful a technique is in the classroom? Does instructional success come only from goals and planning, or can spontaneity improve it? Give an example.

2. All teachers want to have an impact on the future of their students. How can we as teachers integrate such a core intention in our planning? Do we focus on word tenses, facts, and numbers, or should we add activities with intentional meanings that impact the lives of our students? Or might we attempt to do both?

3. Is it possible to use only positive language in the classroom and speak about what we want to achieve with our students? Can we avoid negative comments and harmful intentions? Why or why not?

4. How can we manage the learning goals of large classrooms with fair forms of evaluation?

5. Do the techniques described in this chapter actually improve classroom management and learner engagement?

4

THE WORLD OF ENDLESS POSSIBILITIES

The Educator in Me

Keitumetse Thobani

Keitumetse Thobani was born and raised in Gaborone, the capital city of Botswana. She was awarded a Fulbright Distinguished Award in Teaching to Indiana University in 2016. Currently, she is a high school teacher of English in a government school located in one of the city's low-income areas. Keitumetse's inspiration to write this chapter comes from self-discovering her passion as an educator. At times this journey as a teacher has been challenging, but she deeply appreciates the opportunity to have a positive impact on the growth of her students. She can be reached at keitumetsethobani@yahoo.com.

DOI: 10.4324/9781003213840-5

Comfort Zone

"Do you honestly like teaching?"
"How do you do this every single day? Any motivation?"
"Did you aspire to be a teacher?"

These were the questions I got when I started my teaching career. Fresh from my Bachelor of Arts in Humanities degree and Post Graduate Diploma in Education (PGDE), I happily received an offer for a teaching post. I honestly had mixed feelings about it in terms of the future I had planned, but I needed the job.

You see, when I was about to finish my PGDE, my mother suddenly became ill. As a result, she was in and out of hospital for several weeks. Sadly, after about a month of sleepless nights, emotional turmoil, and horrible pain, my mother passed on. So when the teaching post came about, I had felt a need to start working and be able to feed myself at least. You see, I had become a burden to my three elder siblings, who at the time, were still trying to figure out their own futures. My mother's passing left our lives in a state of utter turmoil and confusion.

Now I guess one of the previous questions has been answered. While I did not aspire to be a teacher, circumstances forced me to be one. Looking back, I am happy that I got to make that decision.

I started my teaching career on a very light note. I did what needed to be done at the time or, rather, with the schedule given. I was punctual for all my lessons, planned well for them, and submitted all the relevant documents on time. In class, I delivered the content as required in the allotted time. When that time was up, I packed my things and said a heartfelt goodbye to my learners. To avoid being in a comfort zone, I had to remind myself time and again that "five more years and I am out of this profession."

Because I was in a rural area, entertainment was extremely limited to pretty much staying indoors or going to the supermarket and then back home. My friend had bought me a motivational book for my birthday which became my daily amusement. I found myself immersed in that book, and every day became different from the previous one. I started going to my workplace and entering my classes with a purpose. I was now viewing things in a different light. With that change in perspective, I became energised, and I started to thoroughly enjoy teaching. I even began doing things differently in my classes. Teaching was now becoming part of me; it was who I was—a teacher who strove for pedagogical excellence. Simply put, I had decided I wanted to be the change that I hoped to see in this profession. That is what is meant by the notion that attitude plays a major role in their life. My attitude was showing me the light that I had not seen before. For this, I was most thankful.

Possibilities—Unfolded

After about three years of teaching in a rural area, I was transferred to a new school in the capital city of Botswana, Gaborone. My excitement level was unmatched.

I thought now was going to be my big break as I was to teach students from a city with much more and better resources. There would be no language barrier (as a teacher of English). And, generally, there would be excellent academic performances compared with what I had seen in the rural school.

Unfortunately, I found that the students in my new school were not as I had imagined. The school was in the part of town that had mostly low-income dwellers. As such, there was minimal parental involvement, and most of the students' motivation was perpetually in low gear, if there was any. They needed a vision of themselves as learners with unique gifts. Because of my already changed attitude, I began to think outside the box on how I can achieve academic success in my classes. I conducted my own research, but I felt pain in not knowing exactly what to look for. For starters, our class sizes were huge (around 50 learners per class), and then our school received a low percentage of the high achievers from the primary school level (elementary). As a result, the classes were mixed ability with huge gaps between the learners. That was a momentous challenge.

There was a school partnership program in the school. This partnership was effectively an exchange program between our school and a school in Scotland. The partnership was sponsored by the British Embassy. Each year, a few learners and teachers from these schools visited each other's schools to exchange culture, curriculum delivery, and many ideas related to the day-to-day running of the school. I was fortunate to have been part of the group of teachers who went to Scotland for the cultural exchange program.

Little did I know that the visit would turn my "impossible" to "possible." In one of the classes, I had observed how the teacher had effortlessly included all students in his lesson. All were doing work according to their ability but focussing on the same objective. It was very remarkable how students seemed to be motivated and were collaborating extremely well during the lesson. The excitement was palpable as I saw the answer to my long unfinished research on how to help unmotivated students in my overcrowded classrooms. After that lesson, I discussed at length with the teacher about my observations and he had shared that he mainly uses differentiation in his classes.

I remember the excitement so vividly. I had already started to see my lessons in a different light. Signs of hope sprung into the air, signalling needed change. Could this be it? Could my dreams be coming to fruition? Alas, the vastly smaller class size issue in Scotland became my mood killer. I started another round of brain cracking. The "how," "where," and "what" were already in play.

The Educator

When I explored the research on differentiation, I soon discovered that I had engaged in practices related to it without even realising it. But there was something lacking in my approach. Clearly, this was not going to be as easy as I had imagined. A Fulbright Distinguished Teacher Exchange Program advertisement was out. I remember thinking that it could be my big break in life that could help not only my learners but also all learners in my country. My research topic was "Improving Quality of Curriculum Delivery Through Differentiated Teaching and Learning." The application was a success, and soon I became one of the Fulbright Teacher Exchange participants based in Bloomington, Indiana. Lucky me!

The vast knowledge I got from the program was immeasurable. Most importantly, my fire to be a highly innovative and successful educator was ignited. During my stay in the United States, I learnt that it was vital to give students choices as we teach. The importance of realising that the 21st-century learner is different and evolving was something that I fully embraced. I realised that with all the differentiation to be done in my classes, I would constantly craft tasks and activities for learner collaboration and cooperation, critical thinking, creative expression, and empowerment or motivation. In addition, I would attempt to integrate technology in different learning activities. I soon realised that motivation could be enhanced in many different ways. My favourite course may have been on Saturday mornings on instructional strategies since it was both fun and educative.

When I arrived back home, I had to start somewhere with my research findings. I still had the same high number of students, so my hopes of doing what I wanted in my lessons were not starting off well. Then I remembered that motivation was my best bet. I had to lose the traditional methods of teaching and try out more contemporary ones. Of course, I did this with baby steps and keeping in mind that students would not absorb everything all at once. Since my learners had extreme variability in terms of academic knowledge, I had to plan my lessons well. Lessons were now more about being cooperative as well as working collaboratively to achieve academic excellence.

With this knowledge and awareness, soon I conducted several workshops for my school on differentiated learning. Amazingly, after that, the Ministry of Education in Botswana invited me to share these ideas with teacher colleagues from different parts of my country. I realized that my advice and ideas would be interpreted differently by different teachers; still, I came equipped to share anyway. I knew that some hearts would be won immediately, and some would still have more questions. Of course, at times, these questions were beyond me, but I would try to resolve them.

I was happy that the opportunity to share my research came at the right time as my country through its Education and Training Sector Strategy Plan (ETSSP) for 2015–2020 had included differentiation teaching and learning as one of the pillars for improving the quality of education in the country. The plan is concentrated on inclusive education and not leaving any learner behind despite their ability or inability. In addition, it seeks to engage learners in the integration of technology in their education.

This is the story of how I turned my work into my passion. I started to realise that students should be given a chance to be critical thinkers instead of being passive in class. This is how I realised my potential as an educator was more than what I had in mind when I started my teaching career. And yes, I do love teaching.

Lessons Learnt and Suggestions

One should never limit their own potential. In loving what you do, you open many closed doors. Most importantly, let us all agree that "one size in class does not fit all."

Reflection Questions

1. How did you feel at the beginning of your teaching career? What were your ideals and goals? In what ways have they changed?
2. What innovative pedagogies have you recently tried out with your learners? What led you to try those innovative pedagogies?
3. In this chapter, the author reflected on how her Fulbright experience transformed her teaching goals and ambitions. Have you ever had such an experience? How often do you take time out to reflect on your teaching philosophy?
4. How do your learners tend to respond to collaboration in the classroom?

5

QUESTIONS THAT MATTER

An Epistle to the Learner

Pratiksha Chopra

Pratiksha Chopra is an English language and assessment specialist based out of New Delhi, India. A former Fulbright Distinguished Teacher, an aspiring linguist, a seeker, and a poet at heart, she strives to bring meaning to language learning in and outside classrooms. Her primary work centers on metacognition and contextualization in language acquisition. She can be reached at pratikshachopra@gmail.com.

Introduction

Disclaimer: I am not here because I have an answer. I am here because I have questions. If you find yourself humming the same tune or spot any traces of yourself in the feelings expressed, welcome to the brigade!

DOI: 10.4324/9781003213840-6

Dear Learner (in me)
Hello!

This epistle is an ode to the year of the pandemic, the times before and after and what I discovered hitherto. It's not just the teacher in me talking; it's the learner as well. It is the archetypal one who is attempting to construct a meaningful view of the world with the wealth of information around her.

We blinked, and the world changed. In fact, the incontestable truth is that perhaps it is just the beginning. It is in such times that we need to craft delicate and delicious questions that matter.

We are facing unique revolutions all over the world. As these revolutions arise, all our long-standing stories are disintegrating, and new narratives are replacing them. We consume mind-numbing content with the swipe-left culture all day, take numerous online courses and webinars, and witness the dance of digitalization turn our lives upside down. Is it just as astonishing to see society spending billions on refining personalization algorithms with services like Amazon and Spotify?

Does it concern and perhaps excite you at the same time to think about whether we are coming close enough to offer personalized learning opportunities in education, where everyone needs a specific learning path, pace, and goal? Has the way we are taught and allowed to learn evolved with the dramatic shifts in technology and automation? History is a testimony to the fact that whenever technology has raced ahead of education, it has led to social change, some large while others are more incremental; that is, until educational systems around the planet were thrown upside down. Remember the invention of the printing press?

It was in 2016, when in the United States as a Fulbrighter and English language teaching specialist from Delhi, India, that my educational philosophy went through an exciting transformation. While I had landed in the United States, I came from a country where the educational paradigm relied heavily on content and limited pedagogical research, on average. I soon realized that I was encountering a new world, loaded with fluid identities, novel sensory experiences, innovative models of education, and brand new jargons, creators, and collaborators. I was in the midst of a storm, caught with endless possibilities as well as the potential for torrential downpours without an umbrella.

To put it simply, I was in the shoes of those new friends around me, trying to filter discourses and adapt them to my needs. But then my teachers appeared. What I discovered was not mine at all; indeed, I realized what it meant to be standing on the shoulders of giants. But what I did with what they gave me was mine. Purely mine; that is until I shared it in this chapter for others to experiment with.

The fact that I am able to share this personally gained understanding with you all in this book bears testimony to the fact that simple shifts in points of view can expand one's comprehension of the potential impact and viability of still emerging educational principles and ideas. I thought about how I thought. Metacognition arrived as a key to understand my philosophical transformations in an inward as well as the outward journey. I think it is magical; how my metacognitive self can turn complex information found in academic texts into bite-sized relishable pieces. Reflective thinking, thinking with structures, and thinking about my own thinking has become the new normal for me and a highly reliable guide to curate future learning experiences for my learners. Such reflective thinking and the emphasis on metacognitive processes is also a very sustainable solution; an approach which I employ to prepare and empower teachers in India to work with linguistically and culturally diverse groups internationally.

Recently, I interacted with a cohort of multicultural, multilinguistic teachers from a Mexican university as part of a teacher training program. The last thing on my mind was feeding them more data, even if it is the new currency. What I wanted them to do was combine the data they already had into a lucid and telling view of their learners and themselves. I wanted them to think first, teach later.

In another training with in-service and preservice teachers from colleges in Delhi, I took up the four Cs routine to teach a novel. It is a text-based routine that helps identify key points of complex texts for discussion that demands a rich text or book. It asks the learners to draw **Connections** between the text and self. It also requests them to **Challenge** ideas, positions, and assumptions in the text. Further still, they should note **Concepts** worth holding onto from the text. And, in the end, these same learners should point to **Changes** in thinking and attitudes suggested in the text. The constructive element of the routine surprised teachers. Classified and labeled thinking can structure that thinking and lead to a unique understanding of the whole text and added depth and dimension to it.

In your everyday life, what do you do when you forget where you parked your car in the parking lot? Perhaps you press your clicker above your head while frantically circling the rows. Or maybe you simply stand there and recreate all that you remember after you parked your car. Do you stand and think? Do you go to the gym and start working out on strength, endurance, or specific body parts?

Soon you may discover that it is not about learning to lift weights; it's about *how* to work with weights. It is not about studying a concept or remembering information; it's about *how* to remember. Knowing the shape and size of a coin does not let you determine the currency; studying *details* helps. Making elaborations helps, as does organizing the data that you gather. Knowing a strategy is not the achievement but applying it to synthesize your understanding definitely is.

We all can multitask easily, my friend. But we cannot fully process two cognitively demanding things at the same time. We, this generation that flips between texts and screens and media like fluttering leaves without pondering what it leads to. This back-and-forth process assumes we are comprehending all those actions simultaneously and seamlessly, but we are not. Consciously training our mind not to focus, while training our eyes constantly to look outward and not inward. At the end of the day, it's the landing wherein we ground ourselves in our experiences, that allows us to gain our footing.

One of the gems I learned during my classes at Indiana University, and that really stayed with me and shaped my ideology was "Thinking in Metaphors." I remember the "Eight Nouns" activity that required me to describe myself in metaphors (Bonk & Khoo, 2014). Who am I? Am I spring, a free-flowing stream, or a firefly? I was pleasantly coaxed into making connections with my surroundings and then reinventing myself. Such an activity was followed by thinking of our workplaces in metaphors. Was my workplace a maze, a pressure cooker, or an airport in motion? I realized metaphors uttered a secret life. They are a way of thought before a way with words. They aren't true or untrue in any sense. They are an art, not science. Metaphors can get under your skin by ghosting past the logical mind and let you feel existence and life-forms directly.

As I write here, I recall teaching a poetry unit to an advanced class at a school in Bloomington, Indiana. The end task was writing a short poem based on a format. The last line of the poem had to be a metaphor. One thing I didn't know at the time was that I would end up saving those samples for the rest of my life. The insight they gave me into the students' minds was indescribable. I do wish that I had the space to include all their lovely and moving poems here. One wrote, "*I was the tall metal tower, firmly grounded; in one place, yet viewing all day.*" Another one wrote, "*I was the owl in the trees; If only I knew what was behind those bright eyes.*" That class was consequential for me in many ways. It was crucial in cementing my belief in the efficacy of metaphors to understand ourselves and others.

People tell you there are tons of defining moments. Every turn is a defining moment. Every text you read or movie you watch is a defining moment. Thinking about what and how you think about them helps you treasure them. Learn to segment and refocus your attention, perhaps stumbling down into using chunks of your brain differently and spontaneously and not what is happening all the time.

I learned prioritizing, eliminating, and refocusing, which proved supportive in coming up with the most profound of ideas, which is exactly the point I am attempting to make; that is, how to construct a meaningful narrative of all that surrounds us as learners and as teachers. Mine was a merger of metaphors and metacognition, creating the perfect scaffold. What's yours, my friend?

Metacognitively Yours

Suggestions

Dear Thinker (in me)

While you navigate the pages of this chapter or any other stimuli in your day-to-day life, use metacognition as an internal guide. Notice when your attention wanes, when your comprehension or your memory weakens or succeeds, when you have/haven't learned something, or when your thinking is faulty. Let that internal guide act and tell you whether you need to transfer your attention, re-read, contemplate or rethink an idea, ask questions, make mental moves, or just reflect.

Reflection Questions

Taking conscious control of your inner voice and ask yourself these questions when faced with a dilemma or solutions at home or in the classroom. Describe this situation and then address the following questions.

1. Does this situation remind me of anything in another unrelated domain of knowledge? If so, where?
2. Is this the first time that I have come across this type of situation or nugget of knowledge? Please explain.
3. If this is a WHAT, then can I explain the WHY? And then ponder the HOW and the WHEN?
4. How can this information be successfully applied in my professional life? How is success even defined?

6

SUN ON THE SNOW

Ad Meliora—Towards Better Things

Remya Parameswar Iyer

Remya Parameswar Iyer invests her life focusing on how to foster learning among her students. She teaches biotechnology at Kendriya Vidyalaya, IIT Guwahati, Assam. Remya has received numerous distinctive recognitions, including a Fulbright Distinguished Award in Teaching in 2014, an Innovation Award for Science Teaching, and the National Teacher Award, the highest award for a teacher in India, for her holistic contributions to the community. She can be reached at riyer1975@gmail.com.

DOI: 10.4324/9781003213840-7

Prologue

Nostalgia is caressing me while memories and words are growing upon me like spring buds and leaves on a tree as I key in these words. Life does not follow any regular symmetry, neither do pedagogical interventions; both involve jump-cuts, zoom-ins, and fade-outs. Therefore, this write-up presents a mosaic of evolving forms and dissolving patterns centered on my life as a practicing teacher.

Silver Lining

On a warm July day in 2004, my aims and desires stretched taut with the clouds across the overcast sky. On that day, I left Cleveland, Ohio, for good to socially settle back in my motherland India. Post my master of science degree in biochemical research at Case Western Reserve University (CWRU), I was expecting to enrol in the doctoral program, when the call came from home—a call so loud and clear that it could not be declined. At the time, I wanted to be a researcher, thanks to some wonderful professors at CWRU.

Reaching India, I found myself lonely in the crowd. Searching avidly to be a researcher, I began to look for positions in different higher education institutions. I knocked on many a door. Unfortunately, such knocks, some louder than others, and frustrating years of desperate searching, proved in vain.

Two years went by. Nothing was falling into place; instead, I was falling into pieces. Life was a thin stream meandering across a desert of hopelessness. My self-confidence was plummeting rapidly, and I knew it was time to do something significant in my life. It was at this time that the fifth edition of Gary A. Davis's (2004) *Creativity Is Forever* came to my hands. This brilliant volume made me realize that the glorious world of creativity is not restricted to a researcher but stretched to humanity at large. How about teaching creatively to children; after all, they are the nation-makers, I thought. In 2006, I applied for the position of a teacher, and was promptly offered a full-time teaching position in a private school in Assam, a state in the Northeast region of India.

Don't Teach

In school, I was assigned to teach biotechnology in Standards XI and XII and biology in Standards IX and X. That would be great, I thought. Here I was, endowed with an MS from the United States and was about to teach well-groomed children hailing from affluent families in the age group of 15 to 18 years. I enjoyed instilling these subjects in the students, taking them to laboratories for experimentation and tinkering and also demonstrating well-known, conceptually rich experiments. Through these innovative teaching practices, highly engaging curricula were unfolding in their minds as a glittering panorama of knowledge; or so I thought.

My teaching bubble was soon to burst. It was six months since the beginning of my tenure at this school, and my students were facing the annual high-stakes exams. Unfortunately, they did not perform very well in the subjects taught by me.

The very next morning, I found myself standing in the principal's room. He was a kind, good-natured man who knew how to bring the best out of the teachers. He exhorted me, "Don't teach lessons; transact." A teacher should not teach! Seeing my disbelieving gaze, and possibly realizing I was a greenhorn with potential, he advised that I must join an in-service teacher training program at Guwahati University, Assam. A yearlong stint at the college made me realize what the wise man had meant.

Riding the Ridges

While studying for a bachelor's degree in education, I realized that there were myriad approaches, methods, and strategies that need to be selected for each class. That year I imbibed different methods of child-centric education. I realized that innovative pedagogy holds an ocean of possibilities for all my students. However, I needed to engage in rigorous study to assimilate all this knowledge and innovative pedagogical approaches and then practice many of them with my students.

I began to involve students in the teaching-learning process and guide them in hands-on experiential learning. In the process, the students began to perform much better while learning more joyously than the previous group I taught. Naturally, I felt a little downcast for my first batch of students who I had somewhat ineptly attempted to teach. The existentialist lament "What's done cannot be undone" struck me to the quick.

To improve myself as a teacher, so that the streak of sadness does not so burden me again, I began attending teacher training programs. During the course of those sessions, I had the opportunity of interacting with other teachers and discuss problems and strategies for negotiating them in classrooms. Towards the end of the first decade of the 21st century, I secured a position in Guwahati as a teacher in Kendriya Vidyalaya; an acclaimed group of schools run by the Government of India.

Beyond the Classroom

This government school presented a different student demography from the earlier one. Some students were first-generation learners, some came from broken homes, and some had learning disabilities. By then, I had come to know the ways of creating an effective, engaging, and inviting learning atmosphere where learners feel welcome with a sense of belonging. I took students out into the wider world where the real action happens to make them better comprehend some of the concepts laid out in their textbooks. For instance, in 2011–2012, when fluoride contamination of water was becoming a major problem in Guwahati, I led the students in finding a solution.

From such enriching experiences, I came to realize that going beyond textbooks and applying classroom learning in real-life situations highly motivate and help students imbibe their learnings deeper. As part of this enriching learning process, the kids presented their findings at the National Children Science Congress. As a corollary of mentoring students to negotiate real-life problems, I was honoured with the CV Raman Science Teacher Award in 2013 instituted by the Department of Science & Technology, Government of India.

Sun on the Snow

The following year, my teaching career took another turn in a most positive direction and one which I am still tapping into for pedagogical insights and novel instructional approaches. It was in August 2014 that I received the Fulbright Distinguished Teacher Award in the United States and I was off to travel to Bloomington, Indiana, and hang out with and learn from many great minds at Indiana University.

Once there, I enrolled in a semester-long non-credit course. This was where I learned the ways of integrating technology into the learning process. Particularly, the use of *TubeChop* came in very handy, as did hands-on, practical experiences in cooperative and collaborative learning. Some four months later, on a cold December afternoon with the sun's rays seeming more resplendent on the snow, I took the return flight to India.

Fortunately, this time I got on that plane with much more enthusiasm than I had when I left Cleveland a decade earlier. I now had an arsenal of creative teaching approaches and was brimming with confidence in how I could use them effectively. Further fuelling those positive emotions, I knew I had a permanent teaching position that would provide ample scope to put my learning into practice. I resumed my position as a full-time teacher and was delighted to observe that students responded to my new ideas and approaches in a most positive way. In fact, their individual learning curves showed clear upward trends, and their achievements of learning outcomes provided me with profound satisfaction. The principal of my former school would have felt validated.

In 2018, I received the Kendriya Vidyalaya Sangathan National Incentive Award for my contribution to holistic learning. The apogee of my academic journey occurred in 2019, with the President of India conferring on me the country's highest award for teachers (i.e., the National Award to Teachers) for my contribution to the community. Later in 2020, being agile and adaptive to ecosystem changes, I upcycled the challenges posed by the adversity of the pandemic into unique opportunities and seamlessly integrated technology into learning. Why not? Integrating technology was no longer considered an add-on but an essential during COVID-19. I did much more than simply teaching the subjects. I used this online and offline blended medium to conduct "Mindfulness" sessions and "Tapping Happiness in Daily Life" sessions for students. These sessions helped them to cope up with the stressful situations that emerged in their lives during the pandemic times.

Ad Meliora

Even after all these years of teaching, when I see the students standing in queues for prayers every morning, I feel blessed at the prospect of positively touching their lives one more time, thereby contributing to the wellness of the planet in my own little ways. It is this sense of satisfaction that, as a joyful teacher, I am instrumental in making the world a little happier and a more beautiful place, and that keeps me going. Subtle disillusions, little niggling worries, and minor physical debilities that stalk human existence are glossed over when I see the bright, wonder-waiting eyes of the children. The immense happiness to find joy in others' happiness is a privilege that is bestowed on teachers everywhere. Words fail me when attempting to express my feelings when I observe the boundless happiness of my students as they achieve positive learning outcomes.

I direct every ounce of my energy into making students autonomous learners. With time, I hope to right-size my identity as a teacher to a vanishing yet vibrant dot. I believe that a teachers' greatest success lies in awakening the inner potentialities in students to become self-learners. With this happy realization, it has dawned on me that a teacher's path to immortality is ensconced in the apparent paradox of eschewing teaching and becoming a co-learner with the students. I grow together with my students every day, one class at a time. The ever-present pointing of my personal compass towards "growth" is the quintessence, the raison d'être, of being a teacher.

Suggestions

From my experience, I think the following cues may help teachers:

- Change is the only constant, and therefore, teachers must have eclectic mindsets to adopt and adapt to changes.
- Realize that there are no good learners or bad learners. They all are learners. As a practitioner of loving kindness, every teacher needs to look deeper into the minds of non-conforming students and help them unravel the dormant goodness in them.
- Help students to learn to live in the moment. Introduce and inculcate mindfulness in every facet of life, not only the classroom transactions but also the mundane daily activities.
- Teach students to self-love and believe that each one of them is unique and does matter a great deal.

- Someone somewhere is doing some work that may be helpful and supportive in improving yourself. Unleash the potential of networking. At times, boldly reach out and make important new contacts.

Reflection Questions

1. How does a teacher adapt classroom practices given widely divergent student demographics? What types of demographic changes and challenges are you facing now or have you encountered in the past? What are your response algorithms?
2. What modes of assessment are possible in remote teaching? What types of formative and summative assessments are plausible when remote teaching? How can these forms of assessment move schools toward active and engaging learning environments and away from excessive reliance on high-stakes exams?
3. Why does it sometimes become necessary to reorient global best practices of teaching? Have you ever discarded any of your successful teaching approaches due to changes in curriculum, student backgrounds, or expectations of your department? If so, it may be time to delve deep into your philosophy of teaching and overall methods and then reflect on ways to redesign these approaches. What did you come up with?

7

FROM ANCIENT HISTORY TO CURRENT PRACTICE

Experimenting With the Pedagogical Tools for Teacher Creativity and Student Empowerment

Nourit Ben David Erez

Nourit Ben David Erez is an English teacher, teachers' counselor, and lecturer for disabled and cognitively challenged students in southern Israel. She is from Kibbutz Kfar Menachem and teaches at Alumim Special Education School for children with slight and moderate cognitive developmental delay. Nourit has given lectures on teaching students with learning differences in Morocco, Israel, and the United States. She can be contacted at nouritbde01@gmail.com.

DOI: 10.4324/9781003213840-8

Introduction

The ensuing chapter documents how a dream for "A Web-Based English as a Foreign Language Course for Students with Learning Disabilities" turned from science fiction to a reality and then a necessity.

Once upon a time, I was a novice English teacher. As customary in our schools, I was given the most difficult classes to teach. That was my initiation; these classes often include students who compete with each other over who is able to throw the chairs the farthest. The more experienced I became, the more I understood their anger and how to try to channel it to learning. Some of them came from dysfunctional homes, some had undiagnosed learning difficulties and, sadly, some had to try and cope with both.

In 2010, I engaged in an online course at the University of Oregon, which opened my eyes to the wonders of teaching with technology. Previously, I used technology as much as I could with the limited facilities (and staff cooperation) available where I taught.

One sunny day, my husband was reading the local newspaper and spotted a Fulbright Distinguished Awards in Teaching (DAT) ad, calling for teachers' proposals to receive a scholarship grant. He called me over and exclaimed, "This is for you. This is going to help you fulfill your dream. Go for it!"

This meant going to the United States for a few months, so my immediate reaction was, "Do you have a mistress? You want some time off?" We laughed and discussed it further. Our youngest boy was 16, and it would not be too hard for my children to be separated from me for a few months (maybe even good?!).

So I did go for it! And, as you will see from this story, I made the right decision.

There were two interesting courses I took during my stay at Indiana University. One was with young teachers and Professor Martha Nyikos in language education, who walked us through the necessities of novice teachers in the United States and in general. The other course was more connected to the specific model I was writing, "A Web-Based EFL (English as a foreign language) Course for Students with Learning Disabilities." In the latter course, we learned many innovative techniques and platforms with which we could teach our students and enhance the level of interactivity, collaboration, and engagement; especially in terms of critical and creative thinking. It was there that I first heard of Zoom!

Don't get me wrong, I did connect with friends and family through Skype or Messenger, but that was about it.

Then reality sat in. I came back to my home country (Israel) full of energy. I desperately wanted to implement what I came up with. I met with officials at the Ministry of Education who told me that my many innovative pedagogical ideas were interesting, but "we don't have the funds to invest in such a pilot." In other words—forget it. Setting up a system of remote and face-to-face learning (what, today, we call hybrid learning) is science fiction and we have more important things to invest in, such as math.

It was a setback which felt major at the time.

A Silent Decision

It did not take long to make a personal and silent decision; I would work in four different but parallel ways. First, I would teach private lessons, using what I learned during my Fulbright experience and continued to learn on my own. Second, I would go back to teach at school, but this time I will follow my heart and start teaching English at a special education school (students with slight to moderate cognitive developmental delay plus learning differences). Third, I would accept the offer to be a counselor for English teachers in elementary schools in my district. Fourth, and finally, I would exercise my risk muscle and develop a website where I can upload materials and refer my students to other sites where they can find suitable materials for their needs.

It is not so easy to go against the tide, but I used all four platforms to advocate the use of digital teaching, by incorporating WhatsApp for recordings and text messaging (for speaking and writing), video creations (for speaking), online games (for reading, listening, and writing) and apps that can bridge gaps for students with learning disabilities such as Read Aloud for Chrome, or Immersive Reader.

In my own school, I did manage to convince some parents to let their children learn with me through WhatsApp, for example, and use their phone as a learning tool and resource. At school, I did not encounter any objection to teach with phones. My students downloaded apps and learned how to use Google Translate. The ones who did not have phones either used mine or formed teams with their peers.

As a counselor, I was responsible for guiding English teachers in eight schools (now, long distance, it is 12). It was a fabulous opportunity to come with a toolkit that is equipped with more diverse tools. I told everyone who was willing to listen (or had to because I was his or her counselor) that they needed to start using models like TEC-VARIETY (see free book, Bonk & Khoo, 2014; http://tec-variety.com/) in order to cater to more students' abilities, knowledge, levels, learning types and, especially, learning differences.

And then COVID-19 came upon us and what was previously in the realm of science fiction became a reality. I am reluctant to say that it was a blessing in disguise. However, addressing this specific topic—English as a foreign language for students with learning disabilities—I believe it was.

My teacher colleagues and I were faced with the reality that our previous pedagogical practices needed to radically change. We needed to find innovative, out of the box, ways to be able to teach effectively.

Suddenly, Zoom is a household name. It is a lifeline for a major part of humanity.

As a teacher, I love to meet my students, whether it be face-to-face or online. In the era we live in, I am delighted to see students any time (when and if they bother to open the camera). I do my best to keep in touch when needed and show them that I care. I also enjoy teaching something new and then sending them to breakout rooms for more attention or group work.

We are almost a year into this new style of teaching and learning, and we still do not have all the answers, and perhaps never will. It is clear that technology is a key factor in keeping in touch and teaching at least part of the curriculum. Many educators would argue it is a bad thing to encourage seclusion and promote the use of screens; they may, in fact, consider it to be permanently damaging. I would argue that everything needs some balance.

The Positives

There are many positive things that have happened due to the pandemic. I list a few next.

1. With different technology tools, I discovered that we teachers could keep in touch with our students and professional colleagues and in a manner that is better than a phone conversation or a written message.
2. I also found out that Israeli teachers all around the country cooperate more than before by using educational technology. Instead of "Knowledge is Power" and, therefore, I/we need to keep our ideas and lesson plans to ourselves, it turned into "Sharing is Caring." There are drives, learning portals, and websites that are exploding with useful content materials where teachers can browse, explore, copy, and adjust to their classes.
3. Teachers and students began to bridge the technological gap between them. I have been telling the teachers I counsel that it only seems like they know less than their students. Children know how to play in the virtual world but are less informed of how to learn there. Israeli teachers I work with realize that they need to teach their pupils how to use these learning platforms.
4. Teachers have to go the extra mile to engage the learners. They have to come up with engaging synchronous and asynchronous tasks. Such engagement can be accomplished by involving their students in creating lesson plans and adjusting them to the different interests and common grounds they can find between all participants (as described in the "TEC-VARIETY" framework, mentioned earlier).
5. As a result of COVID-related teaching practices, there is now more leeway in the ways with which the teachers can teach. Teachers feel they can use a variety of materials and not just books. They are empowered to be creative.

Closing the Circle

Now, the circle is closing. I recently took part in a think-tank, assembled by the Israeli Ministry's Inspectorate. The mission of this think-tank was to come up with a model that enabled teachers to teach several pods of students at the same time from a distance!

The model that came out was very similar to the one I wrote about during my Fulbright experience—blended teaching (i.e., remote and face-to-face), flipped classroom, and loads of technology variety at the ready.

As C. P. Cavafy (1975, 1992) stated in the poem "Ithaka," the longer the journey, the wealthier we get. There is no hurry to get to the destination, as my students and I gain so much from what we learn on the road together.

It is still an ongoing journey. I hope we will all keep learning and preserving the advantages of hybrid learning, for the sake of our students.

Reflection Questions

1. Why do you suppose students reacted the way they did in this story?
2. What motivates the students in this particular class at this particular time? What unique things come to mind?
3. How do you take the previous insights and turn them into an inclusive lesson plan?
4. How and what do you have to do to stay up to date with the latest educational technology innovations that can help your students learn and become capable and contributing citizens in the future?

SECTION 2

Innovative Education

The second section of this book is likely something anyone reading this book is curious about. As detailed in the chapters of this section, innovative education is seen in youth building of urban concept farms, educational programs for incarcerated people in corrections facilities, community health projects, and teacher professional development. And there are likely thousands of such educational innovations happening around the world right now. Suffice to say, it will be worthwhile to take a peek at all five chapters in Section 2.

Chapter 8 is the first in this section on innovative education. It features a reflective piece from Shengnan (Penny) Ma who has recently taught in international schools in Bangkok, Hong Kong, and Beijing. Penny speaks for all educators when she says that teaching and learning is extremely difficult during a pandemic. As she points out, fostering creativity in learning is potentially even tougher for educators at this moment. However, we have all witnessed many successful and innovative teachers who have thrived during this challenging time.

In this chapter, Penny takes a close look at one such success. Specially, she highlights Chris Gadbury to figure out how this visual arts teacher keeps inventing such high levels of creativity within himself and how he finds creativity in his life, and then integrates creativity and creative activities into his teaching and learning with his students. Penny offers us a hopeful message by arguing that you cannot use up the creative juices and sparks within you; instead, she argues that the more creativity you use, the more you will eventually have.

In Chapter 9, Narayani Singh documents an example of project-based learning (PBL) with the Community Health and Environment initiative in elementary school classes in India. Worth noting, this amazing learning story occurred in a school located in the tribal belt in India. The problem that the students addressed was related to an outbreak of malaria and some waterborne diseases. As Narayani

DOI: 10.4324/9781003213840-9

mentions, the project provided students with a platform for exploration where they could observe health problems and identify their causes, find solutions, and suggest preventive measures to affected people. Of course, avoiding proper care of our environment ultimately will cause havoc to mankind. These young people learned that keeping the surroundings neat, clean, and green offers better health for everyone. Solid waste management and facilitating potable water are among the key duties of local authorities for keeping the community in good health. And community safe practices keep many diseases away.

The adopted instructional approach Narayani employed combined cooperative and collaborative learning. She effectively used this PBL activity to nurture curiosity, excitement, and confidence among the learners. In effect, it was a prime example of children ought to be in control of their own learning, deciding for themselves what they want to learn and how they want to learn it.

Chapter 10 builds on this project-based learning theme. Science leader Simon McMillan brilliantly discusses his Urban Concept Farm established at Kaikorai Valley College, which enrolls Year 7 to Year 13 students in the city of Dunedin, New Zealand. In this chapter, Simon details the establishment of the Urban Farm and reflects on how this innovative learning program helps students grasp sustainable agriculture concepts. At the same time, Simon ponders how such activities have impacted his personal development as an educator. Importantly, he provides the bases for why the Urban Farm has been created. Project-based learning and applied learning in different contexts have resulted in increased student motivation and engagement and, as detailed in this literally ground-breaking chapter, they also provide the chance for metacognitive experiences to flourish. Moreover, the success of the Urban Farm space underscores the need to challenge how learning traditionally happens in schools.

In Chapter 11, Mohana Ratnam from the Singapore Ministry of Education focuses on a better understanding of educator practices in developing high-performance teachers. Mohana rightfully suggests that teachers can be empowered to become transformational leaders through engaging in reflective conversations that will help them navigate difficult dialogue with students. Readers will join Mohana in a reflective process in how we can enable teachers to transform practice to embrace technology and pedagogical strategies that could lead to better learning outcomes for students, especially during such a time as a public health issue like the COVID-19 pandemic where home-based learning has become a norm.

Chapter 12, the final chapter of Section 2, is a powerful story of hope and change. In this chapter, Lynnette Brice discusses the transformational potential of emotions in second-chance learning environments such as a corrections facility in Aotearoa, New Zealand. She explores a pedagogy of emotions where one's emotional experiences are made explicit. Such emotions are potentially transformative in enhancing the educational experiences in second-chance education. Of course, there are deep implications for education policy and practice from this approach. The reflective questions at the end of the chapter come from the pedagogy of emotion "kare ā roto," which Lynnette developed in her doctoral thesis.

The chapters in Section 2 are certainly eye-opening and exciting. As you will quickly find out from reading them, the possibility for momentous impact can be found in each of the five chapters found here.

8

"YOU CAN'T USE UP CREATIVITY— THE MORE YOU USE, THE MORE YOU HAVE"

The Story of Chris Gadbury

Shengnan (Penny) Ma

Shengnan (Penny) Ma is a licensed K-6 elementary educator with a master's in teaching Chinese as a second language as well as a master's in instructional systems technology. Penny also has International Baccalaureate (IB) Primary Years Programme (PYP) experience, an inquiry mindset, and a passion to integrate technology in teaching and learning. Currently, Penny is an innovation coach at

DOI: 10.4324/9781003213840-10

Keystone Academy in Beijing, China. She can be reached at mashengnan11@gmail.com.

The World of Chris Gadbury

Chris Gadbury is a Primary Years Programme (PYP) Art Teacher in Hong Kong with 16 years of teaching experience. He is best known for his quirky art videos on his popular website "ArtLesson.blog" as well as for his PYP posters that are used in International Baccalaureate (IB) schools around the world. Chris is also recognized for his illustrated storybook series, which was the topic of his powerful 2019 TEDx talk, where he explained how he informs students about global issues whilst encouraging them to come up with solutions. Chris has designed resources for organisations such as World's Largest Lesson and Managebac. He is a TeachSDGs Ambassador and has recently been commissioned as a sketchnote artist by the United Nations.

I remember the first time I met Chris. It was in a principal's office back when I worked at an international school in Bangkok in 2019–2020. Actually, it was the poster he designed for the PYP of IB curriculum. I was amazed by Chris's creativity and the approaches he chose to present his understanding of education. I wanted to know more. What made Chris tick? How did those creative ideas begin to flow? How did he get them to persist? This chapter explores some of these questions and more.

The next time I met Chris, it, too, was in a virtual space, and that space was Twitter. It was on Twitter that a smile found its place on my face as I discovered that many educators had retweeted, shared, and celebrated his art lesson ideas during bouts of remote learning brought on by COVID-19. Needless to say, I was also one of the teachers who became inspired by his creations. Creativity has an odd way of emerging through such virtual sharing spaces like Twitter. Soon, I started to create my own illustrations and graphic designs with Chris's instructional videos and blog. They offered me a wondrous opportunity to learn from the master without having to sit in a bolted-down desk or perpetually feeling the constraints of an in-class lesson.

I kept wondering why some educators thrive at such challenging times and most others find themselves in the assorted quagmires of frustration and grief. Throughout the year, I was constantly perplexed by this situation. But then Chris shared his story at a webinar session within an online learning community called Toddle that was developed by experienced IB educators. During that webinar, it was like I was living in the age of enlightenment or perhaps traveling further back and taking a most fortunate seat with a renaissance painter. I quickly grasped quite a few insights with regards to creativity, teaching, and ideas. At the same time, I realized that such insights could help educators, as well as students around the world, understand creativity and how we can benefit from using and enhancing it at this pandemic time and beyond.

We all feel stuck by our limitations as human beings each and every day. However, Chris views his limitations as creative opportunities. He exploited his fear of public speaking as a valuable opportunity to practice and refine his presentation skills by performing stand-up comedy in Hong Kong. As Chris told me:

> *To me, stand-up comedy was a way to overcome a lifelong fear of public speaking. I was simply doing something creative (writing jokes) to dilute the horror of speaking in front of an audience of strangers. I'm not sure there are many similarities between stand-up comedy and teaching other than keeping an audience engaged by making your content relatable. When people come to see comedy, they usually avoid the front row as they would rather be a spectator. It's very different from teaching because the learning part doesn't work unless everyone is actively participating and asking questions.*

Another challenge Chris shared is his inability to copy information from the board fast enough. When he started to draw pictures instead of taking lengthy notes, he found success. For example, he took sketchnotes for the United Nations, and he also designed creative posters for IB schools. Per Chris:

> *As a lifelong learner, it was an invaluable experience watching and listening to global leaders, environmental experts, and heads of industry discussing solutions for some of the biggest challenges our civilization has ever faced. As a sketchnote artist, there was an overwhelming amount of information which meant I had to stay completely focused for hours without interruption. It was vitally important that I made an equal visual representation of everyone's point of view. There was always this feeling that one of these ideas may just change the course of history, so I better draw a really good picture of it.*

Effective teaching is easy but boring when we rely on the same plan every day; so it is for learning when we fail to modify our approach. Chris shared his student-led workshop as a prime example of a way to explain learning something in the funniest way possible could bring unexpected outcomes for learners. In this student-led workshop, students were asked to prepare a 25-minute lesson for teaching any topic or subject that they selected. In so doing, students could gain an authentic experience of the relationship between teaching and learning. This unusual instructional approach also illustrates the robustness of authentic learning experiences in education.

As I stated, Chris and I connected on Twitter during the COVID-19 pandemic. I was not the only one to benefit from Chris's creative outbursts. In fact, Chris shared many fantastic creations with other educators on this social media platform. He believed that sharing our innovative and risk-taking practices with other educators requires extensive courage. Nevertheless, the more that we share, the more we can refine our teaching practices. Chris suggested that educators start a blog, make a podcast, or lead a workshop or webinar to present and share our creative ideas and inspirations with the teaching community. In so doing, educators will also gain a new relationship with creativity through their shared intellectual designs that they previously would not attempt, let alone complete. This change in perception of what creativity is and why it is a vital educational life force is potentially transformative. Give it a try.

Advice and Suggestions

Teaching creativity is not easy, but reading Chris's story provides us a fresh and different perspective on how to be creative and how to make creativity work in our teaching and learning as educators. We need to view our limitations as creative opportunities. We need to think of the funniest, most playful, more provocative possible ways of learning something and then use sharing platforms to get feedback and improve our teaching and learning.

Reflection Questions

1.   How is teaching like stand-up comedy to you? Have you ever tried stand-up comedy or contemplated doing it? If so, what were the results?
2.   Have you ever watched someone perform and make a mental list of the teaching or instructional strategies or principles that he or she is effectively using? If so, what tends to be on that list? How has that list changed over time?
3.   How have you used the visual arts for your teaching or your learning? What is your favorite form of visual expression, and why?
4.   Reflect on and discuss one or two people like Chris whom you have met. What are they like? What makes them creative?

9

COMMUNITY HEALTH AND ENVIRONMENT

A Learning Project From India

Narayani Singh

Narayani Singh blends both conventional methods and technology-aided teaching pedagogy. She has conducted various workshops, seminars, induction programs, and in-service training programs for primary teachers and headmasters. From 2005 to 2008, Narayani served at the Embassy of India School, Moscow. In 2015, she received the Fulbright Distinguished Award in Teaching in the United States to work on tribal education, and in 2016, she was a recipient of the National Award conferred by the President of India. Presently, she volunteers her

DOI: 10.4324/9781003213840-11

services to a local government school in Raipur, Chhattisgarh, India. She can be reached at narayani.singh01@gmail.com.

Introduction

In this chapter, I share my experiences of a learning project taken up by the students of elementary classes under my guidance. This project takes place in Kendriya Vidyalaya Bacheli, Chhattisgarh, India, which is located in a deep tribal belt. To foster learning, I adopted an instructional approach to enhance collaborative and cooperative learning among the students, including community participation. This project set a benchmark for innovative pedagogy.

In an Open House discussion, students from elementary classes talked about the common illnesses spread in the community they live in. Malaria and jaundice were the main ones identified. Due to disease and illness, the attendance of the students at this school was also low. As the coach of the project, I suggested that the students get involved in a project to discover the reasons behind the spread of the common illnesses. The students liked the idea and decided to work on it.

A group of volunteers was formed in no time. They were the students from fourth and fifth grades. The name of the project was finalised as "Community Health and Environment." In effect, this project was focused on knowing that community health depends on the environment. I asked students to recall the lessons learned already in environmental studies. Several ideas surfaced, including that a neat, clean, and green environment ensures good health to the people and creatures that live there. The group also mentioned safe drinking water, management of solid waste, and cleanliness to prevent the breeding of mosquitos and flies. One student floated the proverb that "prevention is better than cure." In effect, this idea was a reflection that the immediate prevention of community health issues can also take care of the environment.

There was much excitement in the air. This student enthusiasm soon elevated to a zenith. Further, the break-ups of different learning segments were decided by the group members themselves. Activities included group discussion, elocution on factors deciding good health, essay writing on the role and responsibilities of people, a community survey on solid waste management, and interviews on preventive measures practised by the government bodies. There was also a demonstration by a guest on safe drinking water and purification. And there was time allocated for the preparation of charts on slogans, posters, and models for the exhibition.

When done, the students finally got to make a presentation to an audience of the entire school as well as guests from the community. They were excited to find suitable videos and images for the project. In total, the duration of the project was three weeks. I obtained permission from the school principal to travel to the community for surveys and interviews while collecting the data required and then drafting the suitable findings in a report.

Survey on Potable Water Practices in the Community

Due to the dangers of jaundice as a waterborne disease, survey participation was enthusiastic. These surveys revealed the following:

1. The educated families in the community use water purifiers for potable water such as aqua guards, water filters, and water dispensers. They are aware of safe practices in this regard. These families are sound in health and encounter less ill-health problems.
2. Families with less education or no education often lack safe drinking water habits. Such families consume water directly from the tap or well. They are generally labourers from lower economic status. Their family members are often affected from health problems such as jaundice and typhoid.

In the awareness campaign, students made the community aware of various important aspects such as boiling water before use and storing water in clean containers. An understanding developed: "Drink water pure, get healthy for sure."

Survey on Solid Waste Management

Students learned about various types of solid wastes while working on the project: residential, institutional, commercial, agricultural, and solid wastes from health care. Solid waste is a major threat to the environment and community health. There is a dire need to manage household hazardous wastes and sewage sludge. Such waste and sludge are to be addressed through prevention from throwing away as garbage; instead these can be reused after treatment or recycling. To help in this recycling effort, employees from municipal corporations go door to door to collect sold waste. A mini truck is used to carry the wastes away to be recycled.

The community survey opened students' eyes when they discovered, in spite of municipal corporation efforts, that solid waste was thrown in the open at some locations. Some places are still experiencing garbage piles thrown in the open, causing the breeding of flies as well as mosquitos. In addition, some street animals are disturbing it. Behind some tea stalls, plastic disposal glasses, cups, and plates are thrown. This situation definitely causes foul smells and is a carrier of many diseases. It reveals the pitiful habits and poor mentality of the consumers.

This situation spurs many questions and concerns. For instance, what can these young people do to improve the situation? What can we all do?

A key life lesson learned was that the environment is everyone's responsibility, not only the government's. Apathy will definitely lead the community towards the many-faceted hazards of ill health. In response, the students created a slogan: "Follow hygiene everywhere; keep ill health not to dare."

Probing Interview Findings

Since malaria's root cause is mosquito bites, a team was working to find ways to keep the community safe from the breeding of mosquitos. An officer from the municipal corporation was invited to the school for a talk. He was interviewed on the activities taken up to fight against the breeding of mosquitos. To quench the inquisitiveness of the students, the officer answered questions related to regular sprays of some chemicals and fogging in the vicinity, the names of the chemicals used in the spray, and how it helps in keeping the insects like flies or mosquitoes away. Other items of interest included the frequency of periodical sprays and the longevity of its effect, fogging and how it works, the expenditure for all these treatments, and any known side effects of this approach on the local residents and the workers who are involved in this task. Still, other questions poured in related to the burning of mosquito repellent and the uses of mosquito nets by individuals at home to combat the mosquito problems.

I arranged a demo of fogging and chemical spray in the garden area in the school for the students. Precautionary measures were taken during the fogging demonstration. Videography of the interview and fogging was also conducted by the students.

The elocution activity was coordinated with the co-curricular activities schedule. The topic for the elocution was "factors deciding good health in the community." The main points of this activity were recorded for possible inclusion in the project summary. Winners of the competition were thrilled to receive an award from the headmaster. In contrast, the other group of students participated in an essay writing activity on the "role and responsibility of the people to keep the environment safe."

A group with talents for drawing and painting prepared slogans and posters. The other group, skilled in craft and dexterity, prepared models for the project. A report related to the learning that occurred due to the project was digitally prepared, including all photos and videos.

The Outcomes of the Project "Community Health and Environment"

1. The existence of a healthy, neat, and clean environment ensures a healthy community;
2. Human beings' unsafe activities pollute the environment and cause ill health;
3. Water, air, and land will get polluted by our unreasonable activities so we should be thoughtful in our actions;
4. The environment wants promises towards proper disposal of solid waste;

5. To live a quality life, we should take care of the community;
6. Practices of taking clean food, safe drinking water, rest, and exercise play a vital role in deciding sound health;
7. Nobody should be allowed to damage the environment;
8. Understanding the true meaning of "Health is wealth."

On the 21st day, an exhibition was organised. Parents, principals, teachers, and renowned educationists from the community were invited. The students explained their journey of learning and explicitly revealed the findings of the project through an exhibition. Indeed, it was a great joyful learning experience for the students. It was a proud and privileged moment for me to receive compliments for the innovative learning approach. Successful completion of the project was celebrated. Certificates were issued to the happy students. Thus, the memorable journey of the learning project ended here with wonderful growth of both cognitive and noncognitive abilities among the students.

Advice and Suggestions

Local government bodies should ensure the availability and supply of safe drinking water to the residents. At the same time, people should also be responsible for the proper utilisation of the resources provided to them. To protect the environment, awareness campaign programs should be arranged from time to time through nongovernmental organisations and local civic bodies. A clean and green environment is essential for a healthy life. Environmental protection and its sustainability should be the responsibility of every citizen. As is often noted, "We do not inherit the Earth from our ancestors; we borrow it from our children."

Reflection Questions

1. Do you think a safe environment and community health can operate side by side? If so, how?
2. What kind of awareness programs would you like to conduct in your community for sound health?
3. Can you suggest some preventive measures to ensure sound health conditions in your locality? How might your students get involved?
4. What might a chart of responsibilities for your local community and government look like in terms of environmental protection? How can students influence them?
5. In what ways do you contribute to protecting your environment?

10

METACOGNITIVE EXPERIENCES ON AN URBAN CONCEPT FARM

Local, Project-Based Learning in Science and Sustainable Agriculture

Simon McMillan

Simon McMillan is Head of Science at Kaikorai Valley College, Dunedin, New Zealand. He completed a PhD in sedimentary geology in 1993. Simon

DOI: 10.4324/9781003213840-12

was a Royal Society of New Zealand Teaching Fellow in 2004, the Sir Peter Blake Environmental Educator in 2008, and a Fulbright Distinguished Awards in Teaching (DAT) recipient in 2016. A full-length amputee since 1979, he is a former disabled swimming world record holder. Simon teaches science, chemistry, sustainability, and classes in learning to learn. He has founded and remains the Head of the Urban Concept Farm initiative at his school. He can be reached at simmysgm@hotmail.com.

Introduction

This is a story about the development of an Urban Concept Farm on the grounds of Kaikorai Valley College, a Years 7 to 13 school on the margins of the small city of Dunedin, located in the South Island of New Zealand. The school includes students from different countries and those with special needs, and these students are both integrated into usual classroom programmes wherever possible.

The Farm is focused on embracing learning innovations to meet the needs of our future world. We challenge mindsets about how education can happen for our young people, and how humans interact with the environment. Our learning is focused on science and technology in sustainable agriculture. However, we also apply a cross-curricula approach wherever possible: current examples are in business, Māori, mathematics, and fabrics and materials technology.

In the Urban Concept Farm project, students are learning through inquiry, and in an applied and collaborative way. At the same time, students are building a deeper understanding of content knowledge, and nurturing their thinking skills, mutual respect, and sense of self-worth. Part of our Farm learning links to others, including strengthening community resilience to grow food, building networking partnerships for mutual support across the education sector, practising foundation skills towards career opportunities, and helping bridge the divide between rural and urban communities.

We also observe that our Farm learning experiences serve the affective needs of students. Meeting those affective needs aids students' engagement and motivation to learn. It also results in enhancements to students' self-regulation of that learning. With authentic learning environments like the Urban Concept Farm, teachers are changing their mindsets of what learning can be like in their subject area, and how to change their professional practice to be much more student centred.

Teacher Development

Studying geology gives you a gift: a deep understanding of time—vast tracts of time. I come back to this thought often as I continue to develop as a teacher and as I progress through life. An understanding of time has helped me locate myself in a continuum that endures. Without a doubt, understanding time underscored for me the preciousness of our Earth.

Further, time has helped me appreciate my fellow man and my students for who they are. Here is how. In the 100 years I might live, the people around me now are, as we say, unique: they share the same location on that continuum—one that won't occur again. On its own, this idea, linked to time, focuses me on the importance of empathy towards others.

Endurance, or if you like, persistence or perseverance, are gifts too. I learned to endure, in a hospital bed for months over four decades ago and through disability ever since. I find endurance goes a long way in learning and in commitment with students. Calvin Coolidge, the 30th president of the United States, offered this take on the topic:

> *Nothing in this world can take the place of persistence. Talent will not; nothing is more common than unsuccessful men with talent. Genius will not; unrewarded genius is almost a proverb. Education will not; the world is full of educated derelicts. Persistence and determination alone are omnipotent. The slogan Press On! has solved and always will solve the problems of the human race.*

I like it. These are words with which I can inspire my students.

Persistence and determination to endure show sincerity through commitment. In education, once you have found your way, persist and persist some more. Multiple wins will accrue for the people around you. However, commitment needs a focus.

By late 2014, I had clocked up 18 years of teaching and six as a head of a department. I could rock up to my next class and deliver an engaging lesson with variety for different learners, focused on key science ideas or exciting trends. I had it all pat with a Plan A. Naturally, I had a Plan B just in case and maybe, on a good day, a somewhat push-the-envelope type of Plan C.

Personally, though, I knew I did not know what I was doing. Oops! How many of my colleagues *really* do? What I mean here is that I did not know how kids learn. And if they are not improving, or don't "get" something, why not and what specifically I could do about it in my teaching?

Luckily, while exploring some professional development opportunities in 2015 with the New Zealand Qualifications Authority (NZQA) for Earth and Space Science Scholarship Exams, I came across a key realisation. As I read model answers from teachers to the questions students were to get, I realised they (the teachers) weren't answering the question. The central issue, confirmed by a NZQA colleague, was that the teachers who were tasked with providing model answers to the examination questions failed to show that *they* could think. I understood, too, that if the teachers did not know how to frame their answers to show thinking, how could they teach the thinking skills required of their students to do the same thing?

Learning Through Teaching Thinking

I find that saying that you teach thinking, or that students need to think to learn, yields an underwhelming response. After all, we all *think*, don't we? Coffee or tea? What investment should I make? Surely, we can do more meaningful activities, experiments, or whatever, than just think about it!

I took my NZQA colleague's advice and explored research on the topic. That research continued and developed at Indiana University in 2016 as part of the Fulbright Distinguished Awards in Teaching Programme. The Fulbright programme promotes empathy and understanding of others too and these dispositions align splendidly with what is desirable in a critical thinker. Listed next are key items that I discovered during my time in the Fulbright programme.

A momentous learning point from this research was that many, many, teachers, schools, and institutions of higher learning that you think should, just plain don't teach students *how* to learn. The prevalent (industrial type) model is as follows: here is the stuff you need to know, you remember it, and give it back to me during the assessment when it's time.

Barrier Riddled Knobbly Knee Educational Syndrome ("knobbly knee" for short) is a condition that stifles the flow of best educational practice—like the importance of teaching thinking for learning—across the different tiers of education. The tiers are known to us all: primary, secondary, tertiary, and governmental. The knobbly part is like a knee-shaped or cul-de-sac area along the pathway between the education tiers. These are areas where information languishes due to barriers of all different kinds.

The "across" in this knobbly knee syndrome are the grey zones of education between the tiers. These are the transition points, above and below which and through them too, that have so many intrinsic barriers that best practice knowledge is constricted and is shared to only a limited extent.

By barriers, I highlight conflicting priorities like research versus teaching at tertiary level, the lack of effective conduits or personnel to recognise and supply that best practice knowledge, or even just the excessive workloads of teachers in schools. I maintain that these barriers are stifling our education systems from delivering quality of learning—of deeper understanding *in* learning—for our students. I also want to emphasise that knobbly knee operates both forwards and backwards through those tiers. It is not a one-way street with the tertiary and governmental tiers holding all the knowledge of what to do and how to go about change.

Truly understanding the barriers faced by educators in these tiers is key to improvement in the quality of learning through effective teaching practice. So is the understanding of those educators as learners, in their classrooms or jobs day after day. Enter that word empathy again, throw in the word endurance again, and weld it together with an explicit method, and you can change teaching practices.

A case in point is the teaching of thinking for learning. I had not heard of the teaching of thinking in all my training, and I certainly did not know explicitly how to teach it. I wondered how many other teacher trainees and experienced teachers had. And yet the benefits to students of teaching them the facets of meta-cognition are well documented and pervasive in terms of achievement. Here we should recognise the differences between the teaching of thinking through meta-cognitive knowledge (i.e., the strategies, plans, and tools for how to approach different tasks for different people), metacognitive skills (i.e., the dispositions like perseverance and reflection and self-regulation of and during learning), and meta-cognitive experiences (i.e., any cognitive experience in which thinking skills are explicitly taught or deliberately nurtured) (see also Zohar & Barzilai, 2015).

There are now many methods to teach thinking or at least aspects of think-ing: through a mix of inquiry, questioning, applied learning, cooperative and collaboratively learning, and/or project-based learning—and there are others. I came across Feuerstein when I returned from my Fulbright experience in the United States. Feuerstein and his colleagues recognised the cognitive functions needed by students for effective learning and thinking. Accordingly, they cre-ated the Feuerstein Instrumental Enrichment (or FIE) programme to explicitly strengthen students' cognitive functions and address their dysfunctions (Feuer-stein, Rand, Hoffman, & Miller, 1980). What stood out for me here was the explicit and socially located pedagogy, linked to resources (the instruments) that teachers could pick up and know that *they were addressing* the different cognitive dysfunctions of their learners.

Even more powerful is the learning that accrues from implementing FIE in your school *for your staff*. At Kaikorai Valley College in 2018, the Science Depart-ment implemented the instrument, "The Organisation of Dots"—a typical first instrument of the FIE (Standard) programme—in four different ability groups at the Year 11 level (i.e., students are typically 15 years of age). The following quote is a typical example of what the staff said about their FIE learning experience. Note that the implementation was bridged to literacy and, particularly, writing in science.

> *I saw great progress in some students' ability to think and write in detail for them-selves. Instead of struggling to construct a single sentence they were able to organise their ideas better and write pages of details instead. I changed how I taught some of my year 7 and 8 tasks considering how much information was detailed in a work-sheet; and took (more) time to read through sheets carefully with students. When I design new worksheets, I have found myself carefully considering how much written instruction is required. How much implied and explicit information is needed.*

Metacognitive Experiences

I work at a school with an outstanding natural environment. We have not only a profusion of green space and wooded areas but also a freshwater stream and tributaries that flow through the school. Our location places us on the urban-rural transition. It is in this space that we have developed an urban farm so that students can learn across many different subject areas in a more applied way. This farm learning space—a classroom without walls or a roof—is both liberating and restful, but also stimulating and challenging. And that is not just for the students but also for the teachers and any welcome guest from day to day.

Two of the key criteria for successful implementation of the Feuerstein Programme are what is called transcendence, and the other is called meaning. These are core criteria for FIE, because they are at the core of all quality learning. Transcendence denotes how a learning experience is linked to other areas and goes beyond the immediate: for instance, how a scientific experiment on chemical reactions links to mathematics, agriculture, or technology.

Meaning is the personal and affective link to the individual's learning experience and the sharing of new learning and thinking to confirm or critique one's thoughts. An example might be how a person relieves their indigestion by neutralising their stomach with an antacid tablet (a chemical reaction), and then shares their remedy with others who may offer an alternative and better one in response. These links need to be made explicit during learning by a skilled mediator; the links bridge the core scientific idea of chemical reactions to broaden the idea's application to the students' real world.

The Urban Farm helps establish transcendence and meaning for effective learning by providing multiple opportunities to learn in an applied context. Some of this involves student projects such as in construction of a barn, lamb hut, chicken coop, or compost bins. Other applied contexts include beekeeping or testing water quality and the infiltration and runoff of water through and across soils. In the latter, for example, we have found that the metacognitive experience (linked to meaning) of boys, in particular, is made explicit when using a water bottle to show farm run-off!

Our experiences of learning (yours and mine) are often our focal point for enduring memories and a deeper understanding of our world. My mother chased me down the street with a wooden spoon in her hand after dawdling on my errand to the shops while she was baking. How embarrassing. To this day, I can visualise it, and I developed a whole new understanding of just how fast she could move and how to avoid being a pain in the future.

We often teach words—science is full of nomenclature (especially from biologists!)—by doing word and meaning link-ups. This is pretty humdrum stuff and, no doubt, for many students who have endured it, an uninspiring experience. This learning is functional: associate the meaning of the word with the pattern of letters that go with it and the sound those letters make as the word is said.

A further thinking step is to make an explicit link from the word and its meaning to a visual metaphor that the student develops to remember both; there is so much more creative thinking involved. A next thinking step is to provide an actual experience whereby the word and its meaning are explicitly used in an applied context; one that gives a chance for the student to cement the learning through action. It is here wherein I so often want my students to be, and this is why the Farm as a learning space has been developed.

Contexts for learning that are project based, applied, and active carry the potential for rich metacognitive experiences that students can link to form connections that develop a greater understanding of the world around them, as well as themselves and other students. Importantly, skilled teacher mediators bring out the thinking aspect of the experience by targeted questioning and raising of "the student's self" and how they are relating to others during the project or activity. The reciprocal learning relationship between the teacher as a mediator and the student is crucial, and is the third core learning criteria of Feuerstein (Feuerstein, 1993, cited in Howie, 2019).

Currently, we are building a fence on our Farm. For it to succeed, students have to work together in a team with an instructor. We have placed fence posts, gates, and wire and learnt a lot along the way. Students tell us they appreciate learning this way because they get to produce a meaningful outcome with their friends and learn new skills along the way—such as tying a wire termination knot on a post. Additionally, working cooperatively develops self-worth and is inclusive and relationship-building in its scope. It also builds empathy and endurance to finish the job.

Our world needs empathy. Learning that brings people together, linked to expert mediation of the metacognition taking place behind the learning, builds awareness of one's own thinking and when to call it to action. In effect, such mediation helps provide the scene for metacognition to flourish. Go on. Have a go. May you fashion your own Urban Concept Farm.

Reflection Questions

1. Do you teach to build knowledge in, or understanding of, your subject? If you do, what is your plan, framework, or overriding goal?
2. How do you teach thinking?
3. Do you know what cognitive functions your students are strongest/weakest in? How do you address or can you address their misconceptions?
4. How will you challenge and reinvigorate your teaching practice over the course of your career?
5. If not a Farm space or concept, what other projects or activities could you connect the teaching of thinking to at your school? And how would you link such projects together?

11

EMPOWERING TEACHERS TO BECOME TRANSFORMATIONAL LEADERS THROUGH REFLECTIVE CONVERSATIONS

A School-Based Inquiry and a Professional Development Project

Mohana Ratnam

Mohana Ratnam has been a secondary school teacher in Singapore for over three decades. She is interested in character and citizenship education,

DOI: 10.4324/9781003213840-13

pedagogical content knowledge, and the professional development of teachers. As a Fulbright teacher, she is an advocate for creating caring and enabling school environments that allow for the hearing of students' voices. Mohana received the President's Award for Teachers as well as the National Day Commendation Award in 2010 for her contribution towards student development. She can be reached at Mohanaratnam52@gmail.com.

My Fulbright Journey

It was August 9, 2014, when I left Singapore on a Fulbright Teaching Scholarship to the United States. I remember that day clearly as it was also Singapore's National Day. Never in my wildest dream did I imagine I will make a trip to the United States, let alone on a prestigious Fulbright Scholarship! Just when I thought I had reached the pinnacle in my teaching career, having received the President's Award for Teachers in 2010, I found myself fortunate to be climbing up to and then gazing out with eternal gratitude from another peak of excellence.

I remember very vividly writing down what I wish to do in the four months that I would be in the United States. It was an opportunity to meet great minds and observe exemplary works in meeting the needs of students; specifically, the underserved. Most of all, it was a unique chance to work on a project that would impact schools back in Singapore. I wanted to be able to empower teachers to see things from different perspectives on issues beyond simply teaching the text. Instead, I resonated with ideas related to democratic citizenship from international perspectives. I wanted to find ways to help teachers to begin thinking about ways to create a caring and enabling learning environment that would encourage student voices. In effect, I longed to create timely and meaningful opportunities for students to hear different viewpoints, form and reform their own perspectives, and develop pro-social skills in the process.

According to a Pew Research Center (2014) study, Singapore is the most religiously diverse country in the world. In a country that is diverse in the makeup of its people, I strongly believe in the need to engage students in discussions of issues that are current, relevant, and offer multiple perspectives. I want my students to be comfortable to hear perspectives that sometimes can be different and uncomfortable. Facilitating multiple perspectives that sometimes can be sensitive and contentious has always been on the top of the list of professional development needs of teachers in Singapore.

How can teachers build the capacity to be confident and competent to allow for these discussions to happen in the classroom? If teachers fail to facilitate such conversations in their classrooms, they will likely emerge somewhere else. Perhaps most notably, many perspectives are being shared in social media. Accessibility to information, be it true or fake, is within reach to all. How can teachers build in students' social-emotional competencies such as being self-aware to help students to learn the skills of discernment? How can teachers help students to be open to different perspectives and yet be discerning to know what is right and true? These were some of the many questions that I had at the beginning of my Fulbright journey in the United States.

When on my Fulbright adventure, I could not have been in a better place to find the inspiration as well as the resources for helping teachers facilitate such classroom conversations. The experiences and knowledge that I gained from my classes at Indiana University (IU) provided me with both the theoretical under-pinnings as well as practical ideas on how to create conditions within which to motivate students to learn. Books such as *Adding Some TEC-VARIETY* pro-vided more than 100 activities for motivating and retaining learners online that are equally applicable in face-to-face settings. That particular book and all my experiences at IU were a treasure trove of ideas that I longed to share with my colleagues in Singapore.

Project Goal

My capstone project was specifically a school site-based inquiry focused on a bet-ter understanding of educator practice in developing high-performance teachers. At the same time, it was also a professional development project that was focused on designing materials and activities for a professional development workshop intended for school leaders and heads of departments at both the school and cluster level back in Singapore. In particular, in this capstone project, I crafted a list of reflective questions to guide schools leaders and heads of departments in making work review sessions with their teachers meaningful and purposeful so as to develop high-performance teachers who could lead, care, and inspire students toward the outer edges of learning achievement.

Then-Minister for Education Heng Swee Keat's speech at the 2014 MOE Workplan Seminar emphasized the need for every teacher to be a caring educator who can demonstrate four key beliefs:

1. You believe in your students;
2. You believe in yourself, including a belief that you can do better, that you can keep on honing your craft, and that you will continue to learn and grow personally and professionally;
3. You believe in one another, which includes a sense of caring and dedication to one another;
4. You believe in being part of something larger.

The report from the MOE also focused on the challenges that the teachers would need to navigate given the changing landscape. It detailed the difficult dialogue that the teachers would need to engage with students and parents. The following were some of the challenges highlighted in that report:

- Our students are changing. Primary 5 pupils today are different from Primary 5 pupils just five years ago. They are more precocious, more restless, and more vocal.
- The parents in our community that we are interacting with are also changing. They have different expectations.
- The content of the subjects that we are teaching is constantly changing with new discoveries and new knowledge.
- Teaching is also changing. As teachers learn more about how students learn, teaching pedagogy may improve.
- Demands in the future for our young people are changing with new jobs, new ways of working, new technologies, and new countries in which they will have to go live and work.

All these challenges and changes point to the need to engage teachers in professional dialogue to hone their craft for better teaching and learning. School leaders and heads of departments in Singapore often engage teachers in professional dialogue during work review sessions and pre- and post-classroom observations. Naturally, it is crucial that such dialogues are seen to be developmental in nature and not judgmental.

The effectiveness of the planning, coaching, and evaluation process of a teacher is highly dependent on the reporting officers' experiences and expertise in facilitating quality conversations. Although supervisory conversations lie at the heart of managerial work, the conversation structures used for performance management can vary with the coaching and mentoring styles of the reporting officers.

Most supervisory conversations tend to be directive in nature. Unfortunately, such conversations tend to foster negative results and create ineffective school culture to support quality relationships. It is possible to use positive language to communicate a specific, intentional goal or a standard to be met while affirming efforts and skills. Conversations that focus on positive language provide opportunities for reflective thinking, the generation of solutions, and relationship building between supervisors and supervisees. With the view that commitment is closely connected to the teachers' work performance and their own practice in influencing students' achievement, the coaching and mentoring processes taken by supervisors to promote high self-efficacy in teachers are crucial.

Key Outcomes

Among my goals was to build a training program for school leaders and heads of departments that focuses on engaging teachers in reflective conversations that will help them navigate difficult dialogues that may arise with students and parents. I also wanted such leaders to embrace technology and pedagogical strategies that could lead to better learning outcomes. I elevated my goals even higher as I hoped that this program could result in caring and transformational teacher leaders, which is one of the five teacher outcomes reflected in the Singapore teacher growth model.

Excited from the wealth of knowledge I had gained as well as the rich experiences from the many conversations I had with both teachers and supervisors from IU, I returned to my school, eager to promote the use of technology to enhance discussions in the classroom and expand physical classroom boundaries to include virtual spaces. During this time, I was grappling with what an expanded classroom might effectively look like in Singapore as I trained teachers to take advantage of technology-enhanced pedagogical opportunities. I recognized that to allow for transformative practices in the classroom, I could do this only through engaging teachers and school leaders. As part of these efforts, I continued sharing my Fulbright project at multiple conferences as well as during Network Learning meetings on how we can empower teachers to create conditions in the classroom for students to flourish.

It is amazing how much learning environments have changed in just the past seven years since I came back from the United States. Though there were pockets of innovative educational technology use in Singapore schools in the past, extensive use was slow to take off. Of course, COVID-19 has changed the way we teach today. Life in a pandemic has revolutionized education worldwide. Educational institutions, from preschools through to universities, have experienced sudden and unprecedented disruption worldwide. In Singapore, educators, now forced to teach online, have experienced a steep learning curve in which they often find themselves grappling with the task of editing videos and conducting lessons through digital platforms without the familiarity of face-to-face student contact and interaction. Singaporean educators now need to rise to the challenge to find fresh ways to spark intense periods of creativity and self-expression, opportunities for interest-driven student learning where learners are allowed to pursue their passions, and other innovative ways to heighten learning.

During the pandemic, videoconferencing tools and virtual learning environments became the new norm to ensure the continuity of learning. In 2020, the MOE launched the National Digital Literacy Programme (NDLP) for schools to help students strengthen their digital literacy. One of the components of the NDLP is the introduction of the Personalised Digital Learning Programme for all secondary school students, whereby the goal was for every secondary school student to own a school-prescribed personal learning device (PLD) by the end of 2021.

Such a PLD will truly transform the learning environment as it allows teachers and students to harness technology for greater effectiveness in teaching and learning. The use of personal learning devices for teaching and learning will support the development of digital literacies in our students. Not surprisingly, such digital literacy was one of skills reflected in the 21st Century Competency Framework; the others being civic literacy, global awareness, and cross-cultural skills. While there were systems put in place to bring technology into the classrooms in the NDLP, there was unevenness in the way it was being used in the classroom. To be effective, it required teachers to be pedagogically confident and competent so that students experience meaningful learning in the classroom and beyond.

As I reflect on my professional journey, my capstone project in the Fulbright program back in 2014 provided the much-needed professional development for teachers to engage in reflective conversations to think about where they are now, where they want to be, and how to get there. My goal is to be able to conduct professional development courses that invite educators to redesign their current learning environments to allow for multiple perspectives to be heard and valued not only within the classroom but also beyond. By developing globally networked learning environments (GNLE), educators can promote intercultural competence, experiential learning, and 21st-century skills in character and citizenship education through technology and virtual exchange. I hope to fashion GNLEs one school at a time by creating a critical mass of teachers who are creative, confident, and competent to facilitate rich and engaging classroom discussions as well as discussions outside the classroom that push student thinking to be more socially, culturally, and interpersonally aware.

By sharing with you my story, I could reflect on this six-year journey. The most important lesson I have learned thus far is that there are nuances, caveats, and ever-present rethinking of one's pedagogy in the art of learning; clearly, we educators need to constantly engage in unlearning and relearning knowledge.

Reflecting on the core knowledge gained during this journey, I have learnt to recognize that what got me here will not get me there. I realize that I need to find new ways to engage learners and arouse minds to life; hence, being current and relevant as an educator is vital for me to make an impact in the education world. I also need to continually find new ways to engage teachers in reflective conversations on how we can continue to refine and improve our craft. The educational landscape has most definitely changed in Singapore and around the planet. I beg anyone reading this chapter to ponder how, as transformational leaders in education, we can find ways to create learning environments that support thinking while allowing learner autonomy, inquisitiveness, and interpersonal relationships to flourish.

Reflection Questions

1. How can you capitalize on the affordances of technology to allow for student voices to be heard and felt?

2. What pedagogical practices can you apply in the classroom for diverse views to be listened to and respected, especially on issues that can be sensitive and contentious?
3. How can you create a caring and enabling school environment that allows students to flourish and find success in their intellectual pursuits and curiosities?
4. What opportunities can you create for yourself to engage in continual professional dialogues to talk about your personal beliefs regarding present day issues and seek congruence with professional and national positions?
5. What self-work needs to be done to continue to remain current and relevant in this changing landscape?

12

"POIPOIA TE KAKANO KIA PUAWAI" (NURTURE THE SEED AND IT WILL BLOSSOM)

Affective Spaces in Education—Prison and Beyond

Lynnette Brice

Lynnette (Lynne) Brice received her doctorate in education in 2020 from the University of Canterbury. She is currently Manager, Learner Engagement and Success Services at Open Polytechnic of New Zealand. Lynne is a passionate and scholarly informed advocate for second-chance or disadvantaged learners. Her expertise combines the use of data analytics with positive interventions that impact student success. Previously, Lynnette worked as Director of Karanga Mai Teen Parent College, which won the Prime-Minister's Excellence in Education Focus prize in 2016. In 2015, Lynnette received the Fulbright Distinguished Award in Teaching to study in the United States. Lynne's recent research into the

DOI: 10.4324/9781003213840-14

impact of emotions in second-chance teaching and learning breaks new ground in this field. She can be reached at lynnettepbrice@gmail.com.

Introduction

At the gatehouse, the guard is surly and slow to admit us, much vigorous typing is done on a keyboard we can't see as we stand outside the closed window, slotting our IDs into the thin drawer that slides backwards and forwards below the partition. Finally, after stripping off shoes and belts, we are admitted. We follow the Principal Advisor of Rehabilitation and Learning down a long series of prison corridors to a windowless room where three volunteers and three staff are waiting to be instructed. They look up, stiff and silent, wary.

We are here to introduce the distance learning materials and explain how these volunteers and staff might support prison learners in their studies. We begin with introductions. One man is retired now. "I used to be a scientist," he tells us. "I'm here because I feel I had a very privileged life, and I want to give something back." Another, red-faced and handle-bar moustachioed, has been a farmer, he is anxious, worried that he will be out of his depth, not having had a very comprehensive education himself. The third volunteer is a woman of Middle Eastern descent who explains that she is doing voluntary work while she finishes her social work degree. Then there is the staff; resistance is evident in closed faces and tightly folded arms—my project is additional work for them when they haven't got enough time already. I smile. Not surprisingly, they don't.

I begin the workshop; it's the same workshop I have given many times, teaching staff and volunteers about the programmes of learning designed to build skills in literacy and numeracy and in social and emotional awareness. Each time I will tell a different story, sharing narratives from other prisons—stories of tutors or prisoners and their learning experiences.

Today, I talk about the learner who left school at the age of 12 because of the war in his own country. Now, at 54 and in prison in New Zealand, he is having his first educational experience since then. I talk about how seriously he takes it, how he savors every module, how he builds a rich glossary from every new word he encounters, how he takes each piece of information, each new idea or concept, and mulls it over—chewing it thoroughly before swallowing—asking questions, challenging answers, digesting, and then writing thoughtful, deeply perceptive responses to every task. I tell them about his advice to other learners: "When you do this study—do it well—give it everything you have got."

As I tell the story, I can feel the volunteers and staff relax. I see their arms unfold and feel their anxiety ease as they smile now, warming to this shared purpose. Together, we bring many elements to this assemblage; this foundation education in corrections facilities; this thing we are doing. Cheerfully now, we begin our work.

This story is four years on from my time as a Fulbrighter at Indiana University; indeed, it hard to believe that four years have elapsed since taking the pivotal course "Instructional Strategies for Thinking, Collaboration, and Motivation." I did not know at the time that I signed up for learning about how to develop learning environments that both stimulate critical thinking and creativity and promote cooperative learning and motivation that I would take that learning into some of the most challenging learning environments imaginable: prisons.

Here's the challenge: how can you develop a rich learning environment when you have no control over that environment? How do you stimulate critical thinking and creativity in a grey, windowless room? How do you promote cooperative learning among hardened rivals? From my experience in this and other challenging educational environments, the answer is in the emotional affect generated in those spaces. It is through feeling rather than thinking, through the power and influence of emotions, and in our human ability to affect and to be affected that a richer and more engaging learning environment can be fostered.

> Later that day, I waited for Dave in the central recreation space of the unit. I was surrounded on each side by floors of cells and watched over from a circular glassed station at one end, where three guards monitored a bank of screens that followed the activities of the men inside: a realisation of Foucault's panopticon—a metaphor for disciplinary power through hidden observation. Dave came from his cell down a central bank of metal stairs to where I waited in the noisy recreation area. I wanted to speak to him about a piece of his reflective writing that had brought custodial staff to tears through its raw honesty and deep sadness. Looking around, I feel the inherent tension of this space, where everything is grey; the walls, the ceiling, the floor, the stairs, the metal furnishings bolted to the floor, the men inside. Dave wore a grey track suit, and he had the grey pallor of someone who had been indoors most of his life . . . by his own words:
> . . . Over the course of many years, I've wasted 100s of 1000s of man hours sitting in prison essentially staring at the walls.

Prisons are often characterised as uncomfortable environments: "unwaveringly sterile, unfailingly aggressive or emotionally undifferentiated" (Crewe, Warr, Bennett, & Smith, 2014, p. 57). These views suggest that this experience is the same in any prison space, including the education spaces. Meeting Dave in this environment, I felt the gloom of the colourless spatiality, sensing how it could produce despondency and contribute to feelings of despair and depression. Learners experiencing these feelings could bring them into the learning spaces of the prisons, building a negative field of affect (Watkins, 2011) by lowering energy and increasing tension.

Yet the prison classroom can be experienced as a differently constituted emotional space (Crewe et al., 2014; Harmes, Hopkins, & Farley, 2019). It's separated from the larger institution by practices that enable different ways of thinking and being. Such a classroom space brings with it the presence of noncustodial staff as tutors and volunteers. It also allows opportunities for reflection and alternative discourse and moments of shared learning and rich interpersonal communication.

Goffman (1961/2017, p. 69) points to these spaces within such institutions as "little islands of vivid, encapturing activity" in an otherwise dead sea.

> *While I waited for the guard to bring Dave, Johnnie came over to show me a photo of his children. I had met Johnnie earlier, in a small square room that served as a classroom, one barred narrow window high up the wall, a set of plastic form tables and seven or eight white plastic chairs, nothing else.*
>
> *The tutor, Joanne, and I had followed the group of men as they were escorted by a guard who drew a bunch of keys from his belt to unlock the classroom, then, after slamming the heavy metal behind us, locked us in with the five male prisoners. The men took their seats and opened their workbooks, looking around the room as they did so, taking me in, a stranger from the outside. Johnnie was the smallest man in the room, maybe mid-30s, his small rabbit-like eyes darting nervously from face to face.*

Often, incarcerated learners enter education spaces with a "self-theory" (Yorke & Knight, 2004) of learner identity that has a long-term impact on their emotional well-being. Dave was one of those learners. Johnnie, it turned out, was another. Self-theories are often constituted through past educational experiences and form "fixed beliefs" (Llorens, Schaufeli, Bakker, & Salanova, 2007) that manifest as perceptions of a lack of necessary skills, notable self-doubt, and a sense of inability to learn. As Dave wrote in his reflective journal:

> *My life had gone off the rails at a young age, I was made a ward of the state, and schooling wasn't any kind of priority for me. I was made to believe things about myself which were both harmful and untrue, like I was incapable of succeeding and lacked the smarts to achieve in constructive or purposeful pursuit.*

These subjectivities have developed and are further reinforced through the rules, styles, and interventions found in the cultures of colonised countries as well as the cultures of education and of gang or criminal life, and then, re-enforced in the institutions of correction. Any difficulty with attempts to re-engage in education has the potential to re-confirm those beliefs and lead away from opportunities that will counter any self-theory or call fixed beliefs into question. Conversely, any hope or pride the learner feels may propel their liberation. Dave continued:

> *It has taken me several weeks to work my way through the course material. I've enjoyed the feeling of usefulness and achievement my progress and the tutor have given me.*

There is a spark here, the guiding light of positive emotion that reveals an opening for affect to emerge. As Dave and others make that attempt to re-engage in education, there is hope behind it—hope for change, for transformation, and for a different way of being. Prison classrooms, and other challenging learning environments, can become "affective spaces" (Zembylas, 2016), places of emotional intensity that enhance the potential for these transformations.

> *In the locked classroom, Joanne, the tutor, introduced me to the men. We had decided that she would use the conversation as a way of collecting evidence for an oral assessment that required the men to participate in group interaction. I would ask them about their schooling experiences, and she would note their participation in the interaction and give feedback at the end. I noticed the way Joanne commanded the space and the easy rapport she had with the learners. I also noticed the warmth of her smile and the gentle laughter bubbling behind her words. The men sat quietly, also smiling, laughing when she did and clearly enjoying the interaction.*
>
> *I told the men a little about myself. To ease that introduction, Joanne had already informed them that her "boss" was coming, and they were sworn to be on best behaviour. "We'll be angels, Miss," these tough and heavily tattooed men had assured her. The men took turns to introduce themselves and tell me a little about their schooling history. They were open and friendly, happy to tell their tales of poor school performance and how they were gradually adjusting to academic work in this environment, having decided it was a constructive way to spend their time.*
>
> *One man recounted how reluctant he had been to begin these studies here in prison and how he first thought Joanne "was the devil from hell." Joanne and the others laughed happily at this description. He had only wanted to get out of there, he admitted. Fortunately, Joanne, while holding firm, persuaded him to stick with it and he was now "reaping the benefits," and claiming an increased sense of confidence and pride in his achievements.*

In the corrections environment, inmates can be perceived negatively because of their identification as criminals (Harmes et al., 2019). In contrast, within the prison classroom, the opportunity to meet and mix with those like Joanne and volunteers who enter from the outside to form relationships based on nurturing potential and enabling transformations, contributes to the enhanced emotional zone (Crewe et al., 2014) of that classroom. A confident, experienced tutor understands the fear of education that travels from the past and the hope that motivates the present. The devil from hell sets high expectations at the outset, determines and upholds the rules, commands the space with no-nonsense and then softens, smiles, and laughs, weaving a magical essence within, around, and among these "angels."

As Dave affirms:

> *I found my tutor willing to offer both assistance and encouragement in a life where I have experienced little of either, that helped me successfully navigate the course. It made me feel really good to be doing something productive for myself. I've done more*

for myself, my daughter, and my grandchildren in the last two months than I have in the last twenty years. For the first time ever, I feel proud of myself and what I have accomplished.

When it came to Johnnie's turn to speak, I was surprised by how much he revealed, telling me and everyone else about his anger. He had always been angry, he acknowledged, even as a small child. In his first year at school, in a fit of anger, he had attacked his teacher, resulting in his first expulsion and the beginning of a troubled passage through education. The room was silent and still as Johnnie spoke, the other men listening respectfully.

Johnnie spoke earnestly, telling us that the learning he was doing now was giving him an opportunity to change, it had shown him how to see other people's points of view, and he was understanding how he could apply what he was learning to his own life. He spoke of the changes he was feeling within himself, of his children, a girl of eight and a little boy, his fears that he was letting them down, and how he didn't want them to think of him as a bad person. Because he was small, he told us, he had always been bullied, so he made up for it by being angry and fighting anyone who teased him or laughed at him. "It's just a front," he sadly admitted "acting tough. I think I can change, maybe. I want to be kinder," he announced, looking up at the others.

"But you're the kindest, most caring guy on the unit," stated the man sitting beside him—a big guy, Nathan, who acted a bit of clown, but clearly had the respect of the others.

"Am I?" said Johnnie, tears forming in his eyes.

"Yeah, man, absolutely, you are!" replied Nathan, while the others nodded, adding their assent.

Johnnie looked astounded, then his face opened as he beamed with pride.

Here in this "island of vivid, encapturing activity" (Goffman, 1961/2017), an austere physical environment transformed into an affective space (Zembylas, 2016) through honest, respectful interaction. The classroom, despite its locked door and grim physicality, became an emotionally differentiated zone. Within it, an alternative discourse enabled learners to experience themselves and others differently. Johnnie's pride and happiness were infectious; clearly, we all shared the joyfulness in the classroom and the respect for Johnnie that had emerged. When he later brought me the photographs of his children, he was still beaming with pride.

While strong relationships contribute to the enhanced emotional zone of prison classrooms affect is also harnessed through the learning itself. The way that learning is presented and provisioned; attention to language, representation, colour, and imagery in the learning materials, alongside relevance, context, content, meaningfulness, continuity, and support of that learning are all mighty forces in the creation of affect. In order to make significant shifts in consciousness, learning must incapsulate critical pedagogies that enable these shifts (Smyth, McInerney, &

Fish, 2013). Dave also reflects on changes within himself brought about through new learning:

> *I struggled with some of the work as it was both new to me and challenged some of my long-term beliefs about society and culture. Arithmetic is something I've previously allowed myself to feel intimidated by due to lacking any prior skill in numeracy. It feels good to have completed the maths book because I am now comfortable and confident I possess the skills to come up with a solution to everyday maths problems.*

Dave tells of his inner fight with new learning and of confronting alternative truths. Powerful emotions that might be considered negative, such as anger found in resistance, produce opportunities for transformation, if they are given sufficient space and legitimacy. While emotions and transformations are strongly interconnected, transformations occur incrementally. Of course, multiple emotional experiences may be involved, yielding transformations that travel in many directions. This understanding makes visible the "how" as much as the "what" of the role of emotions in facilitating or impeding personal transformations. In making visible these emotional states and opportunities for personal growth, one can find many paths towards transformation and perhaps even stabilise their variable progression.

In his reflection, Dave concludes:

> *I feel my choice to undertake this course has enabled me to begin moving my life towards a brighter tomorrow and away from the futility and despondency which have been the hallmarks of a troubled life. Anybody who wants a brighter future, to increase the amount of choices they have, or to take a step towards something new, the one thing I know you can do for yourself, which can be a springboard to other opportunities, is learning. Next, I hope to undertake a course on psychology in the hope of gaining insight into not just how others think, but myself as well. The one thing I do know, after completing this course is that it's not beyond me.*

Advice and Suggestions

Making emotions central in the activities of challenging teaching and learning spaces uncovers their influence and reveals vital ways of working with them as knowledge. Making the power and effect—the physicality—of emotions known in these contexts opens untold possibilities for creativity, collaboration, and for enhancing motivation. Emotions have shape and form, which may appear as barriers and challenges or pathways and new directions or both.

Of course, emotions transfer between individuals and groups. They produce movement towards or away from something pivotal in one's life, both current events or memories and experiences from the past. The energy of emotions manifests the affective spaces called for by researchers in this field (Albrecht-Crane,

2005; Mulcahy, 2012; Watkins, 2011; Zembylas, 2016), reconstituting austerity into warmth and well-being, and harnessing the power of relationships. Nurture this seed, and it will blossom.

Reflection Questions

1. What are some ways you could or do bring emotions to the centre of your teaching and learning?
2. How are the emotional needs of teachers and learners met in your present teaching or training context?
3. How are emotions made visible and given space in your teaching and learning context?
4. Can you think of any examples from your teaching practice where strong emotional experiences have prompted transformations for individuals or groups?

SECTION 3

Teaching With Technology

The third section of this book highlights six stories of teaching with technology in Singapore, Saudi Arabia, Morocco, China, Kazakhstan, and Cyprus. In these chapters, you will learn about innovations in augmented reality, virtual reality, online collaboration, social media, e-learning, and much more. However, instead of infatuation with such technologies, the authors of these chapters are concerned with how they can thoughtfully integrate such technologies in ways that motivate and engage 21st-century learners. Simply put, pedagogy matters. It is important to point out that readers thirsty for additional pedagogical practices with learning technology can quench their thirst by reading the many other chapters in this book that also involve learning technology and innovative pedagogy.

Chapter 13 begins the conversation about teaching with technology. In it, Muhammad Nazir Bin Amir from the Ministry of Education in Singapore insightfully points out that one factor that hinders students' motivation to learn is that they may find lessons uninteresting or boring. Drawing ideas from the Relevant, Appealing, Personal (RAP) pedagogical guideline developed by Nazir himself, this chapter shares how teachers in Singapore designed lessons to infuse the joy of learning for their students through technology-based interactive media such as augmented reality (AR) and virtual reality (VR) that are situated within appealing contexts and environments. Stories are shared describing how a teacher might motivate students to delight in learning, as well as how to promote creativity among teachers to teach content (across subjects) in enjoyable ways.

Chapter 14 takes us from Southeast Asia to the Middle East; namely, Riyadh, Saudi Arabia. Here we enter Khadijah Alghamdi's world of teaching high school computer science. Interestingly, she had the creative insight to employ Twitter as a learning tool when it initially came out. More specifically, Khadijah used Twitter to motivate students' learning in computer science courses since many of her

DOI: 10.4324/9781003213840-15

students were already using it. A key focus in this chapter, therefore, is to integrate technology and social media platforms that are widely used by high school students in Saudi Arabia for educational purposes. Khadijah shows how Twitter can be used as a platform to hear from all students in the classroom and improve students' learning and networking.

In Chapter 15, we learn about the evolution of Yassine Abdellaoui as a teacher in Morocco. His journey as an English as a Foreign Language teacher was full of little adventures and a lot of discoveries, surprises and, at times, shocking moments that shaped his teaching skills and helped him to realize how vital the role of the teacher is in building students' personalities and identities as successful learners. At its core, this chapter is concerned with how to move from dull classrooms to ones that sparkle with motivation and innovation. To help readers, Yassine explains how educational technology can play a major role in that transformation. With this chapter, Yassine hopes to inspire other teachers and encourage them not to be afraid of experimenting with teaching tools that might dramatically change the equation in the classroom in empowering student learning.

Chapter 16 takes us to Nanjing, China, where Yan Zhang explores various tools and activities to make English as a Foreign Language (EFL) writing instruction more interactive and engaging. She accurately notes that in 2019, the spread of coronavirus across the world called for a safer teaching platform in EFL classrooms. Under such circumstances, she draws on a review of the process-based writing literature and practical models of group peer review, as well as field notes from American college writing classrooms. Using these reviews, she designed a group peer-review model through Zoom rooms to replace the traditional paradigm of writing instruction in a Chinese university. By combining the second language acquisition theory with peer review practices in a virtual classroom, this approach aimed to inspire new thinking about the future of online process-based writing instruction in EFL pedagogy.

Next, we turn to Shymkent, Kazakhstan, for a description of the use of technology to enhance thinking skills and empathy. Chapter 17 by Begaim Adilkhanova presents an overview of the e-learning environment for Kazakh English as a Second Language learners that she has implemented using the R2D2 (Read, Reflect, Display, and Do) model. One main advantage of such a model is that it aligns well with interactive Web-based learning tools, supporting students' creativity and versatility while enabling an instructor to tailor tasks to individual needs.

A key aspect of this chapter is that it describes how someone can move to another country or part of the world and maintain their cultural heritage through global collaboration and sharing using various technologies, including blogs, email, Skype, Google Docs, and shared online video. Moreover, readers will learn how a Kazakh, who was born in one country but raised and lived in different parts of the world, was destined to meet Begaim online. As you will learn when reading this chapter, they shared the same learning journey from Kazakhstan to the United States. Using that common experience as a base, Begaim and her students also had thoughtful exchanges about cultural heritage and family values through different learning technologies.

In Chapter 18, the final chapter of Section 2, Maria Solomou describes how creative and critical thinking are core skills for our students and future professionals and pillars of innovation and progress. This is the story of Maria's development as an instructor, trainer, researcher, and experience designer, from the time she was at Indiana University Bloomington until today and her current occupation at PwC in Cyprus. As Maria narrates the story of one of her workshops in Cyprus, she reflects on key moments in her professional journey around positioning participants as active agents of change within virtual gaming worlds and the environmental cues, principles, and practices that can rouse to life highly participatory and creative group interactions and activities.

As you will learn, each of these six chapters has lessons about how technology integration can make a major impact on learning and learning across a range of contexts.

13

FOSTERING STUDENT MOTIVATION AND ENGAGEMENT THROUGH THE RELEVANT, APPEALING, AND PERSONAL (RAP) PEDAGOGICAL GUIDELINE

Tech Stories From Singapore

Muhammad Nazir Bin Amir

Muhammad Nazir Bin Amir is a master teacher at the Ministry of Education, Singapore. He received his PhD in education from Nanyang Technological University in Singapore. A passionate teacher who actively carries out classroom research, he mentors teachers in exploring ways to design enjoyable lessons to foster intrinsic motivation, engagement, and creativity amongst students. He is a recipient of the Singapore President's Award for Teachers, the U.S. Fulbright Distinguished Award in Teaching, and is a top finalist in the Global Teacher Prize. Nazir can be reached at Muhammad_Nazir_AMIR@moe.gov.sg.

DOI: 10.4324/9781003213840-16

Introduction

One factor that hinders students' motivation to learn is they may find lessons uninteresting (or boring). This led me to develop the Relevant, Appealing, and Personal (RAP) pedagogical guideline (Indiana University, 2016; Schoolbag, 2014, 2015). This guideline highlights that in designing lessons that aim to motivate and engage students, it is useful for us teachers to take into consideration our students' interests and personal experiences while weaving in content to be taught across the various subjects. Drawing ideas from the RAP guideline, this chapter shares how teachers in Singapore designed lessons to bring about the joy of learning for their students through technology-based interactive media such as videos, augmented reality (AR), and virtual reality (VR) that are situated within appealing contexts and environments. In designing such RAP-infused lessons, teachers brainstormed and developed creative ideas to teach content across the various subjects in enjoyable ways.

Examples of RAP-Infused Lessons

The following is a simple case study of a flipped lesson designed by a team of teachers in a primary school. The team initially brainstormed ideas to teach the topic of "intermediate directions." They found a video on the internet that explained intermediate directions (north-east, south-east, south-west, and north-west) and intended to use the video to teach this content to their Primary Three students averaging 9 years of age (i.e., equivalent to third-grade students in the United States).

I was interested in finding out how this flipped lesson would motivate and engage a particular class of students who were taking subjects at the foundation (or basic) levels and were considered academically lower in progress as compared with their peers. The students were told to go home to watch the video, after which they would return to school the following day to complete a worksheet to demonstrate their learning. The worksheet comprised a map of a playground, and students were told to fill in the sentences with the appropriate intermediate directions. For example, "*the swing is located ___ of the bench*," of which the correct answer would be "north-east."

The teachers discovered that not many students from this class (as compared with students in other groups) were able to demonstrate their learning from the video. They also found out that a considerable number of students did not even watch the video till the end. What are possible reasons for this? When I posed this question to teachers (both those who were teaching this class and others), many mentioned that perhaps this group of students does not have access to the internet or a computer, given that a considerable number of them come from families of low socioeconomic status. This was the initial belief of the teachers.

When they probed further, the teachers who designed this lesson were surprised to find out that it wasn't because the students did not have access to an online device. In fact, many of the students had internet-enabled mobile devices and computers at home. Given this new information, the teachers reflected on the way that they designed this lesson and attempted to engage the group of students again—this time, however, through the RAP pedagogical guideline.

Almost all students went back home to watch the video this time. So what changed? The video chosen this time was Dora the Explorer. In the video, the map from Dora's bag pops out and quickly unfolds, showing her the intermediate directions that she would need to take to reach her destination. The teachers sensed their students' enthusiasm when they were told to watch a cartoon that appealed to them, and also one that they could relate to, as part of their homework.

In terms of motivation and engagement of students, the teachers started to realise that it wasn't just the use of videos that motivated students to learn, but the *choice* of videos that had to appeal to their interests—the element of learner choice was a pivotal consideration in designing the lesson to foster joy and intrinsic motivation to learn the content. The teachers could see how the choice of video instilled an interest in students to *want to* (instead of *have to*) learn the content of "intermediate directions." Students were *emotionally connected to the learning content (affective engagement)*, which led them to be on task in their lesson *(behavioural engagement)* and gain competence of content *(cognitive engagement)*.

Through further reflection and discussions with students, the teachers came to an important realisation. First, they acknowledged that many students who are in academically low-achieving groups (or deemed "academically at-risk") may have social, family, and financial issues and that they may come from home environments that are not very conducive for learning. However, what they found even more interesting is that when they asked the students why they were unmotivated to watch the initial video (as part of their homework), the students did not attribute the reasons to their homes, families, or financial situations. Rather, the students responded with "*The initial video is boring!*"

The teachers eventually realised that using the Dora the Explorer video motivates and engages not only students in academically low-achieving groups but also all other students no matter the achievement level. To say that only students in academically low-achieving groups need such excitement for learning would be incorrect, as *all* students value an enjoyable learning experience. This became very useful in designing online lessons to motivate students engaged in home-based-learning during the pandemic.

The previous example highlights how teachers developed a lesson that is based on the RAP guideline. In designing the lesson, the teachers ensured that the lesson is *Relevant* to the syllabus ("intermediate directions" in English), *Appealing* to the students (in that it has elements of novelty, is multisensory, and is age-appropriate), and *Personal* to the students (in that they can identify and relate to the cartoon character, Dora the Explorer).

The RAP guideline has also been helpful for teachers to design lessons that employ the use of augmented reality (AR) and virtual reality (VR) in teaching and learning. There has been substantial interest in looking at the affordances of AR and VR in teaching and learning, both within and out of the classroom.

On one occasion, I brought teachers and students to several VR facilities as part of out-of-classroom learning experiences. We experienced our Secondary Two students (14 years of age) becoming disinterested in VR fairly quickly (i.e., once the novelty effect wore off) in one facility but continue to be engaged in another facility. While both facilities made use of VR goggles, the key difference was that the first facility was in a stand-alone room, whereas the second facility was in an indoor theme park where students' engagement was sustained over a longer period of time. Teachers began to realise that it was not just the use of VR that contributed to student engagement, but rather the choice of media in the VR goggles, as well as the activities and learning environments that had to appeal to students' interests, which generated their enthusiasm for learning. Lessons learnt from the VR example led to both teachers and my exploring other locations in Singapore that would universally appeal to our students.

On another occasion, I facilitated a professional learning session that involved a collaboration with the Trick Eye Museum where exhibits were displayed and enhanced through AR features. For example, scanning the quick response (QR) code on mobile phones (with an AR app) on certain exhibits made them "come alive," such as polar bears walking on ice and horses galloping on a race track—contexts that teachers believe would appeal to 9-year-old children in Primary Three.

I worked alongside teachers to capitalise on such contexts to design lessons to teach content across the various subjects. I was very happy to see their students not only gaining academic content through such lessons but also enjoying the learning experience, which is testimony that the lessons being designed have both joy and rigour.

Benefits for Teachers

Through the examples shared, teachers realised that it is not the technology (i.e., ICT, AR, VR) that motivates and engages students, but rather the *choice* of media, activities, and environments that has to appeal to their students' interest. In addition, the benefits of fostering the joy of learning to motivate and engage are not only at the student end but also at the teacher end. As teachers, we are motivated to teach our students when we see their enthusiasm to learn through our innovative practices.

What I find interesting in guiding teachers to design RAP-infused lessons is that teachers are able to generate more creative ideas to teach content when the *choice* of contexts is universally appealing. Based on creativity frameworks from Guilford (1959) and Torrance (1979), teachers have been able to generate many ideas *(fluency)*, different types of ideas *(flexibility)*, and new and novel ideas *(original-ity)* for teaching. At the same time, they also developed rich and engaging lessons to teach content across the different subjects *(elaboration)*. This "creativity leap" was especially true when students were exposed to media, activities, and environ-ments that were universally appealing, such as those in the VR theme park and Trick Eye Museum as compared with the stand-alone VR and AR facilities.

Such RAP-infused lessons contribute to students' enjoyment and attitudes in learning, which in turn have had positive effects on their academic performance and self-worth (Amir, 2014, 2021a, 2021b; Ang, 2021). I am glad that through classroom research in the areas of RAP pedagogy, I am able to foster joy and creativity amongst teachers to teach content in their subjects in enjoyable ways. I hope readers of this chapter can find ways to incorporate the RAP pedagogical guideline or modifications of it in their teaching practices and find much success and joyfulness in the process.

Reflection Questions

1. What are some of your students' specific interests? Based on one or more of those interests, how could you employ the Relevant, Appealing, and Per-sonal (RAP) pedagogical guidelines? Give one or two examples.
2. How would you weave in content that you have to teach based on these interests? Think about how you will present content in ways that emotionally and cognitively connect students to the subject matter.
3. Why would your students (particularly those who are academically unmo-tivated) be *driven (motivated)* to *want to* instead of *have to* learn the content through this approach? Bear in mind how you would promote enjoyment and boost your students' attitudes in learning the content through your teaching.

14

SOCIAL MEDIA TO TICKLE MOTIVATION TO LEARN

From Saudi High Schools

Khadijah Alghamdi

DOI: 10.4324/9781003213840-17

Khadijah Alghamdi is a faculty member at Majmaah University in Saudi Arabia and a doctoral candidate in instructional systems technology at Indiana University Bloomington. She is interested in teaching programming and computational thinking to K-12 students and how to prepare computer science teachers to better teach computing in general and programming in particular. She may be contacted at k.alghamdi@mu.edu.sa.

Introduction

In 2005, I started my career as a computer science (CS) teacher in a rural area in Saudi Arabia, where I faced several significant challenges. Some of these challenges were associated with pedagogy as computer science was taught in a very didactic and not interactive way. Making matters worse, CS was not a graded course; consequently, the students were not motivated to learn or participate in the class.

At that time, I taught a course in computer literacy that included basic technology tool competencies such as the features of Word, PowerPoint, Excel, and so forth. Unfortunately, I did not know how to motivate students to actively participate or give their best effort in that class. As I reflected on this dilemma and had a personal conversation with myself, it dawned on me that I could get help from some of the other teachers in the school who were teaching other courses. Soon, I asked several teachers to require students to apply what they learned in my CS class in their other courses, which were graded. For example, instead of students completing their writing assignments in their notebooks, they would now type them using Word and print them out for grading. While many of the students did not have printers in their houses, I noted that they could use the school's printer. Needless to say, I was delighted when I saw students coming to the CS lab to print their assignments.

In 2007, I moved to an urban school in Riyadh, the capital of Saudi Arabia. At that time, the Ministry of Education made CS a graded for-credit course. I was ecstatic! Nevertheless, I faced other issues, such as 35 to 40 students in each CS class who often required much individualized attention, monitoring, and feedback. With so many students, it was hard for me to listen to all the various student voices in CS periods. Also, many students were shy and did not like to talk in front of others.

Thus, I designed a website with all course content in addition to a discussion forum where students could discuss their ideas with their peers and with me. I found that the discussion forum was an excellent space for students to communicate and explain their thoughts. However, not all students had access to the internet in their houses at that time, and many could not access the course website. Despite these constraints, the discussion forums allowed me to hear from the students who were not talking in the classroom.

Years later, in another Saudi school, I encountered a similar problem. Only certain students participated in the classroom, such as discussing their ideas or asking questions, while the rest were passively watching and listening. One day, a student asked me during class if I had a Twitter account. I quickly told her that I had an account and then asked her back if she had one. She replied, "Yes." Not long after, I asked the other students in the class if they had Twitter accounts. Not only did many of them have one, but they also admitted to spending significant amounts of time on Twitter each day.

When I got home that night, I started thinking of how I could use Twitter as a social media platform to hear from all students' voices. I recalled how the discussion forum was helpful with my students in the previous school. Since most students had Twitter accounts as well as access to the internet and their own mobile devices handy, I decided to use Twitter to communicate with students. Fortunately, it was easy to create a Twitter account for school purposes.

I decided to use this account to post anything related to the curriculum that I was teaching and anything related to CS in general. But before proceeding, I had some concerns. I knew that some students did not have internet access or mobile phones. Stated another way, Twitter was not available to all my students. In fact, some students were not allowed to have Twitter accounts. Thus, I decided to set up some rules. First, participation in Twitter was elective. Second, students had the option of creating new accounts or using existing ones. Third, they had to choose the level of privacy that they preferred. In effect, if they wanted their accounts to be private, they could do that, but they had to "follow" me and accept my follow-back request.

They were also required to use their real names as that would help me with grading. In addition to following me on Twitter, every student had to follow at least ten of her classmates based on her choice. In terms of the content to be posted, each student participated in the task each week by doing at least two retweets about either the curriculum content or the CS content. Additionally, they were asked to both reply to one of my posts as well as post something new related to the week's content that was not mentioned. Students who could not use Twitter or who had opted out had the opportunity to choose a different task which had to be discussed with me for approval.

As a result of this Twitter task, by the end of the semester, I was able to hear from all students in the class on the Twitter platform or in the classroom. When I surveyed students to ask them about what they liked and what they did not like about using Twitter in their learning activities, they mentioned several different things. To my surprise and delight, many of them talked about how they were able to network with new people interested in CS as well as experts in the field. Importantly, in the process, they learned about the available robotic technology clubs and had information on how they could join them.

In their survey responses, students also mentioned how they could formulate their questions in a better way so others could understand them better instead of simply asking the question in the classroom and everyone forgetting about it shortly thereafter. To my surprise, my students did not feel shy to ask their questions via Twitter while their peers monitored these postings or "Tweets." Such an atmosphere was vital since their questions opened thoughtful discussions with others. In addition, since Twitter limits all messages to a small number of characters (previously 140 characters and now 280), it helped students to hone all their messages to the central points. It also resulted in more easily and quickly read information compared with reading extended passages from a book, encyclopedia, magazine, or other resource. In reflection, I believe that their ability to effectively read and write in Arabic using Twitter was directly the result of a reduced cognitive load.

At the same time, some students did not like the fact that some of their peers kept their accounts private, causing them at times to not be able to see the whole discussion. As a result, key parts of the discussion were often hidden. Moreover, students found it unhelpful to discuss or understand ideas through Twitter because they needed to verbally talk to explain their thoughts.

Perhaps you will experience different opportunities and challenges when using such social media for quick communication and idea exchange. You might also experience previously unknown benefits with social media like Twitter as learners and teachers around the globe become more familiar and facile with such tools and approaches. If you do, please write to me and let me know about it.

Reflection Questions

1. What do you think of Twitter as a tool to enhance learning? Do you agree with using it at the secondary or high school level for teaching? What about with younger students such as at the middle school level?
2. What do you perceive as the key advantages and disadvantages of using Twitter and other forms of social media in education? How might perceptions and uses of social media change in the coming decade or two?
3. What other social media platforms can be integrated into K-12 instruction? How might such integration be different from the use of a microblogging tool like Twitter?
4. What would you do differently from the instructor in this chapter when using Twitter as a tool for teaching?
5. Often social media technologies such as YouTube and Twitter are blocked in K-12 classrooms. Many times, teachers are not allowed to use social media as a teaching tool in their schools. Have you experienced or seen this issue? How was it addressed?

15

SPARKING INSPIRATION THROUGH MOTIVATION AND TECHNOLOGY INTEGRATION

Yassine Abdellaoui

Yassine Abdellaoui is an English as a Foreign Language teacher who currently works in CPGE "Classes Préparatoires aux Grandes Écoles" (Preparatory classes for engineering schools) in Kénitra, Morocco. He has a master's degree in studies in the English language and culture. Yassine participated in the Fulbright Distinguished Awards in Teaching Program at Indiana University in 2017, where he worked on an enquiry project entitled "Deepening Cross-Cultural Understanding and Breaking Stereotypes Through Video-Inspired Dialogues." He can be reached at abdellaoui.y@gmail.com.

DOI: 10.4324/9781003213840-18

The Beginning of My Teaching Journey

My first contact with teaching in a formal setting was in 2007, right after I completed my BA in English. It was actually in a language center where I was given a chance to observe and eventually teach. That was a golden opportunity that I embraced with much enthusiasm and determination. I have always loved this profession and somehow there I was teaching English in the same language center that I had graduated from a year earlier. Clearly, it was one of life's surprising moments.

Notably, I was pursuing my master's degree while teaching for the first time. I studied teaching-related theories and methodologies at the university in the morning and practiced them in that language center in the evening. It was an amazing start; one that was filled with discovery, fueled by trial and error, and full of personal and powerful learning. I fell in love with teaching because of the freedom it afforded me to decide what might work best for the students. It also offered me a chance to influence and inspire countless others, directly in my classes as well as indirectly through the people my students later interacted with. I learned that a teacher could either make or break a student. The role of a teacher is glorious. In our religion, we say that "a teacher is almost like a prophet."

In the midst of all this positive energy, I soon faced two different educational realities and challenges. Needless to say, such doses of reality come swiftly and often for a teacher.

The teaching conditions in that language center were fabulous. First, the number of students was limited to 20. Second, the high level of student motivation that I felt was palpable; clearly, they were excited to learn English. It is important to note that help from the administration was provided whenever needed. The classrooms were equipped with screens, speakers, posters, flashcards, and assorted other valuable items. The conditions were perfect for a novice teacher who was discovering the world of teaching for the first time. I was entering teaching on a high note.

Unfortunately, I faced the opposite reality too often experienced by teachers when I applied for a job as a public school teacher in 2009 in Ouled Teima, a small town 700 kilometers to the south from my hometown. I soon found that my new teaching situation was entirely different. My classes enrollments at Hassan II High School were about 40 to 45 students, where previously I was teaching just ten to 15 students. In this public school, motivation was lagging or lacking in the majority of students. To make matters worse, the only teaching tool that I had was the blackboard and pen and paper. Help was not always provided in this school when needed.

It was a major shock for me even though I had attended a similar school growing up. This was different. I was in a position of responsibility now where I met more than 150 students every week. These students were my responsibility, along with an overloaded curriculum I was forced to cover. Needless to say, teaching at that school was highly intimidating. At the same time, I realized that my love for teaching is what led me there, and I wholeheartedly believed that this job was my calling.

While teaching at Hassan II High School, I always thought that there was something missing. Should all the lessons be solely about the language I am teaching? Or should students delve into what is beyond the language and learn other skills that can help them survive in this world?

In the small town in southern of Morocco, where I was appointed to teach, most students came from the nearby villages. That meant that the internet was a luxury for them. Since most of them were confined to the area they lived in, they did not have extensive knowledge about the outside world. The only teaching equipment in the classroom that they were familiar with was the blackboard.

I must admit, in my first few class sessions at Hassan II, I felt completely uninspired. If I felt weary of the content, I am most certain that the students did too. The textbooks were dull and lacking in excitement. How could I inspire my students given such boring prepackaged content? The textbooks were full of grammar lessons, vocabulary exercises, and texts that were long and difficult for students.

The only attractive thing about those books was the themes. These themes that promised the students a world of wonders; however, when you flipped through the pages, they looked dry. Something was missing. That missing ingredient is what made the students drowsy and inattentive. Worse, I was quite bored too!

As a young first-year teacher, I could not recognize that right away. What was missing? Well, everything! Start with culture. You cannot properly teach a language deprived of the culture or cultures it comes from. Soon, I realized that learning about new cultures was central to making the students more curious. It will prompt them to compare and contrast, ask questions, and find answers. In the process, they would be employing their critical thinking skills and various other 21st-century skills and competencies.

I knew then that I should not rely thoroughly on the textbook. I should use titles of lessons and themes and craft my own lessons where curiosity and critical thinking should be the priority. The internet was my savior. I started by investing in a video projector. It was not that hard to find ready-made PowerPoint presentations of a whole range of English lessons from experienced and innovative teachers. I was swimming in an endless ocean of lessons targeting the learning of English as a foreign language. It was now my job to find the most relevant and engaging content for my learners.

Surprisingly, I noticed a huge difference in the classroom ambience the very first time that I used the video projector. Even the least careful students were paying attention and curious about what would appear in the next slide. Something inside my head was saying, "The younger generation is more into technology, so why not use it often in the classroom." In responding to such inner voices, I began using more pictures than words and was gently nudging my students to use more English words to talk about the pictures. I found out that the burden was not the English language itself. Motivation was what was missing. When engaged, students will do their best to learn and use the targeted language to voice their opinions.

My classes turned from boring to anything but boring. Was I still at the same school? I began asking myself. Only then did I realize how powerful technology was in a classroom full of students who might not even have a TV at home and probably had never touched a smartphone. Something magical was happening. I may have surrendered the equivalent of several month's salaries, but it turned out to be a solid investment in being a contributing member of the human race. With that one video projector, my options to inspire these students were now endless. If you could engage the students right from the start, you can teach them increasingly challenging lessons. I learnt that there were hundreds of ways to teach the same content. I just had to work smarter and put myself in the shoes of the students.

With technology, we had wondrous opportunities to focus more on culture in our learning. Through pictures and videos, students were introduced to what life is like in the United States and other places in the world. Many stereotypes were exposed and corrected. Admittedly, I enjoy the awe students express when they learn something new about other cultures. We were not only studying the English language but also using it to learn about history, geography, culture, and other information. In addition to enhancing their learning, students were also always excited to come to class.

I realized that I am there to facilitate. Once I found a way to spark curiosity and motivation, students will do most of the work. Educational psychologists call this student autonomy and empowerment. In effect, I learned that I should not only teach. I should inspire.

I knew then that I needed to integrate technology in my instruction for more effective and engaging lessons. Indeed, that is where the Fulbright program comes in. I was one of 18 teachers to be selected to participate in the Distinguished Awards in Teaching Program in 2017. The selection was based on an inquiry project that we had to propose. My main focus was to use technology and to motivate my students to learn beyond their English language lessons. That is why I chose to make inspiring authentic educational videos as a supplement to the textbook they use. Each video handled one of the themes in the textbook and came with pre-watching, while-watching and post-watching activities. In effect, I wanted to look for best practices that would inspire my students and help motivate them to achieve their goals while keeping in mind the curriculum objectives.

I feel most fortunate that my project was selected and off I went to Indiana University (IU) in Bloomington. The four months I spent there were a life journey for me. The experience was beyond my expectations. My project was not the only thing that was given birth to while at IU. A new me was born as well.

Every single experience, from the small excursions and fleeting interactions to the more grandiose events provided irreplaceable lessons that added tremendously to my personal and professional development. What I thought was exotic in Moroccan schools was a humdrum everyday event in the American ones that I visited. I discovered that teachers should be facilitators, and they should definitely inspire and bring the world to the classroom for their students. Most of all, learning should be a fun experience for students.

I discovered that my memorable experience as a novice teacher back in 2007 in Morocco was practiced in many of the American schools that I visited. It was clear that teachers should believe in students' abilities to achieve a certain objective and provide timely and genuine help along the way, have confidence in them, and challenge them. I knew then that I am on the right track. My experience was a confirmation that what I had done with my students was right. Students need to trust their teacher, and that trust should be established by the teacher. Once this happens, the teacher has the power to make a change, and that change can eventually turn into a robust transformation.

With the help of my faculty advisor, my host teacher, the Center for International Education, Development & Research (CIEDR) at IU, and many other citizens in Bloomington and Indiana, I managed in those four months to create interactive videos that were suitable for my students. Videos that were created not only to help them improve their listening and speaking skills, but also ones that could inspire them and open their eyes to a different world where people, like them, also have dreams, and objectives, worries, and ideas to make this planet a better place. For each video, I carefully chose the best resources that would represent the theme of each unit. At the end of each video, the participants were encouraged to ask students a question related to the topic handled in the video to make it more interactive.

What is apparent is that technology, indeed, has helped my students see beyond their language skills and competency goals. These goals have been superseded by global education goals. They now begin to realize that language is a vital component that bridges the gap between them and the cross-cultural understanding of their peers across the planet.

With this experience, I realized that the key to success for my students is to be globally aware. Such a global perspective can happen only if they are open to the world and are willing to share, learn, and produce. That is why my main objective now is to help students become active citizens, both locally and globally.

I can proudly say that the Fulbright program I experienced at IU has had an extremely positive impact on my job as a teacher. The schools I visited, the seminars I attended, the people I met, and the inquiry project I worked on have all contributed tremendously to my personal and professional development. The

Fulbright program gave me the boost that I needed to be more creative in the classroom. All of it has been a life-changing experience par excellence.

After 11 years of teaching, I still face new challenges with my engineering students. My experiences each semester have taught me to adapt my teaching episodes and lessons to the needs of the students. We should thoughtfully and adaptively use technology tools that are available when they serve a purpose. English teachers in Morocco and around the planet are teaching digital natives who are very familiar with technology and yet can be lost in it or distracted by it. Our job is to guide them through that vast jungle of options, potential successes, pervasive challenges, and assorted learning extensions and supplements and provide them with the tools that they need to discover the world around them and build their own futures.

Now that I have returned to my hometown, my new objective is to inspire other teachers by organizing workshops and sharing the humble experience I brought with me from that small town. By the way, that was not the only thing I transported from there. Being appointed in the south allowed me to meet the love of my life, Ilham. We are happily married now. Her presence in my life always reminds me of how I started as a teacher.

As you can see, I have had a memorable journey so far! When thinking about the learning process and day-to-day decisions that I have gone through as a novice teacher, I give gratitude to all the people that helped me to explore this vast world called education.

God bless all the teachers of the world.

Reflection Questions

1. In what other ways could you attempt to promote cross-cultural understanding if technology was not present?
2. On a typical day, are your students motivated to learn? If not, what can you do?
3. How can you use the experiences and stories you accumulated over your life to benefit your students, colleagues, and the local community?
4. Would the same methods work with younger generations of learners?
5. What was your most memorable moment as a student or a teacher where technology was employed? What made it highly memorable?

16

INTERACTIVE WRITING INSTRUCTION IN ZOOM

Yan Zhang

DOI: 10.4324/9781003213840-19

Yan Zhang is an associate professor in the School of Foreign Languages and Literature in Nanjing Tech University, where she has worked for over 20 years teaching a variety of English as a Foreign Language (EFL) courses. Her research focuses on language testing and EFL pedagogy. With academic experience both in the United Kingdom and the United States, she gained rich knowledge in English culture and applied what she had learned to her classroom. As a teacher, she won the first prize in the lecturer competition at university level. She also co-authored books and published papers in top national journals on EFL pedagogical innovations and language testing. She can be reached at shyvia67@hotmail.com.

Introduction

The last decade has witnessed a transfer of Chinese EFL writing instruction from traditional teaching methodology to process-based writing instruction. However, affected by prevailing curriculum designs, conventional teaching environments, and learning preferences, the process-based writing approach fails to work well in a Chinese context.

The key turning point for me was in the year 2019, when the spread of coronavirus across the world dramatically changed English teaching in Chinese universities. The disease calls for safer and more efficient teaching and learning environments. As teachers turned to various online platforms, they found a more efficient form of instruction and an environment that was much safer from which to learn. In effect, as time went by, it became increasingly clear that the traditional paradigm of writing instruction can be replaced by online process-based writing instruction through virtual interactions.

Drawing on a review of literature on process-based writing and practical models of peer review as well as the field notes from my personal experiences in American college writing classrooms, I designed a peer-review model through Zoom rooms. By combining second language acquisition theory and peer-review practice in a virtual classroom, my ponderings in this chapter aim to inspire new thinking on the future online process-based writing instructions in China and beyond.

The Context of Chinese EFL Writing Instruction and Course Design

In traditional Chinese EFL classrooms, writing instruction is optional for non-English majors. Teachers can choose to instruct writing skills in an intensive reading class or just skip it. Most writing instructions at this stage are intended for the College English Test Band (CET-4), a high-stakes English proficiency test, which focuses on three- or five-paragraph teaching methods (Zhang, Wu, Wang, & Zhang, 1995) or relies on writing exercises found in textbooks (Zhu, 2019).

Writing for a specific purpose is typically scheduled to start from the second semester in university study; in effect, it is intended for those who have passed CET-4. These courses can be divided into either general writing or academic writing courses, though the latter is typically preferred by the majority. Unfortunately, there is no systematic methodology for academic writing instruction due to the lack of teacher training and standardized teaching practices. Drawing on this historical context as well as the anti-coronavirus quarantine policy that requires all university students to complete their learning through an online platform, I designed my online writing course.

The instruction of EFL writing, in this case, was conducted among non-English freshmen in a Chinese university. Importantly, the teachers were allowed to choose any desirable platforms based on their needs. My choice was Zoom. I had seen Zoom used when I was a visiting scholar at Indiana University (IU) in 2016 in the IU School of Education. At that time, I was highly impressed by the seamlessness of the instruction in Zoom and the ability to bring in expert guests from seemingly anywhere.

The lessons I delivered in China via Zoom lasted about 90 minutes every week. I had 60 students divided into six groups of ten students each. When using Zoom, I found it important to designate all group leaders and members before class. In the particular lesson described here, I assign an essay to my student through QQ (a popular social media software) with a specific deadline. To keep the momentum going, I try to correct papers and offer brief written feedback as soon as possible after submission. Next, six randomly chosen essays are handed out in class for group discussion, each group being responsible for one essay.

On receiving the essay, group members are required to reflect on and discuss it based on inspiring questions to foster robust peer review. During the discussion, I will slip into different breakout rooms as a means of scaffolding. The discussion will last 20 minutes in respective breakout rooms. When the time is up, all groups will automatically withdraw from their rooms to the main classroom. Every group then shares their answers to various peer-review questions and decides on the final score of the essay based on their discussions. The teacher will discuss the results with students, give proper feedback, and make a conclusion. The whole process is detailed in Table 16.1.

The classroom design of this writing review process combines Wen's (2020) output-oriented method and Li's (2000) process-based teaching guidelines. The former addresses goal-oriented tasks before class, problem-driven methods and scaffolding in class, and excellent sample essay sharing after class. The latter emphasizes broadening the writer's vision, advocating for different critical thinking tactics and skills, and discovering problems through peer learning. Meanwhile, teacher feedback is highlighted during the entire process (Zhang & Cheng, 2020).

The completion of the writing task is divided into three stages—before, in, and after class—which I find amounts to about four hours in a two-week span.

TABLE 16.1 An Instructional Model for Online Process-Based Writing

Platform	Task	Content	Time
QQ group	Assigning a task	An essay	Before class
	Grading the individual essay	Teacher's grading	
	Grouping	Pre-task grouping and leader assigning	
	Group peer-review preparation	Sending selected essays and group peer-review training	
Zoom	Discussing	Group meeting	In class
		Teacher scaffolding	
	Reporting	Reporting and peer grading	
	Concluding	Conclusions and suggestions	
QQ group	Revising	Second draft	After class

Designated assignments refer to tasks from CET-4 and CET-6 exam papers with a requirement of a limit of about 200 words on hot social issues. Brainstorm before writing includes intensive reading, topic-related discussion, and writing instructions on format and argument. After submission of the first draft, my feedback is sent to individual students focusing mainly on the subject, layout, logical thinking, and content.

I keep the essays selected for peer-review purposes. A group leader will be selected from those whose essays scored above nine points (out of 15). They must also have better communication skills and a higher proficiency level of English (based on their CET-4 scores). During group discussion, the teacher slips into the breakout rooms as quietly as possible, records key questions from group discussion, provides proper guidance on peer-review tasks and, during that time, offers reminders, clarifications, and explanations.

At the end of the discussion, the group presentation must address questions discussed in peer-review tasks to see if they achieve the desirable learning outcome. The teacher's summary in the main classroom includes performance on group peer-review tasks, challenging questions raised by group members, and reasons for final scores on selected essays. Of course, suggestions for the second draft are also provided. After class, a revision of the first draft will be assigned. All students are required to prepare for the second draft by reflecting on their first draft as well as drawing on the experience they have gained from the group peer review tasks.

Discussion and Analysis

In such a Zoom-based writing classroom, all tasks aim to foster learning to write in the cognitive process paradigm where writing is truly thinking, rather than write through summary or imitative writing as is conducted in most traditional

Chinese in-person writing classrooms. In addition, during the writing process, I help learners establish short-term writing goals while preparing them for high-stakes exams that they will have in the future.

The leaders in different groups are assigned beforehand by teachers to avoid silent classrooms with no interaction. Leaders with low English proficiency levels too often hinder the communication process due to vague expression and lack of confidence. Properly selected leaders can activate the learners, divide the work rationally, and lead to more positive outcomes overall.

As the teacher, I will mainly scaffold the whole process. As for common language mistakes, the students can locate them by running an error tool on their own. This aims to empower learners and foster the transfer of English skills and competencies within learning zones.

The goal of the group peer-review report is to examine the completion of peer-review tasks over a fixed period of time. This reporting helps the learners understand the guidelines of the peer-review task, the requirements of writing tasks, and the contents of writing instruction. The report revolves around peer-review tasks through question-answer sessions to obtain needed insight into the learning outcomes.

Conclusion and Suggestion

Overall, research from Kong and Li (2013) has revealed that different grouping models have minimal effect on the adoption of peer review and essay revision. However, effective group peer review can be achieved by developing detailed peer-review tasks, scoring criteria, group discussions, and teacher feedback to peer-review tasks. Not surprisingly, students are less stressed through text or voice message because group discussions and feedback are implemented over the network. Communication and interaction are improved; hence, there is enhanced efficiency in peer learning. Naturally, every article submitted for peer review task needs careful selection, including filtering out articles that scored too high or too low to avoid unitary opinions.

Second, the choice of the group leader is critical. Too chatty or silent leaders can have disastrous consequences when it comes to this type of task. English proficiency level can also affect the quality of peer-review tasks. I find it is best when leaders are chosen from those who excel in routine writing tasks, those with high levels of English proficiency as well as solid communication and organization skills. Suffice to say, the teacher also plays a vital role in this process.

In effect, the teacher's role is to assist and scaffold while students take more control over the writing and feedback processes. Teachers guide students in understanding the peer review tasks and the associated task requirements and scoring criteria. Teachers also provide timely access to groups in the discussion. They listen more while interfering less, and they remind students of getting to the point. Finally, teachers clarify the questions intended for peer-review tasks and answer student questions. Some questions from the group are saved for large class discussions. All feedback questions and answers are expected to be in the form of open-ended questions for discussion.

Training is an integral part of the peer-review task (Zhang & Sheng, 2011). It is vital for teachers to answer students' questions to peer-review tasks before breakout discussion groups are formed. I find it is also essential that teachers remind their students during the breakout sessions to comply with task rules. Meanwhile, quantitative evaluation standards are critical as progress markers and springboards toward writing excellence. I have also discovered that the interpretation and application of the CET-6 scoring rubric allow learners to better understand the details of evaluation standards for writing. This type of rubric also helps learners use quantitative criteria to review other people's articles, discuss and analyze their papers, and effectively gain insights into writing tasks to fulfill the curriculum goals intended to improve their own writing skills.

More importantly, peer review under the guidance of teachers shows that students no longer attend too much to language problems; instead, they turn to the content of the essay, the logic of the argument, and various other analytical skills. I view this peer review as a transformation of writing instruction for my students and a revitalization of my own career. No longer must students suffer through traditional prescriptive instruction to learn their rhetoric and logic. They are now freed from such constraints and can support each other to learn new writing skills in the process.

It is an amazing shift in my classrooms toward active and engaging learning. It is simultaneously an inspiration for my colleagues who experiment with their own writing models. The following quotes from my students in Zoom can help to confirm these perceptions.

> "*I was impressed by the feedback made by my peers, who not only help me polish my grammar but also inspire me to explore in the argument.*"
> "*I was impressed by the peer-review process in the breakout rooms, which helps to motivate us and inspire us to bring forward brilliant ideas.*"
> "*I understand teacher's feedback on the problem of comma splice and cohesion by reading my classmates' essays, which are problems I always neglect[ed] before.*"
> "*I come to know the importance of thesis statement and know how to write it after discussing with my classmates and commenting on their essays.*"
> "*Our group leader is great! We complete our task smoothly since she helps to assign tasks properly and raises good questions in our discussion.*"

I hope this case helps to inspire future domestic teaching in the Chinese ESL writing classroom. Drawing on the experiences and ideas from countless others around the planet, the time is ripe for transforming writing instruction from the lower grades through to the upper levels. The curriculum must change. Methods must change. Teacher training is desperately in need of change. No longer can the teaching of academic writing be a one-size-fits-all model. Drawing on the writing purposes of students from various learning backgrounds and proficiency levels, schools as well as colleges and universities need to design innovative teaching materials and methodologies for interactive and engaging writing.

My experiments indicate that the technologies exist in all our hands to develop a new methodology for teaching writing as well as a built-in formative evaluation system. We can use the technologies in our mobile devices to teach analytical writing, practical writing, and academic writing and a wide assembly of process-based writing techniques. It is also essential to establish an efficient peer review mechanism in writing, including online and offline feedback, teacher-student conferencing, and seminars for group peer review.

In closing, I hope that research on peer-review cases, especially long-term research on online peer-review cases in process-based writing instruction, can ultimately lay a solid foundation for the realization of goals set in EFL writing classrooms. When that occurs, we can enhance Chinese university writing instruction as well as systems found in other countries and foster a refreshing new era of process-based writing instruction for all.

Reflection Questions

1. On May 1, 2021, Zoom ended its free trial and started to charge for those who host the meeting, which hinders teaching due to the cost and access issues. Given such changes in policies, how can we guarantee the consistency and efficiency of online learning in future pedagogical contexts?
2. How can successful instructional approaches and experiences described in this chapter be effectively demonstrated to wide audiences at the regional, national, or international levels?
3. Can this model of online writing instruction through Zoom help to develop learner autonomy in the Chinese college classroom? How about in other countries or regions of the world? Can this model help to transform the traditional learning style developed over 12 years in a traditional teacher-centered classroom and promote learner autonomy and empowerment that can facilitate further learning?
4. Writing tasks in national achievement tests like CET-6 seem to be the only relevant assessment for those who attend online process-based writing instruction. How can more efficient formative as well as summative evaluation tools be designed to assess student learning outcomes and generate positive feedback for learners.
5. How can teachers' efforts after class be recognized? This instructional mode requires extra working hours for course design, task assignment, and learner training. How can the teachers' efforts and contributions be quantified rewarded? Should they be? Also, as this instructional model focuses more on teamwork rather than individual contributions, how can individual efforts be recognized to motivate students to contribute more in class?

17

A LEARNING JOURNEY BY BEING FAR AND NEAR

A Lesson Designed in the R2D2 Framework

Begaim Adilkhanova

Begaim Adilkhanova is an English teacher currently working at Nazarbayev Intellectual School of Chemistry and Biology in Shymkent, Kazakhstan. She received a Fulbright English Teaching Assistant award for 2012–2013 which she spent at Indiana University Bloomington in the United States. Begaim's objective is to provide her students with global experiences that can not only increase their

DOI: 10.4324/9781003213840-20

English skills but also build empathy and 21st-century skills. She can be reached at badilkha@gmail.com.

Introduction

A tulip city, Shymkent, located on a Great Silk Road in Kazakhstan, witnessed the third year of Nazarbayev Intellectual School (NIS) successfully operating with gifted children. All these children were scholarship holders which came from the first president of the country, Nursultan Nazarbayev. As a teacher, it was my job to spark their curiosity. As a result, I was thinking of using the CLIL (content and language integrated learning) method related to Kazakh literature and announced "Here comes a hero" as soon as every student settled into the room. That was a phrase of my warm-up activity for Year 11 students at NIS who had just finished the first part of the preliminary stage of writing a rave review.

After a minute of silence, one of my students asked me if they would start a new piece of reading as the word "hero" had nothing to do with the main topic from the previous day's lesson. Indeed, I used the word as a trigger to ignite students' curiosity. I asked them to open their peer reviews written on Google Docs and examine the comment sections carefully. While students were logging into their accounts, I prepared to gauge their reactions to the hero's engagement in the foreign language learning process. There was no doubt that my plan to follow the R2D2 (Bonk & Zhang, 2008) model had successfully planted the seeds of fruitful collaboration in a classroom setting and even beyond it.

It all happened when one of the heroes of a documentary about Kazakh adoptees in the United States kindly agreed to participate in the second stage of my lesson. I was thrilled! All he needed to do was to read and comment on Year 11 students' reviews. For the purposes of making the educational process fun and engaging, his involvement was kept secret from them. Thus, hardly any NIS students knew about my intention to give an unusual reward for their performance and have them collaborate with one of the main heroes of the documentary and an author of the post.

But first, let me explain how I have come across the hero—Rustem (Jordan). He was born by the name of Rustem, and my students would call him a "hero" before having a Skype meeting with him. As mentioned before, my students were familiar with the topic in the Kazakh literature they were discussing with my colleague, a Kazakh teacher. A hero, Rustem, was a legendary hero of the Persian folk epic, one of the central figures of the Shahnameh written by Ferdowsi in the 10th century. For my students, the word "hero" perfectly fit Rustem, as he was a teenager, who was the same age as they were; however, he saw family values quite differently than they did. Moreover, he had something unique in his personality that was worth admiring.

A white blouse. A pair of black trousers. A golden name badge with an NIS symbol . . . my daily uniform lay in a crumpled heap. I was too tired to move them and started checking my emails, hoping not to find any of them demanding urgent attention or action.

Then I switched to my Gmail and found a heart-melting email from Rustem (Jordan), who was born in Kazakhstan and then adopted by an American family. Rustem told me that he had found my email while searching for programs offering the Kazakh language throughout the United States. He contacted me because I was listed as a Kazakh instructor at Indiana University (IU) in Bloomington and co-author of the Kazakh textbook published at the Center of Languages of Central Asian Region. As a result, he decided to email me sharing his thoughts about his dream to reunite with his homeland.

What made this letter from Rustem so special was that we had many things in common. Soon I was reminded of my feelings, after having sung Kazakh songs in Auer Hall within the Jacob School of Music at IU in Bloomington. In actuality, his *background* sounded like a melody coming from the national two-stringed instrument, dombyra. Then I felt his passion for reuniting with his homeland, which brought lyrics of another song I had sung, "Elim menin" (My nation), to my mind. I saw his growing interest in Kazakhstan, which was found in my audience's eyes. Although both of us were born in the heart of Central Asia, we were each fortunate to have experienced life in the United States: Rustem by his upbringing and myself through my Fulbright experience. Finally, not only could we express a yearning and love for the homeland, but we were each able to connect to our own heritage differently.

I was so touched by Rustem and his email that I immediately replied and forwarded his letter to my friends in the United States and Kazakhstan. Later, we managed to do some Skype sessions with the boarding school students from my school who sent some presents that could be considered as symbols of Kazakh tradition and culture. A year later, Rustem starred as one of the heroes in the documentary *Bala*, which was about Kazakh adoptees' life in the United States. Moreover, his posts about life were published and have been translated into Russian in a digital magazine (https://esquire.kz).

Rustem's posts revealed common issues that modern Kazakhstani society has faced. Importantly, Rustem's interest in his homeland were also incorporated in the values taught at NIS, where my colleagues and I attempted to embed them in everyday lessons. At that time, my Year 11 students were the same age as Rustem. They were passionate to see and read a Kazakh adoptee's life experience, which led to his personal growth. When designing lesson plans, I could readily apply the knowledge gained during my wonderful class on instructional strategies at IU. Furthermore, the blended form of learning my hero would provide an excellent space for boosting student's collaborative problems skills within the R2D2 framework: Reading, Reflecting, Displaying, and Doing.

Fortunately, my school, Nazarbayev Intellectual School (NIS) of Chemistry and Biology in Shymkent, welcomed any creative pedagogical ideas embedded in the teaching and learning process. While I made some changes in the lesson plan designed according to the NIS program for Year 11, I maintained the school values of creativity, work, and transparency at the core of my plans. Since most NIS students were mixed ability in terms of having foreign language command, different types of collaboration activities were planned to nurture and support their language skills. For instance, I had my students work alone at first, and then pair up in writing a final product—a "rave review." Following the R2D2 model, there were four stages of this activity; however, since the model is flexible, we went in a different order, namely: Reading, Reflecting, Doing, and Displaying.

To achieve my goals, I showed a documentary titled *Bala*, which was about Kazakh adoptees in the United States. I had students fill in the table with two columns: (1) on the left side of the table, the students would make notes of things they found important (some statistics, one glove lying in the street, etc.), and (2) on the right side, they would record their thoughts or reactions in the form of questions, interpretations, or connections. Upon completing this two-part table, the students were supposed to discuss, in pairs, issues raised in the video and choose three of them to discuss. After having a thorough discussion, they had to choose a single issue that was the most relevant to the video and suggest three possible solutions. To be more precise and better able to speak on the topic, each pair had to prepare a defense of their selection process and their proposed solutions.

At the end of the debate, one real solution should have come to the fore. The second stage was recording the solutions to the chosen issue using a video-based discussion tool called Flipgrid. For this activity, students would think about how their solution might impact one of these people: (1) a Kazakh adoptee, (2) an American couple, and (3) the Kazakh authorities. Indeed, I could track my students' progress through shared Google Documents and chat boxes. By posting trigger questions, students started to make an effective argument with reasonable conclusions. Every participant in these heated discussions had something to say about issues common in Kazakhstan.

The last two stages were dealing with the student pairs engaged in the focused reading of a post published in a magazine and then reflecting on it. For this, each pair had to write a draft version of a rave review. They used some of the dialogue toolkits that they became familiar with during collaboration with other schools on the online collaborative program *Out of Eden Learn*.

While offering feedback on their cooperative work, I was dreaming of the following scenario: I saw my students with Rustem at the reunion dinner table where his dreams and feelings served as a cake and deliciously shared with each of the invited people. In turn, my students and I would drink a cup of tea filled with love, the taste of which would provide each of us a sense of belonging, and then pass it on. Moreover, I felt proud of having such students, as they were Rustem's peers. They were physically far from him and were not raised in the same environment as Rustem; however, at the same time, they felt so close to him.

Keep in mind that all this occurred using the R2D2 model and online tools that empowered communication, cooperation, and responsiveness. Little did they know that their posts that were shared in Google Drive would soon be reviewed by Rustem himself; in effect, not only would the posts be reviewed by one of the heroes in the documentary, but he would personally make comments on them. Talk about an exciting pedagogical activity! Two days after their submission, the final product showed their rave reviews. At that point, voting for the best posts based on the criteria (content, language accuracy, etc.) commenced.

This lesson helped me learn one important lesson: maybe we can fail to *read* minds, *reflect* on our past, predict how attitudes will be publicly *displayed*, and know what to *do* in specific life scenarios; the four key components of R2D2. However, one thing is certain: we can make a tremendous learning journey by being both far and near when immersed in culturally engaging pedagogical activities.

Reflection Questions

1. How did the real-life situations described in the story affect students besides practicing English with a native speaker?
2. Can you suggest a new teachable skill that might be listed as one of the 21st-century skills?
3. What made learners in this chapter develop creative and innovative solutions to real-life problems?
4. How can technology tools help teachers monitor and assess students' social and cognitive skills?

18

IT'S ALL ABOUT THE EXPERIENCE

Technology-Enhanced Designs to Generate Value

Maria Solomou

Maria Solomou is an experience design, consulting and organizational development professional currently working at PwC's Experience Center in Cyprus. She has a diverse background in game design, e-learning, instructional design,

DOI: 10.4324/9781003213840-21

training and development, learning organizations, entrepreneurship, and management. Maria designs and develops interactive, participatory experiences with the application of cutting-edge technologies, seeking to advance creative and critical thinking, facilitate digital transformation and enhance performance in organizations. She has a master's degree in education, technology, and society from the University of Bristol and a second master's as well as a PhD in learning sciences and instructional systems technology from Indiana University. She can be reached at msolomou@mariasolomou.com.

A Journey Full of Powerful Experiences

As I turn off the interactive screens, the virtual reality (VR) glasses, and the hologram, I catch myself singing along with the loud background music "clap along if you feel like a room without a roof-a . . .". My energy levels are still hitting the ceiling. "What a workshop!" I think, and smile. Suddenly, I pause and look outside the window. Vibrant orange, pink, and red colors on the Cyprus sky. At this point, I lower the music volume and pour myself a cup of coffee. Then I make my way to the couch in my attempt to enjoy the last few minutes of the sunset. "It was worth it!" I think.

It was worth it, not because of the sunset—well, OK, that was great—but because of all the energy I had absorbed from my interactions with participants of a design thinking workshop I was delivering over the past couple of days. If you are reading this, it probably means that you are into learning and development and are likely intrigued by emerging technologies as well.

This is a story about that particular moment, out of many, wherein I finished delivering a workshop in Cyprus and I felt ultimately rewarded! A story that has its foundations in my life experiences, my work, and my beliefs about using technologies to enable people to think critically and creatively in all areas.

Since my childhood, I have loved playing computer games. I found them to be such fascinating contexts of action, without realizing why. Growing up, that hobby started to affect my vision of what I wanted to do in my life. By the time I completed my first degree, I knew I was going to combine learning and games in my career. My challenge was, "How can I implement games and virtual worlds to create memorable experiences for people?" "How can I exploit the value of emerging technologies to engage people in ways that they are immersed in a situation?" "How can I turn abstract knowledge and information into practical, valuable, and memorable experiences?"

During my studies at Indiana University Bloomington, I was curious to learn ways of incorporating emerging technologies to enhance creativity as well as critical thinking. As a result, I took a couple of classes on emerging technologies, instructional strategies, creativity, and motivation. One of my realizations was how much, as a society or as an organization or institution within it, we need creative and critical thinking. And so my answer to the previous questions is to position people as active agents of change, like in the games we created with members of the Quest Atlantis design team at Indiana University over a decade ago, in ways that enable learners to realize the consequences of their actions and imagine creative, bold, and innovative solutions.

When it comes to creativity and innovation in the workspace, we tend to characterize ourselves as either creative or not creative, depending on the ideas we generate, the design preferences we have, and even our mood and habits. What I mostly hear from people in the business world is along the lines of "I'm not creative, I'm an accountant!" or "Why should I care to be creative? Isn't that a different profession?" There seems to be a conceptual misunderstanding about what creativity is since most people associate it with art. Creativity is more like a skill that helps us bring value to what we are doing. And when combined with critical thinking, it drives innovation.

What has become highly apparent every day in my journey is that creativity and innovation are enhanced by the organization's leadership (Hughes, Lee, Tian, Newman, & Legood, 2018); this is especially true in the workplace. What leaders need to do is inspire others! Usually, it is a challenge to convince people that they can be creative and that devoting time to innovation is no waste of time. Why wouldn't it be a challenge! In most societies and within most educational systems, we have been nurtured from early childhood to take most things for granted. We rarely challenge the validity of information, knowledge, or abilities. Until recently, rarely were learners induced into the process of understanding the "why," imagining the "what if," and conceptualizing ways to achieve the "possible."

Back when I was at Indiana University, we had developed an online 3D game for youth centered on creativity. We wanted to look into the ways participants engaged with creativity. Accordingly, we explored user perceptions on whether creativity is a structured or completely unstructured process. We were also curious whether it lies solely in each individual (cognitive theory) or if it can be the result of collaborative interactions and inspiration by the context (social learning theory).

Professor Kylie Peppler and I had adopted a systems-based approach to creativity and a sociocultural constructivist approach to learning to highlight how creative ideas emerge from our interactions with others (Peppler & Solomou, 2011). We created a narrative (based on Ayn Rand's novel *The Fountainhead*) in which there were two protagonist architects, one (Peter) giving absolute freedom to players to build any type of building they liked in their plot, and one (Howard) requiring players to follow particular guidelines to create their buildings. Impressively, players from both architectural teams had built remarkable buildings, each with its own character and each portraying the story of the interactions between the players and between the players and the non-player characters (NPCs).

Our analysis of the discussions within the virtual gaming environment provided clear evidence of the value context and collaboration have on creativity, as well as on critical thinking and argumentation. To me, that was a turning point. I had to create the right conditions each time to facilitate interactions and enable people to combine creative and critical thinking. And that was the case in the business workshop I was delivering at work here in Cyprus.

Another study I conducted around ways of designing online communities to operate as learning organizations showed that elements such as teamwork, leadership, planning, common vision, accountability, and responsibility are core to the success of such organizations (Solomou, 2014). That particular study was developed within the virtual gaming world of Quest Atlantis. There, users were organized in groups to solve different challenges and quests in their gaming missions to reach a valued treasure. Obviously, positioning these users in active ways and enabling them to work as experts defines their sense of responsibility and accountability. Having a common vision sets the ground for teamwork and leadership.

Creativity thrives in such contexts, as there is an open and transparent culture. Imagine how current professionals would think and interact if they were set up to think creatively and critically. Innovation would thrive in organizations! Part of my mission was exactly this—to enable my participants to combine creative and critical thinking, convergent and divergent modes of idea generation. And here I am at PwC Cyprus's Experience Center, working toward that, only this time with adults.

A few days before the workshop at work, I was having a discussion with Mr. Jones—the company executive—about digital transformation and creativity. For the workshop that I was organizing for his employees on ways to improve processes, I wanted to get a better understanding. To my question about how the company responds to the industry demands, he proudly responded,

> *Our people follow specific processes in all departments, from HR to financials to operations. Most of our people have been at the company for more than five years. They know their job and they do it well. All the years we have been in the market, we have been doing well. Our approach works, the way we have been doing things works. We bring new technology in when necessary and we try to keep production rates high. I want my employees to have a voice, be engaged, and take the organization to the future.*

I followed up: "How often do people in your company experiment with new ideas, explore new technologies, or investigate new solutions?" Said Mr. Jones, "Our focus is on delivering results." Clearly, Mr. Jones is very focused on his company's vision. As the conversation progressed, we established that it is important for organizations to move alongside progress and the client's needs.

The two-day workshop with Mr. Jones and 15 of his colleagues is about to start. Loud, energizing music is playing in the background. Participants are finishing their coffee, getting ready to take places. "Mr. Jones, we are doing this workshop, but I'm telling you once again, I'm not doing overtime work for the things that will be left behind!" stated a couple of participants in a teasing way. "There is value in our work, there is value in our development," Mr. Jones responded. Mr. Jones represents those C-level executives that apply transformational and inclusive leadership to enhance their employees' engagement. He sees the long-term value of learning and development, even though most of his employees find it difficult to escape the somewhat fixed way of processing things. For yet another work-shop, this was the bet to win.

We are about 45 minutes into the workshop, and participants start to write notes on the interactive screens detailing different challenges that they face at work. Perhaps this was made somewhat easier for them since we had already established that everyone left their ego at the door. And from the ideas pouring in on the monitors, it was clear that this attempt to foster an open, sharing-focused, and honest environment to work within was seemingly successful. At its core, this workshop positions participants in active ways so that they bounce between creative thinking and critical thinking at each stage. However, this was indeed a challenge for the participants, especially for the first couple of hours.

The role of the facilitator at this point is crucial—she must enable participants to think in particular ways and process information through different techniques and lenses. She must also help participants to generate ideas—lots of them—and then discuss, expand them, evaluate them, and adjust them. Then she needs to help them pick the most appropriate one and process it in relation to the ideal solution to their challenge.

I demonstrate some VR scenarios to immerse them into the challenge and understand it from different perspectives. We then use the interactive screens to work collaboratively. During the dance between creative and critical thinking, participants must be open to all ideas. Such openness to new ideas and flexible mindset creates a stage wherein when it is time to evaluate team ideas in relation to the challenge, participants are able to cluster them, set criteria, and process their value and feasibility. Technology, in this case, becomes a significant tool for enabling people to unlock specific corners in the two hemispheres of their brains, namely, both for sparking creativity and for enhancing critical thinking. By the end of the day, each of the teams had dived deeply into the challenges and understood them, defined them properly, and ultimately applied several ideation techniques to generate potential solutions.

The second day is dedicated to teams polishing the finalist solutions that they generated and prototyping them. Imagining how the implementation would be, creating user journeys and prototyping enabled teams to identify "bugs" and make improvements to their solutions. As participants work to the sound of the energizing music, I wander around the teams to get a sneak peek of their proto-types. It is exciting as they are about to present them in the plenary. One of the teams asks me to create a hologram of their data: "*If we send you these, could you please create them into a hologram? But don't mention it to the other teams . . . We have to have the best solution presentation and the hologram will make our description so much more powerful!"* A feeling kicked in at that moment—I am a proud facilitator who somehow turned the participants into creativity machines! Gamification worked. Immersion worked. Silos have been broken. I smile. "But of course!"

I call each team by their name and say, *"It is now time to share the solutions you prototyped and tested. All solutions are work in progress; however, we can all understand your concepts and how they work. So let the presentations begin!"* As expected, each team had its own, unique way of presenting its prototype. Hologram, Legos, and mobile application prototypes were just a few ways to express creativity in communicating a solution. Mr. Jones was astonished: "Colleagues, never before have we come up with so many solutions to challenges. And, never before have we had a robust understanding of what it means to solve the right problem. Bravo!"

The workshop is reaching an end. Happy faces greet me as they exit the room. Positive feedback and wishes to come back for more soon. What more can a trainer ask for? As if it was intentional, the clapping song starts playing. Is it for them? Is it for me? Whatever it is for, it definitely feels "like a room without a roof-a . . ."

Reflection Questions

1. Are you using the appropriate technology tools and all available resources for your particular learners and content?
2. How does the use of the technology tools that you access, evaluate, and utilize in your teaching and training actually facilitate creative and critical thinking?
3. How do you best induce your learners in different situations so that they live a memorable experience?
4. How can your learners apply the skills and competencies emphasized in your courses in their own situations?
5. Do your learners actively participate in the course and make substantive contributions that impact the course itself and their own lives? How does your course encourage such active learning through learner reflections and decision-making?

SECTION 4

Pandemic Practices

Section 4 chronicles how the pandemic altered, restructured and, in some cases, transformed the educational practices of teachers around the planet. While just five such stories from teachers in Singapore, Finland, India, Korea, and Mexico are found in this section, they each provide interesting tales of what teachers were able to accomplish during the pandemic and what types of instructional adjustments were easier than others.

Chapter 19 comes from Edwin Chew, a geography teacher in Singapore. Edwin shares his personal journey related to teaching his secondary school-age students during a turbulent year marked by school closure and the subsequent adoption of online teaching for all classes. While his story demonstrates how online learning platforms such as Google Classroom can be successfully adopted, it simultaneously warns of the distractions afforded by uncritical adoption of new technologies and the importance of maintaining our focus on student well-being and progress. While Edwin found most of the technologies tools that he used during the pandemic to be immediate in terms of impact and effectiveness as well as quite empowering, many such tools and resources were being deployed long before the pandemic hit. According to Edwin, teachers must be supported in forming online communities where they can reflect on the intersection of creative pedagogy and empowering technology.

Chapter 20 discusses "learning in lockdowns" and how to create learner-centered classrooms that are sufficiently safe and well structured during a public health emergency. In this chapter, Maija Heikkilä from Finland discusses what to take into consideration when moving from face-to-face to online classes. Maija describes the basics of what a teacher has to consider when planning online or face-to-face classes so that they are well organized and promote active learning. In essence, this chapter aims to make readers think about their own values and

DOI: 10.4324/9781003213840-22

conceptions of learning. In addition, it emphasizes the importance of collaboration in language learning and how to promote it successfully when online.

Chapter 21, the middle chapter of Section 3, deals with how information and communication technology was fruitfully utilized to supplement teaching-learning activities when the COVID-19 pandemic extensively wreaked havoc on schools around the world. As principal of a residential school in Mahe, India, Rathnakaran Kozhukkunnon Othayoth shares how he encountered and overcame various hurdles in establishing and facilitating virtual classrooms, which had replaced the traditional classroom in his country during the pandemic. Rathnakaran also recounts how his experience as a Fulbright teacher stood him in good stead in facilitating a smooth transfer to online learning in his school, in particular, and his organization, in general. His story offers hope and optimism to anyone dealing with sudden emergencies at their school or organization.

Chapter 22 discusses Jeong-Ae Lee's personal experiences in the fast-changing field of education in Korea due to the COVID-19 pandemic. As Jeong-Ae discusses in her chapter, schools are continuing to provide positive educational activities despite needing to rely on distance learning during these troubling times. Like preparation in all educational systems, what is vital during emergencies like the COVID-19 pandemic is the development of innovative teaching materials and the revitalization of teachers' learning communities. While many teachers are struggling, Jeong-Ae suggests that we can wisely overcome this crisis and more effectively communicate with students to adapt to the new normal era.

The final chapter in Section 3 describes a teaching dilemma that turned into a business opportunity. In Chapter 23, Samuel Arriaga recounts the many challenges he encountered as the head instructor of the TOEFL iBT and the GRE prep courses in Mexico when forced to move from a face-to-face to an online environment at the start of the pandemic. His experiences as a Fulbright scholar at Indiana University a few years earlier were a key factor in helping him cope with and adapt to this unforeseen challenge. This chapter describes some of the pedagogical methods he selected and the various successes that transpired.

As all these chapters show, the pandemic had wide-ranging effects on schools across the world. In spite of the myriad obstacles and challenges, through determination, support, and ingenuity, many educators were able to design highly successful activities that they can now build on.

19

CHICKEN OR EGG?

Achieving the Right Balance Between Technology and Pedagogy in Online Learning

Edwin Chew

Edwin Chew is a secondary school geography teacher in Singapore. His interests lie in fieldwork and the use of technology in geography. His work centres on continuous professional development, mentoring, and curriculum innovation.

DOI: 10.4324/9781003213840-23

Edwin was awarded a Fulbright Distinguished Award in Teaching at Indiana University in 2017. He can be contacted at chew_tec_heng_edwin@moe.edu.sg.

Lessons to Learn

Despite the almost overwhelming consequences of COVID-19, this global crisis has also been an extraordinary time for learning. As a profession, we have come to learn how adaptable and resilient we as teachers can be. We have also been shown, in a way none of us would have ever anticipated, the central importance of teaching and learning for our students. With the closure of schools during this pandemic and the subsequent shift to online learning has also come the realization that our students enjoy and respond positively to innovative and engaging methodologies. I have also become aware that the innovative and enjoyable aspects of my face-to-face classrooms must somehow be preserved via online platforms, tools, and resources, at least in part.

This is an account of my own reflective practice. In this chapter, I briefly describe the novel and, at times, exhilarating turns of my own journey of continuing professional development throughout this extraordinary period. With everything seeming to be in a state of constant flux, it was inevitable that my own practices and the norms that I had come to take for granted also required significant changes to fit these momentous times. Would a virtual classroom still be appropriate for the methodologies and approaches that I had used in a physical classroom with real walls, marker boards, and chairs? How would online teaching be different from face-to-face teaching? How would my students be affected, and how could I ensure that they continued to perform to the best of their abilities? In short, I needed to make certain that, as teachers, we were managing the new technologies to support us in continuing to deliver the best learning outcomes for our students whilst avoiding the pitfalls of a technology-driven pedagogy.

Virtual Classrooms, Real Students

We have been fortunate in having had some, albeit limited, opportunities to enjoy face-to-face teaching with our students as COVID-19 lockdowns have been imposed, lifted and, most recently, re-imposed. In that time, it became starkly clear that our students, and their parents too, were as anxious about the impact of school closures as we were ourselves.

In 2020, at the outbreak of the pandemic, full home-based learning (FHBL) had been a struggle as teachers grappled with the exigences of virtual classrooms and were learning to understand and use several new e-learning platforms. Everyone in the educational community wondered how we would cope in the months ahead. We received intensive training in e-pedagogy and e-assessment from the Ministry of Education, Singapore. It soon became clear that the Google Classroom platform was to become the new medium of interaction with our students.

And yet, what might have become overwhelming was rendered less so with the acceptance that, despite a virtual presence, our students remained as real as they have always been. They continued to require effective teaching in order to make steady progress in their curriculum subjects, which were learned best through peer-supported activities and relied upon teacher assessment and feedback to help them become independent learners.

Our task then became to effectively navigate these real and virtual classrooms, which would impact our planning choices and decisions as experienced teachers. One certainty, however, remained; we would continue to try to provide our students with the best learning opportunities available. Fortunately, during the pandemic, technology existed to deliver our lessons. As the French might say, "*Plus ça change, plus c'est la même chose.*" In other words, what goes around, comes around.

In this case, teacher responsibility for students' overall learning progress and well-being remained the driver within the virtual sphere in which we now found ourselves working. Coherent lesson planning, structured activities, valid assessments, and sound feedback continued to occur in Google Classroom. Perhaps they are even more vital if we are to convince our students and their parents that, as a profession, we teachers are more determined than ever to deliver the highest standards of teaching. As proof, my colleagues and I will use new technologies to re-open our classrooms for effective learning in the virtual sphere during COVID-19 and beyond.

Collaboration, I have always believed, is key to successful learning outcomes. Opportunities for teamwork, social interaction, and dialogue should perhaps become an even higher priority if we are to mitigate the isolation that students, trainee teachers, colleagues, and we ourselves experience during such a pandemic or other educational emergency. We need to find innovative pedagogical methods that access technologies, tools, and virtual classrooms for online collaboration within a particular class, as well as strategies that are robust and powerful for global collaborations with other classes around the world. When successful, it becomes apparent that mentoring, teaching, and reflective practice can be maintained even when we are forced to rely on virtual spaces instead of physical spaces.

A Personal Journey

I began working face-to-face with my students in January 2021, introducing them to the Google tools and features related to Google Classroom that they would need to become familiar with during FHBL. For me, it was important that students were confident in working with Google Classroom as this would become our only way of continuing academic progress in my geography classes. I was convinced, above all, that subject knowledge, understanding, progress, enjoyment, and success was, and would continue to be, the driving force behind my students' use of Google Classroom and that this should not become diluted or compromised by the technology we were using to support their remote learning.

For myself and my students, our familiarity with the software helped ease this transition to remote learning. Nevertheless, there remained a number of significant differences and obstacles that we needed to overcome. My aim was to re-create the same collaborative environment in my Zoom classes as seamlessly as possible. I worked through the design of different activities for online collaboration, such as brainstorming ideas in Google Jamboard since I knew from experience that students learned much more easily when they worked together, sharing ideas and supporting one another's learning.

As adults, we may be more familiar with online learning, studying for further qualifications in our own out-of-work time, completing training modules required for our jobs, or simply choosing to study a subject or follow a course that fits in with our own interests. For our students, however, this would be a very different and novel experience. I forced myself to remember that they had not chosen to register for an online geography course. Therefore, it was my responsibility to ensure that there be no qualitative difference between their online and actual classroom learning. I wanted students to be equipped with the knowledge and confidence that would help them continue to enjoy their learning and to make progress in the subject. Whilst the goalposts had certainly shifted in terms of *how* students were now taught, the goal of *what* they should be taught remained unchanged.

In my work as a mentor to newly qualified teachers, I have discovered that the best way to learn is most often through networking. At the outset, FHBL seemed to challenge this notion in every way; students would be working in isolation in their own homes, thereby making group activities, shared discussions, and the exchange of ideas and data interpretations somewhat problematic. At times, it seemed as though each day and each lesson within each day presented a new challenge. However, I discovered a wealth of resources available through the Student Learning Space learning platforms, the Education Technology Department Division in the Ministry of Education in Singapore, SgLDC Designers (i.e., a community of Singapore learning designers coming together to share, learn, and design learning experiences with information and communications technology for the 21st-century classroom), and other online educational tools that would help me achieve my overriding mission of conducting collaborative and engaging online classes with my students.

Using online collaborative tools, such as Zoom breakout rooms, gave students who might otherwise have contributed little or nothing to a full-class meeting ample opportunities to work together on specific tasks, express their ideas, and learn from one another. The use of Google Jamboard allowed me to monitor how well they performed and provided me with feedback to plan revision or extension work for individual students. I was also able to assess how well students had understood the work at hand and how I should plan for the next and subsequent lessons in the sequence. Given my overriding high course quality goals, I felt fortunate that this technology tool also allowed me to interact with students so that I was able to provide timely and pointed feedback and participate in their discussions, thereby helping them maintain pace in their work. This practice also ensured that everyone remained focused and felt included despite their apparent isolation.

Chicken or egg? Online learning tools and technology have certainly provided us with a new range of innovative and exciting teaching methodologies that can enhance students' learning. Using online technology, the learning environment can be immediate, familiar, and empowering. However, if these technologies are to be successful, many other methodologies, tools, and resources that enriched our classroom lessons before the onset of COVID-19 should not be overlooked. Robust lesson planning and work schedules that prepare for incremental progress and are relevant to both the most and least able students remained essential. As with any instructional situation, when teaching in FHBL, teachers still must consider the pace, interest, feedback mechanisms, and use of sound and other multimedia elements. And they must make a judicious choice and use of free and open educational resources as well as incorporating effective and consistent classroom management strategies.

Wellness and Our Teacher Community

The shift to FHBL in May came with a slew of challenges. We were working in uncertain times, with no clear idea how long these new measures would remain in place. Given such uncertainty, it was important to accept the changes happening around us and become involved and pro-active by taking our own voyages of self-discovery through e-learning. In effect, teachers in Singapore and around the world had to recognize that this was an opportunity for creating new and effective ways of teaching.

I fully accepted that this was no easy task, and I had times when frustration kicked in. However, I learned that by reaching out for support from colleagues and by working collaboratively with them, or by seizing the opportunity to enhance my own practice by searching online for advice and examples, I could help ease what was, at times, a quite difficult journey. We are, after all, humans and not AI bots and agents!

Understandably, as educators, we want to explore all the available e-tech tools to decide what is highly effective and to give our students the best range of opportunities and experiences possible. Of course, this emphasis on helping students shine is very laudable; perhaps it is an inherent trait of those who choose the teaching profession. However, we face inevitable time constraints and other limitations that force meta-reflection and reconsideration on our every move. To provide successful online learning, we have had to become familiar and adept with the technologies presented to us. Unfortunately, too often, these have been served up in quite daunting portions.

I found that sometimes I attempted to learn too much and explored too many educational technology tools and resources. In such moments, I came to realize that perhaps, by doing this, I may have been compromising the time I should have been directing towards the content and presentation of an individual or planned sequence of lessons. It was difficult to put aside an article when reading about a new online tool even when realizing that I still needed to prepare the content of the next day's lessons. At times, I slipped into burning the midnight oil and then some! Needless to say, the endless work hours were not sustainable, and I soon adopted the mantra that it is always OK to accept common human limitations. Of course, such acceptance is valuable and quite prudent, as we must care for our own health and well-being.

Effective teaching is well planned and executed. Using multiple tools in our online classes and conducting classes with a new platform every session does not make online teaching more effective; rather, it may cause confusion and panic for ourselves and our students. We should keep the curious discoveries to ourselves and let our students focus on their learning instead of constantly attempting to figure out how to use the inexhaustible supply of online e-learning tools so readily available.

We need to give our students clear guidelines around online class rules and expectations, including how and when they can contact us; after all, FHBL should include the rigours and standards of the non-virtual classroom. Most importantly, we must continue to ensure our students' journey as independent and autonomous learners. As teachers worldwide discovered during the pandemic, online education allows learners to take greater responsibility for their own learning. Accordingly, within the FHBL environment, it becomes even more vital that we, as teachers, focus on continuing to plan for such self-directed learning and monitor its success.

We can achieve this goal by keeping a vigilant eye on the pedagogy and not letting ourselves become blindsided by all the user-friendly online technology at our disposal. Our accumulated experience as educators remains paramount as we develop online cognitive tasks and assessments to support students' learning. Perhaps the question after all is not necessarily which came first, the chicken or the egg, but rather how mutually dependent they are, the one upon the other. As shown in the following student quotes, both innovative pedagogy and thoughtful use of technology are vital to student and teacher online learning success and sustainability over time.

Student Reflections

On the whole, during course evaluations, comments about FHBL were generally positive. A student expressed sympathy for her teachers: "During the last few days of Full Home-Based Learning (FHBL), it must have been difficult for the teachers to be assigning work to us, students." Another student described some benefits of virtual instruction:

> *Mr. Edwin had given us a Weather Instruments handout as well as online quizzes to help us out with studying for Weighted Assessment (WA) 2. This was very useful as I could access this set of handouts from anywhere, and it could really save a lot of paper. And it would allow for a quick last-minute revision that we could access from our mobile devices.*

Student comments on the ease of use were also common. As one student put it, "As I began to explore the various options in Google Classroom, notes were uploaded into Google Classroom which were accessible for all of us . . . This made it easier for us to understand instead of hearing the teacher telling us what we had and needed to do."

Many students remarked about the power of tools for collaboration and brainstorming like Google Jamboard. For instance, "One of the memorable uses of tech tools that enabled my writing and collaboration with my classmates was to use the Google Jamboard in framing our thinking before writing." Note that Google Jamboard is a cloud-based app that enables visual collaboration between users in real time; a highly valuable tool for remote teaching and learning.

Such tools also offer opportunities for perspective taking, as exhibited in the following learner comment: "As we had to work in groups and be receptive to feedback given online, I learned to pause, think and respect others' points-of-view." Such a tone is apparent in this quote as well: "What I had discovered is that there were ideas being bounced and generated which allowed us to populate the whiteboard. In addition, I realized that the use of Google Jamboard gave me confidence in planning and conceptualizing my thoughts."

In effect, students had also learned to feel comfortable within their new online communities wherein group work, in general, was well received. One learner stated: "Working in groups remotely is very different from working in the class-room as we had to respect each other, and everyone had to contribute and par-ticipate. Visually, it helped me as I could connect the dots and was glad that my classmates gave input towards the essay assigned."

A sense of community also seemed to provide motivation for some students working in isolation at home as indicated in this final quote.

> *Online classes may be boring, but you will find yourself being extra productive with a bit of self-motivation, either before, during, or after class. Alongside that, we were also able to explore the different online platforms that could help us with learning during the HBL lesson. Online tools such as the Google Jamboard, which are help-ful for mind maps and note-taking.*

Summary

The move towards a blended learning approach needs to help students develop the capacity for independent learning and not simply be used to replicate classroom teaching in the virtual medium. One of the key lessons learned is the need to redesign the learning experience around technological affordances and to avoid replacing face-to-face lessons with virtual talk-and-chalk lectures. When well designed and matched seamlessly with effective instructional methodologies, online e-pedagogy tools and technologies offer exciting ways to enhance and facilitate students' learning beyond the current exigences of COVID-19.

Reflection Questions

1. Ask yourself: how critical am I in the selection of e-learning tools and materials? Is my decision-making process affected by my own knowledge and understanding of these technologies? If yes, how so?
2. When teaching online, to what extent am I able to discuss ideas, concerns, and experiences with colleagues and share best practices and success stories? How are these opportunities to share pedagogical ideas and actual experiences impacting my own practice?
3. How good is my time management in a working-from-home situation? Do I need to draw up my own timetable to achieve a healthy work-life balance?

20

LEARNING IN LOCKDOWNS

Creating Safe, Structured, and Student-Centered Classes During the Pandemic

Maija Heikkilä

Maija Heikkilä teaches English as a foreign language for students ages 12 to 18 at Helsinki University Viikki Teacher Training School in Finland. She is also a teacher trainer for preservice teachers who are studying to become English

DOI: 10.4324/9781003213840-24

teachers at the University of Helsinki. In addition to teaching, Heikkilä also works as a teacher training coordinator for the English Department at Viikki. She also has experience in adult education. She can be reached at maija.o.heikkila@ helsinki.fi.

Values and the Concept of Learning

As a teacher trainer, I always talk to my student teachers about the importance of establishing their own teaching philosophy. What do they think good teaching is? How can that be achieved, and how do they know they have achieved it? When I reflect on my own teaching or plan an academic year, all the activities, tasks, assignments, and pedagogical choices rest on my beliefs and values of what good teaching is and how it can be achieved. In fact, each module and every single lesson boils down to those deeply held beliefs and values.

My personal standards of quality education are based on the values, beliefs, and conceptions of learning described in the National Curriculum of Education in Finland. The National Curriculum is, most importantly, a set of values in education, together with guidelines and goals that should be reached. However, it does not specify what you should exactly "do" to reach those goals. Thus, teachers in Finland are required to do a fair amount of organizing, planning, and structuring themselves on how to reach the goals and follow the guidelines set by the National Board of Education. In other words, it is the teacher's responsibility to plan and organize and also to assess and evaluate students' learning as we do not have standardized testing in Finland. Teachers in Finland have extensive freedom in what to do in class, but it also comes with plenty of responsibility. As a teacher trainer, I always say to my student teachers that being a teacher means that you will need to make many pedagogical decisions to reach the stated goals set in the curriculum. However, how you accomplish them can be done in many different ways. The approach undertaken should reflect your values, beliefs, and the concept of learning that you believe in.

Such bounded freedom within mandated curriculum goals came to be as important as ever in March 2020 when we were given a three-day notice from government officials that they would be closing schools and all teaching would be conducted online for the foreseeable future. This was a historical situation in a country that values education above all else. The only time in history that Finland has ever closed its schools was during the Second World War. We do not close schools because of snow days or bad weather, so the country-wide school closures were quite remarkable. The announcement gave us three days to plan and organize all our classes online. During the early days of the pandemic, I really thought about my values and what good teaching means online. I also reflected on how to maintain students' well-being; in effect, I wanted to make sure that, in addition to learning, my students were also feeling safe.

Student-Centered Learning in Online Classes

One of the essential values of my teaching is that learning should be active. A second essential is that students should use English as much as possible. In addition, I believe that communication, cooperation, and collaboration play an integral part in my lessons. In language learning, it is vital that the students are able to practice their spoken language skills in every lesson. In other words, in my classes, we spend a fair amount of time doing paired or group activities that promote my students' communication skills. We play board games, debate, discuss different topics, engage in role plays, and practice communication in different types of situations. We also practice new vocabulary and grammar with different types of spoken activities.

Clearly, active learning and collaboration were vital in my online classes. To achieve high levels of collaboration, I created different channels for our online platform where students would be able to complete oral activities with their partners or in groups via video conference. My online classes were structured so that we started with activities and games that were completed together as a whole class. Then they would move onto the channels to complete tasks in pairs or in groups. Finally, a small part of that class time would be allocated for independent work. Such a structure became to be a common thread in all my online classes.

One of the key concepts when promoting active or student-centered learning is the ratio of student versus teacher time in class. In my face-to-face classes at school, I always make sure that I have designated most of the class time for active and engaging learning while attempting to minimize teacher talk. This emphasis on student-centered instruction becomes even more important in online teaching, where student voice and engagement are extremely critical. In online learning, opportunities for students to work together and collaborate become even more important than in a regular class. Successful collaboration at a distance offers the student a chance to socially interact outside of their family structures. As a teacher, you want to make sure that even those students who might not have many friends and social connections can still feel a sense of belonging and have a chance to interact with other people in your class.

Lesson Structure and Planning

Another aspect of teaching that is crucial when planning are the routines and the structure of the lesson. For instance, I usually start my lessons with a fun game of revision about what we have learned previously. This technique is easily transferred to my online classes as the online lessons also start with a fun game of revision. Moreover, I also want to plan my online lessons so that they will be as similar as possible to my in-class lessons at school.

At the same time, I thought that this approach would create a sense of security as students realized that even though they are at home and even though the world around them might be in chaos and quite scary at times, our lessons and things that we do in class would remain more or less the same. That sense of security and feeling of being safe when you are learning is crucial. Suffice to say, if students are not feeling safe, they cannot concentrate on learning. Moreover, in classes during the lockdown, we never discussed the pandemic. I avoided directly discussing the pandemic as I wanted to give them a reprieve from such negative circumstances. I want my students to enjoy and have fun in class.

Lessons Learned

It is time to look back now to the time when the announcement to close the schools was made by the government. In reflecting on and evaluating my pedagogical decisions and my approach to teaching online, I realize that I managed to succeed because I was able to follow my teaching philosophy and values. Later in the spring of 2020, when the schools were opened for the last two weeks of the academic year, I collected some feedback from my students about their experiences from the lockdown. I felt fortunate that many of them praised my online classes for being easy to adjust to and that learning English was easy and fun. Comments from these students included kind words that "English classes were well-planned and organized," and that "English classes were one of the best online classes."

Now that we are in lockdown again, I tell my student teachers how critical it is to think deeply about what is essential in teaching as they are planning their first remote lessons. For instance, they must take into consideration students' sense of security during this global crisis. The most important question to think about when planning to teach, whether it is online or in-person, held with preschoolers or adults, or is self-paced or teacher dominated, is what good teaching means. The answer should be at the core of every lesson, module, and course you are planning. Your values and emphasis as a teacher might change over the years as you gain more experience and learn to assess and develop your teaching strategies and approaches. Nevertheless, the core philosophical questions on which you base your plans and activities remain the essentially same.

Reflection Questions

1. What are the values that you base your teaching on? Have there been any recent changes?
2. What is your conception of learning? In what way has it changed during the past few years?
3. What kinds of strategies would you emphasize in online classes and why?
4. What makes effective online teaching, in your opinion, and how is it different from face-to-face instruction?

21

ACTIVELY ENGAGING STUDENTS IN INDIA DURING COVID-19

A Former Fulbrighter Finds Hope

Rathnakaran Kozhukkunnon Othayoth

Rathnakaran Kozhukkunnon Othayoth is the principal of Jawahar Navodaya Vidyalaya, Mahe, India. During his tenure in the United States as a Fulbright Distinguished Award teacher, he interacted with many teachers and teacher educators to identify best practices in integrating information and communication technology (ICT) in teaching. He is the recipient of the National Award for Teachers from the President of India and the National Best Principal's award by Navodaya Vidyalaya Samiti. He is one of the resource persons for training teachers in mathematics education and ICT integration in India. He can be reached at rathnanko@yahoo.com.

DOI: 10.4324/9781003213840-25

Introduction

"Are you from China?" It was surprising that a person wearing a face mask should be asked such a question by his co-passenger. It was the month of February 2020, and I was traveling to Delhi. I was the only person onboard wearing a mask, of course, by personal choice. That was the time when the first COVID-19 positive case was reported from India; a medical student from China tested positive for COVID-19 on his arrival to his home state Kerala.

Everything has changed now. Everyone in my country, like everyone elsewhere around the globe, wears a mask, probably more by medico-legal enforcement than personal choice. Yes, we are fighting an all-out battle against a tiny villain, the coronavirus. The whole scenario of daily life has changed. The impact of this pandemic is felt in every field and in every moment, be it in people's attitude, their living conditions, or in their educational pursuits. You see it in the healthcare sector, manufacturing and production sectors, administrative fields, service industry, and so on. You name it! The question is one of "to be or not to be"! And undoubtedly, we prefer to take the side of "to be."

The education sector was one of the worst affected, particularly in our country, as online teaching had not been a regular practice here. In fact, I had the first meeting on the Zoom platform when I was at Indiana University (IU) Bloomington in the fall of 2017 as a Fulbright scholar. My professor had invited me for an online meeting of a special class guest of his, which I was thrilled to attend. I attended many similar programs with this professor, and he always brought in prominent guests from places around the world. I was not just learning interesting content and ideas from these researchers and scholars, but also I was learning a whole new pedagogical approach. These Zoom sessions brought a level of excitement and energy that I fully welcomed.

This novel experience motivated me to experiment with online meetings with my teachers in India during my stay in the United States. It all started just for fun. In retrospect, I never thought that these meetings, which first came as a digital luxury, were destined to become a normal platform for the classroom teaching-learning process in the whole of my country in general and find use in my school in particular. In fact, as part of my Fulbright program, I was working on an inquiry project on the topic of information and communication technology in learning mathematics using open resources, using different research tools such as interviews and interactive sessions with my professors at IU and the teachers from different parts of the United States. I was hungry for ideas and innovations.

Then it happened, and I have not looked back. It was my first experience to be added to the Canvas platform as a student for the course. That fall, I was auditing a course at IU called "Instructional Strategies for Thinking, Collaboration, and Motivation." The experience I gained from my interactions with the professor and my fellow scholars was quite enlightening as it opened up an entirely new world of communication, interaction, and collaboration on a global scale. For me and my fellow educators in India, it was a previously untapped treasure-house of knowledge. The teaching methodology followed here was remarkably different from the traditional ones we had been using back in my country. I was increasingly fascinated! Knowing how to use technology effectively and meaningfully in the teaching-learning process has paved a new way in my thinking and interacting with children, which I am vigorously practicing on my return to India.

Coming back to where I started this story, COVID-19 started spreading over the whole country. To contain the spread, a lockdown was first introduced in my state, Kerala. It most certainly was an unprecedented and unheard of experience for everyone. Normal life came to a grinding halt. Schools were closed, and we were all in a state of dilemma and confusion. That was the third week of March 2020, just when the annual exams were around the corner. There would be no exams. Instead, parents were asked to come and take their children back home. Ours is a residential school, one among a chain of more than 650 schools across the country, named Jawahar Navodaya Vidyalaya. It is run by the government of India for providing good quality modern education to talented students predominantly from rural areas. Unfortunately, once all the children left for home, the campus, usually a hub of curricular and co-curricular activities, had a deserted look. Soon I was wondering how to go ahead with my pedagogical ideas and experiments and what to do next.

As the principal of the school, the onus was on me to formulate further plans of action according to my superiors' directions. It was at this juncture that my Fulbright experience and exposure to online collaborative tools and systems like Zoom came to me in a flash. With a brimming smile on my face, I scheduled the first online meeting with parents and students in the third week of March For most of them, it was their maiden experience with such technology, and they were all thrilled to see each other virtually.

After that single meeting, there was no looking back. Frequent synchronous conferencing meetings were then carried out. Students were advised what to do and how to come to terms with this unprecedented situation of a lockdown. To help with their emotional states, I requested that they practice yoga, which they were doing during the stay in the school. In addition, I suggested to the students that they help their parents with their household chores. I also recommended that they devote a little time to some small kitchen gardening and enjoy their stay home. So far, so good. Still, I knew their learning was suffering. As the saying goes, an idle mind is a devil's workshop. There were abundant opportunities for students to be influenced by unnecessary things and picking up undesirable habits.

I decided to take the online meeting to the natural next step in the process, namely, online teaching. Given this necessary shift to online instruction, I requested that some of the teachers enroll in online classes on an experimental basis. At that time, I purchased a pen tablet as it was absolutely essential for my subject, mathematics. Amazingly, almost all my teachers bought their own pen tablet and started getting acquainted with it gradually. Online teaching offered a different experience for all of us. What we discovered was the thrill of teaching this way. In fact, in some cases, we felt that online teaching was better than regular physical face-to-face teaching. Why better? Well, the teachers found and shared a dazzling stream of open educational resources and tools for teaching like GeoGebra and Desmos in mathematics and many other resources for other subjects.

In the first week of April, I received a call from Navodaya Vidyalaya headquarters asking me to explore the possibilities of using Microsoft Teams for online teaching. My experiences at IU with Canvas were a tremendous help in exploiting this platform. I was excited and had many meetings with the officials of Microsoft Teams. Soon, a "tenant," as Microsoft names it, was created to host Microsoft Teams for free for my school and was named Jawahar Navodaya Vidyalaya, Mahe. Thus, it first started with my school, and then taking a cue from us, the other schools in my state Kerala followed suit.

And now Microsoft Teams is being employed in several schools in different regions of India. I am delighted that I have been chosen to coordinate the rollout and implementation of Microsoft Teams. As indicated, Microsoft is providing this platform free of cost to Jawahar Navodaya Vidyalaya. I also had the privilege of organizing different meetings, including a number of principals' conferences in different regions of the country using this platform. My hope is that online learning experiments and the use of different instructional strategies for enhanced thinking, motivation, and collaboration can perhaps be integrated throughout India.

The whole teaching fraternity slowly started going online: discussing, interacting, teaching, testing, meeting, and attending workshops and seminars. Now this online experience has come to stay and take roots. It is a paradigm shift in my country from offline mode to online mode. Notwithstanding the initial glitches, teachers in my school, as well as those across India, have adopted online teaching methods. It was a challenge for everyone to reach out to the children in online mode, and it was a different experience for the whole teaching-learning community.

Many of the students in my school are from rural backgrounds. Now looking back, it is genuinely incredible that we could reach out to all of them. Those students lack the necessary internet connectivity and technology gadgets. However, they were contacted individually by our teachers, who supported them by providing them with alternative learning resources such as printed materials, dedicated TV channels (e.g., DD Gyan Darshan), and various radio programs. All this changed the mindset of the teachers as most of them started enjoying this new method of online teaching and learning. It was a substantial paradigm shift in the methodology and process of teaching. As I reflect on what we have accomplished during the past year, I feel immensely indebted to my Fulbright experience for enabling me to extend a helping hand to my organization and my nation in this hour of direst need.

When writing this, our country has embarked on a massive vaccination drive, perhaps the largest in the world, given India's population index. There is now hope, despite recent massive COVID-19 outbreaks in India, that this pandemic too will pass soon. I can see the light at the end of the tunnel. This light will hopefully shine some paths for more exciting pedagogical experiments at my school and throughout Kerala. I cannot wait to get started or rebooted.

Reflection Questions

1. How can the experience you have acquired in a different cultural milieu be integrated into your classroom teaching and learning? What challenges do you foresee, and how can they be best addressed?
2. In the next five or ten years, how far do you think technology can influence academic exploration and vice versa?
3. What could be the author's objective in narrating his experience in the given context?
4. How do you think the author succeeded in helping his colleagues and students overcome their inhibitions and apprehensions about the new method of teaching-learning? Do you find his ideas and methods practical? Could you implement them? Why or why not?

22

ONLINE EDUCATION IN A KOREAN ELEMENTARY SCHOOL DURING COVID-19

Focusing on My Experience Using Blended Learning

Jeong-Ae Lee

Jeong-Ae Lee has been an elementary school teacher in South Korea for over 20 years. She has a master's degree in computer education from Hanyang University. Currently, she is teaching fifth-grade students in Busan. In 2018–2019, she was a visiting scholar at Indiana University. She is interested in collaborative

DOI: 10.4324/9781003213840-26

learning, coding education, reading education, and Positive Discipline in the Classroom. She can be contacted at aecom92@gmail.com.

Pandemic Reactions

After spending the 2018–2019 academic year as a visiting scholar at Indiana University (IU) in Bloomington, I returned to work as an elementary school teacher in Korea. Just four short months later, after the first confirmed case of COVID-19 occurred in Korea in January 2020, the virus began to spread among people in earnest. Because of this unprecedented situation, the start of the school semester was delayed. Since the start of school that spring could not be postponed forever, the Korean Ministry of Education began school online. This was the first time that online education emerged in K-12 education across Korea. As a result, there were significant changes and adjustments for students, parents, and teachers.

To successfully open the school, the Korean Ministry of Education provided guidance and support to deploy and use various online platforms and technology tools. Among the technologies and resources were the E-Learning Center and EBS (Educational Broadcasting System) online classes, which made online courses so that schools could conduct classes in one-way or two-way modes.

As someone who has worked in an elementary school for more than 20 years, this sudden change was quite disconcerting when online classes suddenly appeared as the main method of education. At first, I gasped as I had a lack of experience in teaching online classes. Simply put, I did not know where to start. My school also urgently set up a task force team. Following the Ministry of Education's guidelines, members of the task force team helped reorganize the curriculum, set up plans to build an online environment, and purchased equipment such as webcams and dual monitors. Unlike other schools, which just decided to engage in similar types of fully online classes across grade levels, first and second graders in my school used EBS online classes to utilize various contents, whereas with third to sixth grade students, my school decided to use contents from the E-Learning Center and two-way real-time classes via Zoom. Overall, this switch to e-learning was a most daunting task since it forced most teachers to conduct classes online all of a sudden without being prepared.

Much of education in Korea is regimented and standardized—the schedules, the courses, the assessments, and so forth. As a result, switching to a totally new educational delivery structure was a shock to the system. There was much to be done in a short amount of time. First, teachers in the same grade learned how to use the online platform and Zoom. They also dug in and learned related programs one by one. Due to the nature of an elementary school, where homeroom teachers have to teach almost all subjects, it was impossible to create all the necessary course content for an online environment. As a result, each of the teachers in the same grade took charge of one or two areas and then created and shared the contents. In addition, an online environment of sharing news and educational content among teachers across the country was extremely active, and extensive advice and support were consistently provided.

The first online session began with a mixture of feeling quite burdensome, high pressure, and lofty expectations for the new class. In the case of the fourth graders who I taught, four classes out of my six classes a day were one-way online classes focused on content utilization and task solving, while the latter two classes relied on two-way interaction using Zoom.

At first, only the learning environment was changed due to the pandemic, but the actual format and content of the classes did not deviate from the traditional methods. This was unfortunate. Soon teachers were posting learning-related videos and assignments on online platforms, which the students watched, and where they solved tasks and submitted assignments. Feedback and lecture-style classes were given during real-time classes. However, due to the characteristics of elementary school students, they tended to lack sufficient self-study skills, and they also displayed short concentration spans. Both issues made online learning especially difficult.

It was evident to me that there was a need for different learning strategies for my elementary school students. Soon I was designing many activity-oriented classes. Students who lacked the power to do things on their own found online classes especially difficult. Such students displayed a lack of seriousness in learning and solving tasks and tended to quickly lose motivation as well as attention. Therefore, after online class sessions, I frequently had to interact with parents to consult about students' learning attitudes and academic conditions via a phone call, educational SNS, or some other means. In effect, teachers had no choice but to spend a hectic year preparing for in-person classes, preparing online class contents, giving feedback on the various learning results, giving perpetual counseling, and receiving training on the use of various technology tools and programs.

At the start of 2020, online classes began without enough time for proper preparation. Fortunately, after much trial and error, the online delivery system became relatively stable in the second semester, and we were able to wrap up the year successfully. Based on this success, in 2021, our school, which is an oversized school with more than 1,000 students, decided to conduct both in-person classes and online classes. Importantly, online classes were fully two-way classes using platforms such as Zoom. Along with Zoom, our school is currently purchasing tablet computers for students and installing electronic blackboards to support blending learning. At present, teachers are also learning the meanings, methods, and examples of blending learning and applying them to actual classes.

My Preparation and Activities

When at IU, I attended classes on emerging learning technologies and instructional strategies. In these classes, I was able to learn methods and strategies for engaging in online learning. In fact, I honestly didn't think there would be any chance for me to actually use these methods in Korea. However, due to the pandemic, the situation has changed, forcing teachers in Korea and around the world to employ online learning and blended learning techniques akin to what teachers in Hong Kong and Singapore went through in 2015 to deal with the MERS outbreak as well as SARS 12 years before it.

For example, I applied blending learning in my social studies class with questions such as "How did people in the past improve human rights?" On the day when we had an in-person class, we went through social studies textbooks to check the meaning and importance of human rights. Students also searched for additional people who strove to improve human rights in the past. In addition, we found books related to human rights and had homework to read those books at home.

In the next remote class, we wrote research papers with the information from the book and online research. It contained a picture of the person and their name and nationality, a brief explanation about that person, and what he or she did to foster human rights. We uploaded the papers to Padlet, which allowed students to share their work and provide peer feedback. Importantly, I allocated time for discussions of these papers using Zoom breakout rooms.

Frustrations and Achievements

Whether you were a student, teacher, or parent, there were some serious challenges as well as noticeable achievements in this novel educational environment during the pandemic. First, adopting new devices and platforms was a major challenge. Students, parents, and all the education stakeholders needed a period of adjustment to the use of these tools and devices. Many parents had a negative view of the situation. One of the reasons for their pessimism was that since they expected that their children would need to use computers for many hours, they would be easily exposed to games, YouTube videos, and other distractions. Next, in addition to the pressures of the new teaching environment experienced by teachers and students, the additional information provided to parents about the course contents and progress added a layer of stress on everyone.

In addition to the frustrations displayed by parents, many teachers also did not view online learning positively. Overall, the decline in students' academic performance was clear; especially students who previously had average or below grades. These students suffered the most, as shown in their dramatic academic declines since they were not used to self-directed learning. A major challenge in the online classroom was overcoming individual differences in student digital skills and capabilities, attitudes toward learning online, and overall sincerity and seriousness.

For schools, there was no proper teaching manual for situations like COVID-19. As a result, many educators experienced a year of dramatic confusion. My school had to make rapid decisions about many issues and challenges on its own as came up. Teachers and administrators had to determine the online teaching environment and methods that fit the school situation and then establish detailed guidelines while following the Ministry of Education's policies and guidelines.

Along with these challenges, some interesting things have also been discovered. For instance, the pandemic gave me the opportunity to observe various aspects of students that I did not witness at school. Before the start of the real-time class sessions using Zoom, all the students in our class were able to get to know their friends by taking time to introduce their emotional statuses and reasons for such status. Interestingly, one student introduced his pet parrot on his shoulder, which drew much excitement and amazement from his classmates. Such introductions eased the awkwardness of the online class and students became more intimate with each other.

After the creation of an environment where online classes are viable, it has become possible to cope with suddenly dangerous situations and emergencies. For example, the day after a heavy rain, an emergency occurred at school. The previous day's massive rain left the school's electricity out, which made all systems, including computers, unusable. The school quickly switched from in-person to online classes. Fortunately, teachers were able to use their personal devices to conduct online classes without any problem. In effect, experiences during the early days of the pandemic can have a positive impact on school adjustments months or years later caused by other emergencies.

I should also point out that online classes, which were considered something way off in the distant future for teachers, were here all of a sudden today. This fast emergence of online learning elevated the need for digital literacy for both students and teachers. Teachers are learning how to use devices such as video cameras, dual monitors, and tablets for their online classes. Additionally, they are learning how to use Zoom, Padlet, Google Classroom, and digital textbooks for interactive and engaging online classes. In addition, a large teacher community (LTC) has been created to share their knowledge, experiences, and discoveries for their own professional development. Importantly, this online community of Korean teachers is growing and developing together by finding better teaching examples and optimal teaching models.

Moving On Post Pandemic

In this difficult and stressful time where we face a global health crisis, with thoughtful planning and extensive support, schools are continuing to provide positive educational activities. Despite the many struggles, there are countless learning successes due to the devotion and creative abilities of Korean K-12 teachers who are preparing exciting and engaging course materials for various online systems and revitalizing LTC. With such skill and dedication, Korean teachers (as well as fellow teachers around the world) will wisely overcome this crisis and be able to adapt to the post-pandemic era.

I can't wait to see what education in Korea and around the world evolves into during the coming decade. It will be a quite memorable journey. Thanks for reading about my journey thus far.

Reflection Questions

1. How does one know if there is a learning gap when learning remotely? What does the phrase "learning gap" actually mean? How can it be observed or measured?
2. What are the potential causes of learning gaps between students in remote classes and face-to-face classes? How can any gaps be resolved?
3. What are some of the challenges that teachers face in conducting online classes, and how can they overcome them?
4. What do you think are the most emphasized basic skills and capabilities for teachers after COVID-19? What about for students? How have these skill expectations and requirements changed?
5. What are a few of the most important learning principles, key concepts, and innovative ideas for teachers and educational leaders to keep in mind after COVID-19?

23

MOVING FROM FACE-TO-FACE TO ONLINE ENVIRONMENTS IN MEXICO DURING THE PANDEMIC

Samuel Arriaga

Samuel Arriaga has a BA in educational management and a master's degree in school innovation. He was awarded a Fulbright Distinguished Award in Teaching in 2016. He has worked as a language teacher for more than 20 years. In recent years, he has created a couple of online educational platforms for public universities and another platform for the U.S. Consulate in Mexico. He can be contacted at arriaga.samuel@gmail.com.

DOI: 10.4324/9781003213840-27

Introduction to Language Certification

I am a Mexican citizen who has worked as an English language teacher for over 20 years in my country. Here in Mexico, as in other developing economies, there is a growing interest in studying abroad. I was among those interested in such an international experience. Fortunately, through a Fulbright award, I had a chance to learn new teaching methods in the United States.

I was lucky: not all study abroad candidates are comfortable in taking language certifications like the Test of English as a Foreign Language (TOEFL) or the Graduate Record Examinations (GRE). In other words, a large number of potential candidates are willing to apply for an international scholarship and potentially change their lives but fail to grasp the requirements such as the well-established certifications. Their questions vary from "what the test is about" and "where to take it" to frankly not knowing anything about it.

In response, the General Consulate of the United States in Mexico decided to offer a preparation course starting in 2019. Notably, this program aims to develop candidates' language abilities prior to their actual tests. I understand this history since I am the head instructor of the TOEFL iBT and the GRE prep courses.

The Pandemic

One of the TOEFL prep courses started at the end of February 2020. The course was to be taught in a face-to-face environment at a local public building a few miles away from the Consulate of the United States in Mexico. At first, everything proceeded normally; however, a couple of weeks after starting to offer such prep courses, I received a startling phone call from the administrator of the building. He said, "*Starting today, you can no longer teach the course here.*" Somewhat shaken, I kept silent and was thinking and hoping that it might be a kind of joke since we are talking about a course sponsored by the U.S. Consulate. Then the administrator added, "*I am not kidding; you'd better take a look at the local government resolutions.*"

So I read the paper that day and realized that the pandemic was, in fact, affecting all kinds of activities across the Mexican territory, including the academic ones. At that time, the local government established that no more than five people could meet in one place. In addition, all public buildings and schools were permanently shut down, and other measures were set in motion to protect citizens.

As a head instructor, it was my responsibility to inform the U.S. Consulate of any changes in the program. Moreover, it is up to me to come up with a solution in case something goes awry. And now that is exactly what happened!

Coming Up With a Solution

Before telephoning the Press and Culture Office of the U.S. Consulate in Mexico, I decided to take action and conducted a quick research review of online learning platforms such as Blackboard, Canvas, Google Classroom, and MOODLE. In the end, I happened to decide to use the same online platform that we had at Indiana University (IU) back in 2016 during my memorable Fulbright program in Bloomington, Indiana. And I started to recall the tools and features of Canvas.

Soon, I started deploying the Canvas platform and was thinking about the opportunities ahead. As soon as I finished creating the contents of the week that I was to teach, I contacted the U.S. Consulate. I explained to them that due to the pandemic, I had created content on an online platform from which students could now take their classes online. With this platform, I was able to set instructions and add various interactive and collaborative activities that include audio and graded quizzes with up to five attempts. The quiz items were randomly selected for each attempt from an item pool. I could also post announcements, deadlines, and welcome messages to help personalize the learning experience during these difficult times. At that point, I scheduled the first synchronous sessions, and I shared the link with the Council.

During the first and second weeks, I made some adjustments to the learning environment. For instance, instead of Zoom, students felt more comfortable on Skype, so we utilized that tool. In addition, before a quiz or a Word document assignment, a couple of messages were shared with students, one on WhatsApp and another via email. In that way, students were free to choose either a mobile phone or a personal computer to work on the assignments.

Results

As the weeks went by, students kept working on the platform and attended some 80% of the synchronous sessions. During these weeks of content and course adaptation, the representative from the Press and Culture Consul made no comments when he visited. Instead, he was basically observing and obtaining feedback from students. Fortunately, in the end, he made extremely positive comments about what we were doing with the TOEFL prep courses. He shared the following words during the graduate ceremony:

> We are currently running other academic programs in Mexico; for example, we have a course for journalists who wish to increase their English language proficiency. And because of the pandemic all courses needed major adjustments, I am glad to say that Professor Arriaga had an immediate response. We did not have to wait, and his experience was useful for you as students, but then, we happened to learn from these strategies and to take part of this knowledge to other areas of our own. Professor Arriaga managed to build up a robust platform, a tool that has been an intuitive one. And as I contacted some of you guys [he referred to my students] you have recognized his work and his knowledge.
>
> We do thank you, Professor Arriaga, for such a thorough response, and we also thank all of your students for having completed the program.

Conclusion

I am part of the generation of Fulbright Distinguished Award teachers at IU, where I learned technology, educational policy, and learning strategies, among other topics. It was a highly valuable experience that continues to pay dividends during the pandemic and hopefully far beyond. Perhaps most importantly, I learned that we could help create a better world no matter the sociological, economic, and health-related issues and conditions; many thoughtful and creative solutions can be found and tested.

At this time, I continue working for the U.S. Consulate as an external instructor. In addition, after the experience highlighted in this story, I decided to launch my own business. Now, instead of teaching one or two courses, I create online courses of the English language for educational and training purposes. In addition to helping with desperately needed university courses, there are hundreds of elementary, junior high, and high schools that need better and more intuitive user courses, tools, and systems. Clearly, the journey has just started.

Reflection Questions

1.   During the pandemic, many of us educators have moved from a face-to-face to an online environment. What has been your experience? What challenges did you have to overcome? What challenges remain?
2.   In this online education journey, we have realized that there are more robust, more user-friendly, and more attractive courses, tools, and platforms than a single teacher can often offer. Are school districts investing in training and in software, or do they need to start hiring specialists like graphic designers, programmers, instructional designers, editors, and content developers so that better online courses can be created?
3.   Are administrators providing incentives and support to help build stronger online courses and programs? If not, are teachers demanding better software, enhanced training, and other related needs?
4.   How have students and administrators responded to the contents and activities that you implemented? What has been your biggest success? How do you share your successes and failures with others?
5.   What unique opportunities are there to teach language skills online? Have you experimented in this area of online language learning as a teacher, tutor, or learner?

SECTION 5

English Education and Collaboration

As we move to the second half of the book, Section 5 is centered on English education and collaboration in language learning. Each of the chapters could have also found its housing in Section 2 on innovative education or Section 6 on active learning strategies. English educators and language teachers in general have been leading educational reform movements for decades with initiatives like the process writing approach, writing as thinking, and writing across the curriculum. In terms of educational technology, there was also IBM's popular "Writing to Read" program in the 1980s and 1990s. Notably, each of the chapter authors in this section is exploring ways to activate learning in the language education classroom. There is much to learn and extrapolate from their ideas even if you are firmly planted in other disciplines or specialty areas.

We open this section with a fascinating chapter from Chaoran Wang. Chaoran recently completed a dissertation that explored an innovative approach to teaching English in China. In Chapter 24, she introduces us to a model of how synchronous hybrid instruction provided English learning opportunities for rural children in an under-sourced Chinese village school. The synchronous hybrid class adopted a dual-teacher model with a weekly synchronous English instructor and a local classroom teacher. In this chapter, Chaoran shares her story of working as a voluntary online English instructor for the village school, introducing her experiences, challenges, struggles, and hopes of working with rural Chinese children. Chaoran also reflected on how, as an overseas language teacher, she made use of online spaces to provide innovative learning experiences for rural students.

The ensuing chapter story in Chapter 25 takes place in Thailand. The author, Apapan Sailabada, is the head of a demonstration school in Bangkok. In this role, Apapan makes a bold attempt to understand how the language classroom in a Thai context can potentially shift from highly "teacher centered" to one

DOI: 10.4324/9781003213840-28

rich in "student-centered" pedagogy by instilling various collaborative strategies into teaching and learning. Collaborative learning seemed to be the answer for her learner-centered challenge since it required students to conduct activities, share ideas, and work collaboratively to successfully complete tasks and activities. Examples of these activities included role play, think-pair-share, and jigsaw.

However, amid the public health breakout of the COVID-19 pandemic in the spring of 2020, the field of education was disrupted and those in it immediately shifted to online and blended forms of learning. When the classroom shifted online, collaborative learning hopes and ideas soon morphed into individual forms of learning. Such a change was not suitable for young learners, especially in the language classroom. However, when students return to the new normal classroom scene in the future, Apapan hopes to foster those moments of intense and engaging learning wherein her students can collaborate and share ideas and knowledge with each other in physical settings once again.

As shown in Chapter 26, Xiaoxiu (Anne) Wang is filled with creative ideas for teaching English in China. One of those ideas, "English Reading Series of Classes for Ninth Graders," Anne invented to offer her classes online. Through reading or watching different passages and videos about current events or what Anne calls "Live Classes of Lives," she encourages her students to understand the importance of learning English. Anne's approach also cultivates in them a sense of patriotism while attempting to enhance students' social responsibility so that they can learn from the resulting life-related textbook in this pandemic period and perhaps far beyond.

Instead of learner collaboration and interaction, Chapter 27, the fourth chapter of Section 5, explores language teacher collaboration. Here, Sanna Leinonen asked us all how we can make students active learners and become better teachers in the process. As we all know, the way the teacher works in the classroom affects the way students feel about themselves and how comfortable the classroom feels in general. According to Sanna, for teachers to be able to create a collaborative learning atmosphere in the classroom, they must have experienced it themselves. In this chapter, you will learn about how you can build such a collaborative teaching and learning environment, including a description of the steps that tend to come first.

In Chapter 28, the final story in this section on English education and collaboration, Hyun-Ju Kim details her teaching days before and during the COVID-19 pandemic. One day, she asked her students to write a reflection about the course, Language and Culture, which made her ponder her teaching. As a result, Hyun-Ju decided to pilot flipped learning pedagogy with her class at Dankook University in South Korea. Based on her results, as both an instructor and a researcher, she strongly suggests that flipped learning classrooms and activities should systematically apply best practices for successful active learning in online and offline contexts.

As indicated, each of these chapters makes you ponder the common or traditional instructional approaches that you might rethink in the near future. Perhaps these changes will be truly transformative. Let us hope.

24

ENGLISH EDUCATION ENABLED BY TECHNOLOGY

Story From an Online Teacher for an Under-Sourced Village School in China

Chaoran Wang

DOI: 10.4324/9781003213840-29

Chaoran Wang earned her PhD in literacy, culture, and language education from Indiana University. Her interdisciplinary research agenda examines the issues of online/hybrid language instruction through the intersecting perspectives of language studies, sociocultural theories, open educational resources, and various educational technologies. She is a multilingual writing specialist and an assistant professor of writing at Colby College, Maine. She can be reached at chaoranwang314@gmail.com.

Instructional Approach or Strategy: Online/Hybrid Learning

It was a hot, humid summer day. After teaching the third-grade English class completely online for a year for an elementary village school *(cunxiao)* in China, I finally got an opportunity to visit the school. I was excited, but I did not tell my students that I was going to visit them because I wanted to give them a big surprise.

Several years ago, I started to work as a voluntary online English teacher for a non-profit educational organization that builds hybrid classes for students in rural Chinese villages. I was assigned to teach at this village school where there were no English classes due to the lack of qualified teachers. Therefore, I became the first-ever English teacher for the school, and one of the first-ever online teachers. When I realized this fact, even more energy poured through me. I could not wait to see them in real life.

To create those hybrid classes for the school, the non-profit that I worked for built a computer lab and recruited online teachers from urban Chinese schools and abroad. Voluntary online teachers like me were nonpaid. We met with the class once a week. Whenever there was a hybrid class, a local teacher took the kids to the lab where they could interact synchronously with me through a large projection screen. I taught the class using a video conferencing software called *Zhumu*. There were 22 students in my class. Soon, I would be in their classroom from Shanghai over 1,100 miles away; during this trip I took a three-hour flight, followed by a two-hour long-distance bus, and then a one-hour taxi ride.

I could still remember my first day of teaching. I was nervous because I had never taught online to a group of students before. Once I turned on my video and greeted them, I was delighted to find that my students all waved their little hands at me. I was also surprised to find that although many of my students were very shy, they were eager to learn. As I taught at a distance, I was mainly concerned about two things. On the one hand, I was not sure what I sounded like in the actual physical classroom. On the other, I could not see the students sitting in the back of the classroom clearly enough, and I desperately wanted to interact with and engage them all.

Such common teacher observations, which were vital in helping me adjust my teaching on the fly in a face-to-face classroom, were not available to me in this hybrid class. Was I clear? Did they seem to understand me? Should I stop and repeat things, or should I move on? Therefore, throughout the entire class, I made attempts to initiate more verbal responses and body moves from my students than I normally attempted in a face-to-face class. I adjusted my standard instructional approach so that I could be in better control of that distant class. Luckily, my students were very active in giving me their responses and reactions. When the class ended, I said, "Don't forget I am Ms. Wang! See you next week!" They all waved to me and said in a cheerful tone, "Yes, we won't forget!"

The local teacher, Ms. Chang, was also with us during the entire class. After the class ended, she chatted with me and told me that she found her students were surprisingly active during my online class session. Although Ms. Chang did not teach English, she was interested in learning with the students. She normally sat in the second row and passed around microphones whenever I called on a student. Sometimes she helped with clarifying my instructions to the students. Throughout the semester, she confirmed with me that the students were so enthusiastic about the hybrid English class that they asked her whether I could teach them face-to-face and meet with them more often. My students' passion always drove me to provide the best instruction that I could as a teacher.

After a semester's worth of online teaching, I became increasingly interested in learning more about my students as individuals—something I found extremely challenging to do online because there were no other means to contact my students once our English class ended each week. I kept wondering what their school and surrounding community were like. What was their everyday life like? How did they learn English outside the hybrid class?

I asked these questions to the headmaster and to Ms. Chang while they were showing me around the school. Both mentioned that many students lacked confidence speaking in their regular classes, but the hybrid English class allowed them to practice speaking and communication skills. They also expressed that the greatest learning challenge that my students had was related to their family backgrounds. Because most of my students' parents had migrated to work in cities to feed their families back in the villages, there was no parental involvement in the students' everyday life. Their parents were employed in blue-collar jobs in cities because they wanted to provide better living conditions for their children. All this was of deep concern to me as their teacher and as someone who was in a doctoral program in the field of education in the United States.

I was not aware of how my students' learning was influenced by their families until this school visit. I was shocked by how hard it was for a rural student to succeed with the scarcity of home learning support and parental companionship. Ms. Chang mentioned that 60% of the local students dropped out before they finished middle school. Many went to other communities and cities to seek job opportunities. It was also not uncommon to see groups of middle school students skip classes and immerse themselves in internet bars playing games. Ms. Chang was concerned that a teacher's efforts could hardly have an effect when parents did not play an active role in their children's education, either due to their absence or because they did not know how to provide appropriate guidance for the children. As a result, the paucity of educational materials and teacher resources in formal schooling and the dramatic changes in contemporary rural family structure are combining to enlarge the gap between rural and urban education in China. Such disparities were quite alarming to Ms. Chang and to me.

Ms. Chang's words made me wonder what kind of hybrid classes could better support my students given their backgrounds. Obviously, a class that seeks only to provide students with knowledge is not enough. My students must encounter more than streams of definitions, punctuation and grammar rules, and sentence procedures—they also must come into contact with a teacher who cares about them as a student *and* as a child. They needed not only quality learning resources but strategies that could help develop effective learning habits and positive attitudes as well. They could definitely benefit from interacting with talented educators and role models who engage with them to build their confidence, interest, and long-term dispositions toward learning. These young people should be provided meaningful classes that put their needs at the center, instead of being imposed with curricula and standards prepackaged and predetermined by people in an educational center or institute over a thousand miles away. Overall, they needed an educational system that could help them succeed and excel.

The class bell rang. The students were having their break now. As I was walking toward their classroom, a few students in the corridor were staring at me. To be honest, I could not tell whether they were my students, because, as I mentioned, I could not see many students' faces clearly when I was teaching online. I waved to them and said hello. Suddenly, one of the students jumped and questioned with caution and excitement, "Are . . . are you Ms. Wang?" I smiled, "Yes! I am Ms. Wang. I am here to visit you. Are you surprised?" They danced and jumped. We laughed and walked happily together to the classroom.

My appearance suddenly became the biggest news in the school. My students all gathered around me and were so eager to ask me all kinds of questions. Their eyes were glittering on their small faces. It felt like a get-together with good friends or a family reunion after a long-time separation. Happiness was spewing all over the classroom. Outside the door and the window, I could see the corridor crowded with students from other classes curiously watching what was happening. All of a sudden, a little girl asked me, "Ms. Wang, how long will you stay with us?" Like all reunions, there had to be a time to say goodbye, but I was surprised that my student had already thought about me leaving when we just met. It was at this moment, Ms. Chang's words about student families came back to my mind. I was hesitant and sad to say, "I will leave tomorrow." While speaking, I dared not to look at her eyes. She responded, "No, that's too soon! Ms. Wang, could you stay longer?" A few other students also held my hands and asked me not to leave. I hated to break their heart, but it was not easy for me to travel all the way here.

You might wonder what happened after my visit. First, I decided to make my class more engaging and meaningful for my students. For instance, I incorporated more authentic learning materials and activities that could make my students see the power of their learning. For instance, I took them to live video-streaming tours of Kroger, one of the largest American grocery stores in my college town, so that I could teach them with objects and they could practice the vocabulary while experiencing a foreign culture online. I brought guests to my class so that they could practice communicating with someone with the English dialogues that they just learned. I attempted to break in the limits of space and textbook materials and make use of the flexibility of distance learning and the affordances of technological tools.

I also built more connections for my students outside the hybrid classes. In fact, to this day, even though my students have graduated from the village primary school, I am still in contact with some of them from time to time. Students who had access to cell phones added my WeChat number to their parents' accounts. We chat once in a while. They share with me their stories and their feelings about middle school lives. In return, I encourage them to keep up with studying and making new friends. I share with them my stories of how I overcame all kinds of challenges when I was a young student at their age.

We have truly become online friends. They now view me as a friend, a mentor, and a role model. I am lucky to earn their trust and become a distant companion outside their classrooms. Certainly, there is a long distance between my former students and me. Yet our teacher-student relationship is long lasting.

Advice and Suggestions

1. Create opportunities (e.g., virtual hangouts, face-to-face visits, and social gatherings, if available) to get to know your online students as individuals. Get to know the backgrounds of your students so that you can adjust your teaching to provide more meaningful and relevant assignments and activities for your students.
2. Online classroom spaces can be more flexible and should not be confined as fixed spaces defined by the learning platforms. Rather, think about ways to expand your online classroom spaces (e.g., virtual tutors to an interesting place, guest speakers that connect multiple spaces, online apps, and social networks that could build more connections and interactions with students and amongst themselves).

Reflection Questions

1. What are the biggest challenges that you have encountered in online/hybrid teaching? How have you attempted to overcome those challenges?

2. What strategies have you found that work best for your online/hybrid class? Why do you think those strategies work in an online or hybrid model and might not be as effective or powerful in the face-to-face classroom?

3. How would you create opportunities to learn about your distance students' backgrounds, attitudes, habits, and needs?

25

HIGHLIGHTING COLLABORATIVE LEARNING IN LANGUAGE CLASSROOM

A Story From Thailand

Apapan Sailabada

Apapan Sailabada is the Head of the English Department at Chulalongkorn University Demonstration School in Bangkok, Thailand. In 2021, Apapan received her PhD in English language teaching from Language Institute, Thammasat University, Thailand. Her academic interest areas are teaching language to young learners and material development for language teaching and learning in

DOI: 10.4324/9781003213840-30

primary schools. Apapan has many years of teaching experience in primary and higher education settings. She has mentored numbers of undergraduate English majors in their field practicums. She teaches full-time and serves as a special guest lecturer in the Faculty of Education, Chulalongkorn University, Thailand. She can be contacted at apapantao@gmail.com.

Introduction

A teacher stood in front of the classroom. Her eyes looked carefully around the class, and she nodded her head gently like a signal. The students stood up and greeted her. It only took a moment for silence to fall across the classroom as everyone was waiting for her to give permission for them to sit down. Then the class can start.

That was the first memory that popped into my mind when I reflect back on my primary school years. From this recollection, you may think that someone forced the students to say and act this way. But no, this is a typical traditional classroom greeting routine. Obedient. Respectful. Disciplined.

Far beyond what the title of this chapter suggests, the opening paragraph briefly hinted about what it was like to grow up in a Thai classroom. Obedience is the keyword. Be respectful toward your teachers. Strong discipline for classroom management. As you can see, it is unrelated to the essence of collaborative learning in the language classroom, the topic of this chapter. Of course, there was a reason behind the opening paragraph: I wanted to pitch in the context of my background in the traditional Thai classroom where the authoritative figure is the teacher whose primary duties are to give instruction and teach and then later assess that learning. The students sat in their individual seats, repeating the patterns that the teacher wrote on the board. "Repeat after me" and "Copy these lines down in your book" were the two main instructions I remembered from my English class. Still, I enjoyed and loved English class very much. There was a small chance, if any, that students were allowed to work in groups, or move freely as they wished across the classroom. Stay in your seat, be good, and listen to the teacher.

Back in the old days, the teaching approach was "teacher centered" and involved never-ending spoon-feeding information to students. In my attempt to overcome this challenge and ingrained expectation, I added what I considered effective strategies for teaching, to move away from "teacher-centered" to "student-centered" instruction. You may say that I set my heart and re-programmed my brain to teach differently from what I was accustomed to.

I graduated from Indiana University (IU) in Bloomington in 2014. On my graduation day, my mind was still thinking, should I stay or return home to my family? As you might have guessed, I chose the latter. Once back in my hometown of Bangkok, I decluttered my emotional issues and told myself I am ready to embark on a new journey; I must get a real teaching job. I decided to apply for the teaching position at one of the top primary schools in all of Thailand; namely Chulalongkorn University Demonstration School (CUD-Elementary). The school is one of the well-known demonstration schools in Thailand due to its strong academic reputation and for receiving many national awards for outstanding teachers in distinguished departments.

My course experiences at IU and interactions with peers and professors there definitely strengthened my passion for becoming an effective language teacher. I desperately wanted to teach English in a different way than I was accustomed to. I came back to Thailand realizing that I now had a "one size doesn't fit all" mentality. There are many substantive challenges that I am willing to address to create a collaborative learning atmosphere in the language classroom. It was clear to me that I had an approach to teaching, which was different from the highly traditional style in which I was taught. I wanted to make learning more fun, like what I experienced during my graduate studies at IU. I wanted to inspire my students to learn and use language to communicate, not just teach for passing tests. I wanted to provide choices and create opportunities to learn.

At CUD, teachers can bring in fresh teaching ideas and cutting-edge teaching methods and try out their theories in the classroom. CUD is known for being the "laboratory school" where every new teaching idea can be experimented with and piloted. I was like a flower in springtime that is blossoming with ideas for how to make language learning more fun, interesting, and meaningful. I wanted students to walk away from my class with a positive attitude toward the English language.

Truth be told, my highest goal was to have students fall in love with English just like I had done, not just learn a bunch of language rules, procedures, and other academic knowledge. It is a motivation-filled classroom with passion-based learning and passion-filled pedagogy that I brought back from my graduate study at IU wherein I received a master's in language education. But now, I was faced with the ultimate challenge: how can I make it happen here at CUD? How can I operationalize my ever-flowing ideas to make an impact with these inquisitive young minds in Bangkok? Could collaborative and engaging learner-centered activities be the answer? If so, which ones would I choose and when? Each night those thoughts entered my head, and I went through streams of paper in the morning as I wrote them down in assorted color pens and then I saved them in neatly organized notebooks and folders in my home office. But where would I start?

For about the decade prior to the COVID-19 breakout, my priority in teaching English as a second language to Thai students was to try using different collaborative approaches and other strategies that I found effective for my classroom. This is when I came up with the abbreviation AEC. Here, "AEC" is no longer an abbreviation for "Asian Economic Community;" instead, A is for "Active." E is for "Engaged." And C is for "Collaboration." I started to adapt strategies based on my AEC notion ("Active, Engaged, Collaboration"). I began to think of bringing different activities into the classroom such as role play for Active, think-pair-share for Engaged, and a jigsaw for Collaboration.

Role play challenged the students to step in and take the role as the character from the story. I usually based the role play activity on the unit's reading. I would divide the students into small groups and then have students from each group read their lines out loud after I read the narration. Role play enhanced group work and strengthened individual responsibility (of their own lines!). The intuitive collaboration happens when everyone helps one another to read their lines correctly to perform well. Thai students are very shy to express their personality and action. Role play helps them overcome social anxiety and their inertia. Everyone has to be active because everyone is responsible for the group's success. Often after class, I hear the students praise their friends, "I like how you say that line in class. It was so funny." This made my heart brim with joy.

Think-pair-share emphasized cognitive processes that enabled the students to think about the assigned topic quietly in their minds before pairing and sharing their ideas with their friends. Thai students liked to work with a partner who, in effect, is a friend who can help them. Speaking in front of the class, if done alone, is a most embarrassing moment that most Thai students dread. Their affective filter skyrockets and they fall silent. Thai students were afraid of making mistakes and embarrassed of their accents. Strategies like think-pair-share help to lessen students' anxiety because they first share their ideas with their friends, in pairs.

Many times, I heard that such pairs continued the dialogue and enjoyed their conversation. Practice makes perfect. The more they practice using the language, the better language user, they will become.

I have always been an enthusiast for collaborative learning. Jigsaw is the first activity I set my eyes on when I first started teaching. In the jigsaw activity, the students break out into small groups and have to place the right sentences one after another in order to complete the paragraph. The paragraph can be taken from the extensive reading section or a simple story. The students work together collaboratively to arrange the sentences into a correct paragraph. Adding in a time limit increases the excitement!

However, when the COVID-19 reached its peak, the school had to close and switched to online learning. This was a sudden disruption in teaching and learning. Everyone at school was underprepared for this sudden challenge. No more active and engaging interactions in the classroom; in fact, no one was in school. Soon, everyone shifted their lives to online forms of living and learning.

It was a challenging time to shift abruptly from on-site to online as my colleagues and I had minimal experience with online/distance learning. Countless teachers had to spend most of their time in front of the computer, tablet, or mobile device, to prepare and serve their online teaching. The students in my class were primary school-age children who were too young to rely on online learning from 8:00 in the morning to 3:00 in the afternoon.

Zoom was the only application that I used to teach my online class. I "Zoomed" with my students once a week to wrap up and to maintain some kind of interaction. It was quite difficult to maintain everyone's attention online during our 50-minute Zoom sessions. We spent almost two months relying solely on online learning. Near the end, I could tell that everyone—students, teachers, and parents—were completely worn out and wished that the pandemic would end soon so we could all return to our normal lives. Fortunately, near the end of the semester, the situation significantly improved, allowing schools to be re-opened if they followed strict guidelines so as to avoid additional COVID-19 outbreaks.

COVID-19 disrupted the education process at all levels. We are all going to have to perpetually learn to adopt new ways of living and learning, in both formal and informal learning pursuits. Teachers should prepare for challenges and be opened to continual changes. We can still engage in collaborative language learning; it just needs to be online or blended at the present time. As I experiment with collaborative activities like a virtual jigsaw, online think-pair-share, forms of Web-based role play, and other interactive, engaging, and collaborative activities, I hope to find and foster those passionate moments of learning joy among my students. And I truly hope that they may evolve into repeatable and sustainable episodes resulting in sheer love of the English language. COVID or no COVID, I hope to report back in the affirmative soon.

Reflection Questions

1. How might students react to learning English or other languages in person after learning online for a year or two? How might their relationships with friends and teachers be affected?
2. How much do you relate to the classroom experiences that the author mentioned earlier in the chapter? Do you feel familiar or surprised with the traditional classroom style? Please give justifications for your answer.
3. What are some other active learning strategies that enhance collaborative learning in the language classroom?
4. What kind of formative and summative assessment approaches could be used to foster collaboration among young learners in a foreign language classroom?
5. What changes do you see in terms of technology advancement that could shift the current education paradigm?

26

LIVE CLASSES OF LIVES

English Reading to Ponder Life, Social Phenomena, and the Fate of the World

Xiaoxiu (Anne) Wang

Xiaoxiu (Anne) Wang is the head of the teaching and research group of English in Shanxi Experimental Secondary School. She was named the Famous Teacher

DOI: 10.4324/9781003213840-31

of Shanxi Province in 2020. For more than 20 years, she has been teaching in junior high school and devoting herself to researching English teaching methods that are highly engaging and relevant for Chinese students. She can be reached at 2407202785@qq.com.

Live Classes of Lives

"We see the virus raging around the world. But here in China, we see the fearless figures of the medical workers, the gatemen who help people take temperatures, the delivery men that keep our lives as normal as possible. We are in a great motherland and a great era. Being aware of this alone is enough to make a person to tears," Jitian Wu noted, after reading the passages about people all over China fighting against the coronavirus.

"English is our bridge to communicate with the world. With this tool, we can better express our ideas to the world," wrote Zhaotong Zheng when she read the passage about Fu Ying, former vice minister of foreign affairs.

"The difference between losers and winners may only be the courage to face difficulties." This wonderful quote comes from Miao Wang who shared his idea after watching the animated short film *Piper*.

All these amazing thoughts come from my "English Reading Series of Classes for Ninth Graders." And there were more, many more, that would evoke a range of emotions from the tugging of a tear on one's face to the ever-extending warmness of a smile. These early teenagers are making connections with the English language. Such connections to humanity had increasingly special meaning during the pandemic.

To stop the spread of the epidemic on the campus and to ensure the safety and health of teachers and students, according to a notice issued by the Ministry of Education in China, all schools in the spring semester of 2020 had been postponed. In an attempt to deal with the crisis, local education departments organized schools at all levels to conduct online teaching in as orderly a manner as possible.

The important measure of "Classes Suspended but Teaching Continues" is not only the emergency response to the epidemic, but also an acknowledgment of the possibilities of Internet Plus Education. As a junior high school English teacher, I made preparations and quickly formulated the teaching goal (4R principles): (1) regrowing up in the epidemic, (2) reverence for nature, (3) respecting science, and (4) responding to disasters scientifically. These emotional goals cultivated a sense of patriotism among students. In effect, such goals were also attempted to enhance students' social responsibility so that they can learn this life-related textbook during this special period.

For instance, we read the passage titled "Why are bats so 'poisonous' and not themselves?" to understand the virus. Another article from *China Daily Bilingual News* reported the National People's Congress Standing Committee had made it clear that all wildlife on the protection list of the existing Wild Animal Protection Law or other laws were banned from consumption. This report strengthened students' awareness of protecting the environment and living in harmony with animals. "How to Prevent Novel Coronavirus" from *China Daily* with pictures gave students timely scientific knowledge of epidemic prevention in English.

People from all walks of life have made selfless contributions in the fight against the epidemic. Students read the passages "Farmers from Henan donate one hundred thousand pounds of green onion," and "Alumni from Wuhan University who are studying in America work for 30 days and nights to help collect the supplies for fighting against the virus" from *China Daily Bilingual News*. They also watched the inspiring speech from Jessica Liu, "We are all fighters."

In rich and colorful forms, such stories let teachers and students in front of a computer screen shed tears for all the ordinary people and touching stories of help and support, including all the great medical workers. It was a highly moving experience for me as I contemplated the value of online teaching and learning. In fact, I constantly reflected on my pedagogical approaches. Such articles and speeches awakened in my students the importance of learning English so that they could better understand and interpret the trending societal news around them.

What's more, there are articles such as "Fifteen Sentences Worldly to Remember in the Epidemic," "Heroes in harm's way," "Foreign Minister Wang Yi's speech at the Munich Security Conference in Germany," and a CGTN (China Globe Television Network) anchor's English comment "In the darkest time, the best hearts." The abundance of factual information in the real world teaches children to view events and the world in a rational and dialectical way. They were learning English through actual lived experiences. Stated another way, through the stories of the lives of others, they were embedded in rich contexts for learning English.

Some of these shared experiences had highly emotional themes. For instance, the Disney animated short film *Piper* let the children know that we need to have the courage to face difficulties. Along with courage often comes hope and thankfulness. For instance, to pray for the people of Wuhan and all of China, students learned and sang the heart-warming song "Blessings" by Laura Story, which won a Grammy Award in 2011.

Students also shared and exchanged ideas using an online tool called DingTalk. In their DingTalk groups, they could practice their written English and reflect on what other students had stated. In effect, they were learning from the various media and tools around them. When you enrich the senses with such multimedia, you empower students and help blaze many avenues for learning.

Listed next are details of my operating processes and procedures.

1. Take full use of the advantages of network teaching. Personally, I make a concerted effort to take advantage of the diversification of information available for teaching and learning. I also try to keep pace with the times and use current events in the news. In addition, I continue to develop my teaching resources.

2. Combining my teaching experiences and the characteristics of ninth-grade English, I designed the "English Reading Series of Classes for Ninth Graders." This content contains bilingual and illustrated text resources and audio-visual resources that are available for my students to access online.

3. During the teaching process, activities involving reading, watching, displaying, and communicating were constantly on display. Students in different groups explored information, exchanged ideas, and shared notes. All these are components that reflect the "English Reading Series of Classes for Ninth Graders." Such components not only aroused students' passions to learn English, but also inspired them to think about life, social phenomena, the fate of the nation, and even the world. Students were internally motivated to learn more by exploring and reflecting on personally chosen resources and topics, not coerced into it with a teacher-centered model dictating what they were to learn.

Advice and Suggestions

1. Materials must be selected and arranged. For selection, it means different forms of learning, including passages, videos, speeches, or songs as well as the degree of difficulty of the materials. For arrangement, these special classes should be planned together with the normal textbook learning classes.

2. Reading tasks must be made available for students of different levels and abilities.

Reflection Questions

1. How can recent events and news foster student learning of English or learning in general?

2. How can you select articles and speeches that are suitable for your students to read and listen to? What cautions would you have about using online news?

3. In addition to knowledge and information, what else do you need to teach your students?

27

STUDENT COLLABORATION STARTS WITH TEACHER COLLABORATION

Sanna Leinonen

Sanna Leinonen is a co-author of a high school English language textbook series called Culture Café. She has taught grades 1 through 6 and grades 7 through 12 in both traditional and blended settings and worked as a department head in a community college. Sanna works with a diverse group of students and colleagues, Finnish and international, which has resulted in her becoming an expert in English language learners, special education, professional learning communities, and collaborative learning, to name a few. One of her foundational teaching practices entails student-centered learning. Sanna was awarded the Fulbright

DOI: 10.4324/9781003213840-32

Distinguished Award in Teaching in 2017. She earned her MA in English at Tampere University and the teacher of special education certificate at the University of Jyväskylä. She can be reached at leinonen.sanna.k@gmail.com.

Introduction

Was it the silly hats? Was it the shared lunch? Or was it the amazing ideas I learned when in a class at Indiana University (IU) that made me spend my Saturdays during the fall semester of 2017 on the IU campus. In the process, I missed so many things I wanted to do, like going with my Fulbright teacher friends on a field trip to Louisville, Kentucky. If you were not there, you would not know. But life and success as a teacher are all about choices, and I made mine.

Collaborative methods in the classroom have been my passion for as long as I can remember. However, until my experiences as a Fulbright teacher in Bloomington, I did not fully understand the power of collaboration. With high hopes, I returned home to teach English and special education at Ylöjärvi High School near Tampere, Finland, and this is what happened:

> *I've arranged the chairs of the classroom into a circle. The students come in and stare at the arrangement. They don't know where to sit before I tell them to take any seat. They look at me, don't say a thing, and sit down. I sit down, say "Good morning," and wait for a response. There is none! No "Hi," no "Hello," no nothing. The usually talkative students shut up in this setting.*

My plan was to pilot some of the collaborative methods I had learned in Bloomington. The tactic described earlier was meant to be the "fishbowl" technique I had learned the previous fall when I skipped the field trip. OK, no bowl there, just dead fish. If you have ever met any Finns, you know that we are quiet. We do not like to talk and definitely not in a foreign language until we master it superbly. The curriculum in Finnish high schools has previously had a strong focus on individual student learning and their passing the matriculation examination. With such an exam focus, learning and teaching have been lonely jobs. Students sit in neatly arranged rows and answer when the teacher asks a question. Today, there is a change toward more collaborative methods, but the change is slow.

In fall 2016, high schools in Finland started to work with a new core curriculum, and we were taking a huge step into a new direction. The new core curriculum emphasized cooperation, student-centered methods, problem-based approaches, and the use of technology. In spite of these initiatives, Finnish students too often continued to languish in an educational system where they were told what to learn, how to learn, and when to learn. Unfortunately, their Finnish teachers were not using these new methods of learner empowerment. What I want to do in my classes is teach the students to take responsibility for their own learning and become more aware of themselves as learners. I strongly believe that when students "own" their own learning, it becomes more meaningful and interesting.

I asked myself, how can I accomplish my goals of making students active learners and become a better teacher in the process? That is the question we teachers ask ourselves constantly. After our teacher training stints at a Finnish university, the development of our own careers is usually left to ourselves. However, Finnish schools do not usually have enough resources for continuous professional development. And as we all know, the way the teacher works in the classroom affects the students and the way they feel about themselves. It also affects how comfortable the classroom feels in general. For the teachers to be able to create a collaborative learning atmosphere in the classroom, they must have experienced a collaborative learning environment themselves. We are the ones who can change our work and the school. We are the experts of our own teaching practices. We know our students, the school, and education in our context. What I realized after the fishbowl incident is that we teachers need to start collaborating and experimenting with active learning pedagogy.

Where to start? First, we need to decide if we are talking about cooperation or collaboration. In my opinion, there is a big difference. **Cooperation** can be defined as working together to accomplish a goal or set of goals or achieve a certain set of skills or competencies, such as helping everyone on a team learn to solve simple division problems. A cooperative task can often be divided among the participants so that each person is responsible only for their own part of the task. We teachers have numerous staff meetings where we decide who does what and design guidance for team functioning.

Collaboration entails working and thinking together to accomplish a shared goal such as editing a book like this one or crafting a technology tool tutorial or guide. In addition, it is vital that collaborative team members freely share knowledge among team members. Successful collaboration requires participants to share knowledge in interaction. Collaboration requires dialogue throughout the process to have a shared vision and a goal.

As you can see from the title of this chapter, I am all in for collaboration. In language learning, "working and thinking together" is essential for the students to learn the language. Sure, they can repeat sentences after the teacher and learn phrases by heart, but to truly know the language, they have to be able to use it as a tool to reach a goal. And what is the goal? Communication with others, of course!

Second, teachers need to experience collaboration, working and thinking together, themselves, to be able to use it. What I have done in many schools since IU Bloomington and the horrible fishbowl incident after I returned back to Finland is to start a teacher teaming process. What this means is that teachers form small teams for collaboration. The idea is to **think and learn** together. These team meetings are not normal staff meetings where there is an agenda and teachers decide various everyday issues. Instead, these are meetings for learning. Put away your laptops, your phones, and sit in a circle and talk. It is surprising how fast ideas, problems, and innovations arise in these "no-agenda" team meetings. There is always someone with a question or an idea to start the dialogue.

Where to find time for this? My recommendation is that you look at your normal staff meetings. Are they all really relevant? Could you make them shorter somehow? Don't attempt to change the whole system at first. Take baby steps.

How are my students doing? Great, I think. I still use the "normal" communicative textbook exercises and we don't sit in a circle all the time, but I have learned from the teacher dialogues that I need to give my students time. Time to talk. Time to raise questions. We simply need to allocate time to stop and hear each other.

I have also thoroughly enjoyed the dialogues about teaching and learning that I have had with my colleagues in my school, as well as the dialogues in other schools where I sometimes participate as an educational coach. There is so much we teachers can learn from each other!

Advice and Suggestions

1. When you meet with your colleagues for the first time, don't talk about school. Get to know each other. Talk about your family, hobbies, weekend plans, pets, and so forth. The better you know each other, the more trust, respect, and shared understanding you build.
2. The second time you meet, talk about rules. The four basic principles of dialogue are expressing yourself and your feelings genuinely, listening to others without judgment, respecting and honoring one another's point of view and, finally, suspending judgment. How do you make sure this happens?
3. The third time, agree on a goal. Remember, you are there to think together and learn, not make decisions. After these initial steps, you are ready to dive in!

Reflection Questions

1. What does collaboration mean to you? How have you seen it effectively enacted in your classrooms or in those you have observed or participated in?
2. What kinds of roles should there be in a collaborative group? What roles do you volunteer for and why?
3. How could we as teachers implement collaboration in a classroom in engaging and inspiring ways?
4. What do you think are the most important aspects of collaboration? And what are common barriers to success?
5. What do you see as key differences between cooperative learning and collaborative learning? What are the similarities? How do the differences play out for younger and older age groups?

28

TRANSFORMATIVE LEARNING? YES, POSSIBLY IN A FLIPPED CLASSROOM

Hyun-Ju Kim

Hyun-Ju Kim is a professor in the Department of British and American Humanities at Dankook University in South Korea, where she teaches undergraduate

DOI: 10.4324/9781003213840-33

and graduate courses in TESOL, language testing, and applied linguistics. She received her PhD in foreign language and ESL education at the University of Iowa in the United States where she was awarded the T. Anne Cleary Psychological Research Scholarship and Rolland Ray Award for her distinguished research on educational measurement. She currently serves on the Korea Association of Teachers of English (KATE) board as well as the Korea English Language Testing Association (KELTA) board. She can be reached at hyunjuk@gmail.com.

Face or No Face? Doesn't Matter!

As seen in the chapters of this book, in Korea and around the world, an educational paradigm shift has been underway for several decades. In fact, there are noticeable changes in educational environments all around me. Adding further fuel to the paradigmatic changes, the COVID-19 pandemic situation around the world made educators seriously reconsider their preferred educational paradigm or theoretical approach for instruction. I did too.

Teachers at all levels had to teach over the internet regardless of their goals and backgrounds, whether they wanted to try it or not. In the end, all educational institutions in South Korea needed to be equipped with special hardware and software for e-learning classes. For example, my institution, Dankook University in South Korea, was equipped with Canvas as an e-learning system for asynchronous communication and coursework. For the synchronous side, Dankook decided to offer a Zoom account to every professor and instructor so that the classes could run as smoothly as before.

Through student-centered teaching and learning in these online environments, the hope was that students could have a positive learning experience. In fact, being able to effectively learn online is now a core competency in Korean society that all teachers must cultivate for a successful life. Learning online is no longer a future dream or vision; it is now!

Fortunately, student-centered practices, though not pervasive, are increasingly common in Korean education. If one were to visit Korea, you might hear people talk about the need to improve teaching and learning methods in Korean education. More specifically, teaching methods such as flipped learning, cooperative learning, project-based learning, and internet-based learning are being experimented with across different grade levels in Korea.

All these discussions among Korean educators (and educators around the planet) are fundamentally seeking ways to get learners to actively participate in classroom activities; in effect, they are espousing the concept of active learning. To foster active student learning, it is necessary to change the roles of teachers and learners according to a more constructivistic perspective. In a constructivist classroom, teachers are the facilitators of learning who encourage and support students' active participation and deep conceptual understanding, resulting in their learning important concepts.

At the same time, using such a constructivistic framework, students should initiate learning and actively participate in classroom activities with help from teachers and classmates. When successful, the social interactions among students and between teachers and students will be more active and engaging; in a word, such classrooms are more exciting since the students are empowered and have some choice and autonomy in the learning environment. As this occurs, students will become more responsible for their learning. In addition, they will hopefully become more open minded and collaborative, including listening to various opinions and thoughts from others. When active learning approaches are effectively designed and monitored, each student is given license to construct meaning and organize useful and authentic knowledge by respecting other learners' arguments and opinions.

Active learning is a practical teaching method that emphasizes a more learner-centered and learner-focused education. Activities in active learning are intended to engage learners and voluntary learner participation throughout the learning cycle. Among the more prominent and important learning principles involved in active learning include learner's individuality, choice, self-directed learning, and an integrated experience-oriented education; in addition, active learning often entails interaction-based learning between learners and between a teacher and a learner. When employing these key learning principles, teachers might utilize strategies such as small-group discussion, presentations, problem-solving activities, and exploratory learning activities. Specifically, at the university level, active learning is practiced in a variety of ways and is often employed in engineering departments. However, it can be applied in any discipline or course if the teachers are well-trained in the pedagogies and instructional strategies for engagement like flipped learning, collaborative learning, inquiry-based learning, and project-based learning.

Since 2016, I have taught Language and Culture as an undergraduate core course in the Department of British and American Humanities at Dankook University in South Korea. The students in this course, most of whom are Korean along with several Chinese students, are all English as a Foreign Language (EFL) learners. These students want to acquire knowledge about the relationships between language and culture while improving their debating skills as well as their English proficiency. Over the past few years, I have realized that a semester course meeting three hours a week is not enough time to teach the content of this course. As a result, I have felt challenged to teach this course in a totally different way, which is called a "flipped classroom."

Flipped learning is generally used to change and perhaps even transform existing teaching and learning methods. Students in a flipped classroom learn the contents of the lesson outside the classroom before the topic is discussed in class, usually via online video lectures. Discussion of the topic and enrichment activities take place based on the degree of student understanding of the online lectures. Needless to say, the role of the instructor is vital in a flipped classroom approach; instructors must be careful not to intervene too quickly or heavily since then the students might decide not to take the initiative to self-direct their learning from the video lectures. In effect, instructors must be patient and tactful in providing timely and genuine support for learners in a flipped classroom. A dominant and demanding teacher-centered approach will severely lighten to potential impact.

Typically, teachers in a traditional teaching method are faithful to their role as one-way communicators, while learners passively acquire knowledge that teachers deliver in the classroom. However, in flipped learning, students try to understand the concepts by watching the online lectures and then share their learning and new understandings in the classroom. If they haven't fully grasped the concepts, they can solve the problems through discussion and other support from an instructor or classmates. In addition, students can watch online lectures as many times as they need before the class session. Simply stated, in this teaching and learning method, students are taught how to interact with other students more naturally and effectively.

This method of teaching and learning positively affects individual learners' zone of proximal development (ZPD) and enables individualized learning for various levels of learners. Therefore, when effectively conducted, flipped learning is less likely to have a negative impact on the learning process, which all too often occurs in traditional teaching methods. In effect, distinct gains are made in learner comprehension by altering the role of a teacher to one of helper or support giver in the classroom.

In a student-centered symposium in my class, students raised many thought-provoking educational issues and led a discussion as well as a debate. Through this activity, presenters, debaters, and listeners all obtained some benefit. Presenters gained a greater understanding of the issues because they were well prepared for the discussion, whereas debaters received opportunities to speak their thoughts and ideas logically and thoughtfully. Finally, listeners could listen with an open mind and evaluate what was right or wrong. In the end, I found that these student-centered teaching and learning methods helped all students at various levels engage actively in interactive classroom activities and maintain a high level of participation over time.

The Results

Based on these theoretical backgrounds and perspectives, I attempted to examine the effects of active learning in a flipped classroom in an English major course at a university in Korea during the fall semester of 2019. The results of the study indicated that students liked active learning in a flipped classroom and considered it highly effective in learning the contents of the course. The following quotes are excerpts from interviews with the students. For example, one student in this flipped classroom stated:

> "I think the biggest advantage is that it can maximize our participation when it is done well. Also, it was very good that we could organize and develop our thoughts through discussions in class after being prepared well by watching recorded lectures."

Another student argued the following in terms of flipped classrooms:

> *"Participation in class increases because I know the contents before class. Also, it's very efficient because I can re-catch the part of the lecture that I missed during the class."*

In terms of the video recordings, one student felt as follows:

> *"Because we watch video lectures in advance, our concentration increases during the real class. I think our knowledge has been deeper and deeper as we've studied in this way."*

Many students talked about the logistics of a flipped class and the change in interaction patterns resulting in rich student–student dialogue. For instance:

> *"I think the best thing is that we can take the class in advance and talk together to establish the concept further in class. Also, it's good to keep listening to the recorded lecture even after class."*

Importantly, the students also recognized that active, participatory pedagogy is beneficial to their learning, as noted in the following quote:

> *"It can lead to active participation of students, I believe. I think that's the best thing of this kind of class."*

Given the didactic, teacher-centered traditions of Korean education, such quotes are exciting and reveal an educational transformation is underway in Korea and, most likely, in many other regions of the world. The following is a more comprehensive quote regarding the flipped learning approach:

> *"Unlike other traditional classes, I could understand the contents better because I think I was able to get the contents in advance and then could confirm them in class. Especially, small-group discussions, student-led symposiums, debates under the professor in class were very effective in understanding the concepts, I think."*

As shown in the previous quotes, students displayed positive perceptions and attitudes for active learning in a flipped classroom. In fact, they indicated that they preferred to take that type of class again in the future. Such results challenged me to research this new teaching method. I know teaching always brings great rewards but contains many challenging experiences, especially during the pandemic. I had never previously attempted or even seen flipped classrooms before. Fortunately, my eyes soon opened up to the benefits of such flipped learning approaches to teach university students. I was able to become a better communicator, facilitator, and instructor for my students, and, ultimately, this teaching experience transformed my perspective on teaching.

Honestly, I did not know much about the flipped learning approach and other forms of active learning until I audited a critical and creative thinking class during my sabbatical years at Indiana University (IU) at Bloomington. Currently, I'm applying active flipped learning in my online classes, which I am calling online flipped learning. I feel that this new approach is working well, too, in these online courses.

Now, I would like to end this short article with sincere gratitude to the people at IU. Without timely and innovative pedagogy on display at IU, I might not have conducted these class experiments where I ended up rethinking my teaching approaches. And I might not have changed my educational paradigm from a teacher-centered online to a highly learner-focused one. And you can do such rethinking too!

Reflection Questions

1. Do you have experiences with flipped classrooms in online learning or face-to-face contexts? If so, what happened? And what would you do differently today?
2. How can you design class activities to keep your students engaged in online flipped learning contexts? What specific steps, stages, or tips would you recommend?
3. What might be effective ways of assessing learning in flipped classrooms?
4. How could teachers who are reluctant to use flipped learning approaches perhaps be convinced? How might they be more effectively trained?
5. What other active learning strategies and approaches do you prefer besides employing the flipped classroom and why?

SECTION 6

Active Learning Strategies

In Section 6, we turn to the topic of active learning strategies. You might be wondering what took us so long. Well, as should be obvious by now, this entire book is filled with instructional strategies for active and highly engaging learning; some are focused on creative thinking and innovation, whereas other chapters home in on strategies for cooperative and collaborative learning as well as motivational ones. Many of them also entail forward-thinking ideas related to technology integration. That is not surprising. As explained in the preface and Chapter 1, these topics were part of a course on instructional strategies that all the chapter authors participated in. As shown in these chapters, most of them have returned to their native countries and have attempted to operationalize many of the ideas from that course.

We begin this section with a story from South Asia. In Chapter 29, Marina Basu reflects on her highly regimented educational background she experienced in India and contrasts it with the highly open and expressive curriculum she found herself in early in her teaching career, which effectively transformed her perspectives on learning and the role of the learner. In her chapter, Marina contrasts Education 1.0 and Education 3.0 classrooms based on her varied experiences as a student and later as a teacher and teacher educator. The overriding focus is on nurturing creativity through the use of active learning strategies meant to foster higher order thinking; notably, many powerful instructional strategies are detailed in this chapter. Marina shows that active learning helps learners of all ages to be engaged and motivated. There is less need for direct instruction as active learning strategies can scaffold team learning, creative thinking, and critical thinking.

Next, in Chapter 30, we head to the southern hemisphere for a fascinating story weaved by Sutapa Mukund in Wellington, New Zealand, regarding how to hook students into science with highly engaging activities. As you will see,

DOI: 10.4324/9781003213840-34

Sutapa finds problem-based learning (PBL) aligns well with her student-centered pedagogical approach. PBL allows students to explore authentic problems. Such real-world problems often drive the learning process as learners are motivated to contemplate and explain potential solutions to the problem. To solve the problem, students are encouraged to work in collaboration with others. This approach allows learners to share diverse skills within a team environment.

As Sutapa argues, PBL meshes well with project-based forms of learning as learners often work over extended periods of time on a specific project to either solve a problem or design an outcome. Both problem- and project-based learning approaches are intertwined and encourage learners to master 21st-century skills toward future-focused learning. These learner-centered instructional methods allow learners to be bold and curious while challenging them to move outside their comfort zones and adapt to a rapidly changing world. Importantly, a snapshot of both these approaches in a science context is offered in this chapter.

We travel to the northern hemisphere in Chapter 31 from Tarja Mykrä in Finland, which is known for its excellent education system and high achievement scores such as on the PISA. Tarja also notes that Finnish teachers have extensive freedom to choose the instructional methods and procedures that they want to use.

As an example of this freedom, Tarja discusses a technique that has taken root recently in Finland that utilizes positive phenomena as a starting point for learning and has proved to be highly successful. In fact, phenomenon-based learning as an instructional method has been embedded in Finnish core curriculums from preschool to upper secondary education. Tarja cautions, however, that phenomenon-based learning requires extensive preparation, collaboration, coaching skill, and plenty of positivity and passion. Perhaps most essential is the creation of a safe learning environment where learners are free to ponder, experiment with ideas, and make mistakes.

Heading back to the Down Under, in Chapter 32, Fiona Jeffries from New Zealand explores the use of a digital platform, *Actively Learn*, with a group of New Zealand high school students. A summary of her fascinating and highly important research study reveals ways students can be supported to deepen their reading comprehension. Instructional technology provides a means for students to engage in their reading and respond with deep thinking. According to Fiona, with digital reading being prevalent in the 21st century, learning to read with a "thinking brain" is a skill that needs to be practiced in order to avoid skimming, grazing, and shallow reading that too easily occurs when reading in a digital space. In effect, the focus is on how digital tools can support comprehension depth instead of promoting surface-level behaviors when reading.

In the last chapter of Section 6, we once again journey north. This time we find ourselves in East Asia or, more specifically, Tainan, Taiwan. In Chapter 33, Jhenyi Wu uses local contexts to attract students' interest and engagement via involvement in globally important environmental issues. Jhenyi discusses methods to better engage undergraduate students so that they transfer their motivation from mobile games on smartphones to fully engaged classroom discussion. She asks whether such students be further motivated to take real actions. This chapter addresses such questions in an active learning classroom, which attempts to step out from a local city environment in Taiwan to similar situations around the world and then back again. Such authentic problems and scenarios help students connect local problems and issues to the larger world and, in the process, there is hope to improve some aspect of society.

After reading these chapters, you might ask yourself, what active learning strategies have you seen teachers use in the past that motivated you toward peak performance? You might also ponder on the ideas in Chapters 29 to Chapter 33 that you now might want to implement or extend in new directions.

29

"WHY WEREN'T WE TAUGHT LIKE THIS?"

Introducing Creative Strategies to Indian Teachers

Marina Basu

Marina Basu is a doctoral student at Mary Lou Fulton Teachers College (MLFTC), Arizona State University. She has been a teacher, curriculum developer, and teacher educator for several years. For her Fulbright project, Marina created a teachers' toolkit for fostering mathematical thinking. Her current research focuses on creativity, elementary mathematics teacher education, arts-based research, and non-Western educational paradigms. She is the lead editor

DOI: 10.4324/9781003213840-35

of *Current Issues in Education*, an international open-access journal published by MLFTC. She can be reached at marinabasu@gmail.com.

Introduction

One of my first encounters with creativity was in middle school; more specifically, during a "unit test," we were asked to write a story that started with a specific prompt. I enjoyed the rare opportunity to craft my own story rather than complete a comprehension exercise from a textbook. Being an avid reader from an early age, writing fluently was not a problem for me. I no longer remember the prompt, but I do remember the enjoyment of my writing flowing along with the ideas, resulting in several pages of narrative.

Imagine my surprise on discovering that I had received a score of zero for my story. Overcoming my usual timidity, I was perplexed enough to go up to the teacher and ask her the reason. "A story has to have dialogue, and your story has none," was the teacher's reply.

Yes indeed. Walking back to my desk, I realized that the books I loved reading did indeed have dialogues in them, but no teacher had ever taught us how to write a story—we had simply been assessed. Years later, when reading Gabriel García Márquez, I also realized that there were many ways to write a story. "Must have dialogue" defines a story rather narrowly and excludes some brilliant literature! But to return to my middle school days, I realized at the time that creativity meant following a structure that someone else established, rather like the art classes that I never attended but had heard about—you had to copy an outline and perfecting the drawing implied that you were "good at art." With these previous experiences, I, unfortunately, kept creativity confined to the arts and literature in the real world, and to excellent imitations of already created forms in the world of schooling. I also came to the conclusion that I was not creative.

Let us fast forward several years to when I took on the role of the teacher in a real classroom. This classroom was quite different, however. While as a student, I had sat in highly regimented rows wearing a crisp uniform, the school where I taught had no uniforms, tests, or even textbooks. Instead of a preset curriculum tied to yearly examinations, the teachers collectively planned the curriculum for the elementary grades; each day brought opportunities to try out something new. The pedagogy was based on the educational philosophy of Jiddu Krishnamurti; schools following such pedagogy are hereafter referred to as a "K-schools." As such, we had no formal assessments; instead, we wrote a narrative report at the end of the year based on our observations about the child in the learning environment, her interactions with peers, her inclinations, and her aptitudes.

From my first year of teaching, an interesting anecdote stands out that, in some ways, was my second significant encounter with creativity. Keep in mind that this was my first year in that school. Accordingly, I was discussing my observation notes with my mentor teacher before attempting to write narrative reports for specific children. I was puzzled by "inconsistencies" in a particular child's writing abilities, and I brought it up in our discussions: "Palash knows when to capitalize his letters and ends his sentences with a period, but in creative writing, his sentences run on and he seems to forget all the writing conventions!" I exclaimed.

"Why do you want him to focus on capitals and punctuation if he's doing creative writing? Don't you want him to be in the flow of writing and focus on his ideas?" Those questions from my mentor teacher jolted me out of my habitual ways of thinking about teaching and assessing—the same kind of habitual thinking that I had been subjected to as a learner during my school years. None of my ideas had mattered to the teacher, nor the rich vocabulary that I had used in writing my story. The only thing she noticed was what was not there—in my case, dialogue. And here I was, years later, falling into the same trap. The only thing I noticed was what was not there—writing conventions in the context of creative writing.

I was fortunate that my mentor pointed out my flawed thinking. At the same time, I was also fortunate that I was teaching in a K-school, where students and teachers alike had the freedom to learn, explore, create—and not be tied to the state-mandated rigid curriculum that most schools in India have to follow. From that first year of teaching, I fumbled my way into understanding and nurturing children's creativity in myriad ways, without preconceived ideas about "good English" or "correct spellings" or even preconceptions of "creativity" coming in the way.

We created our own chapter story books. This was exciting for students and teachers alike! In addition, we crafted an anthology of poems as well as a field guide for ants and restaurant menus with invented food items. We composed haikus and diamantes. And we wrote *pourquoi* tales and tall tales. I devised games to get the creativity flowing—drawing words out of a basket; using these random words, we had to make up a story, however, silly or goofy or unrelated those words seemed to be. We worked in groups, in pairs, and individually. While I continued to invent ways to nurture creativity in the classroom, it was the students who were engaged creatively and generated myriad memorable learnings and discoveries. What I came to realize is that all these activities involved extensive trial and error, continued unlearning of what had been indoctrinated in the past, and the willingness to make mistakes as well as try something new.

Ideas from teaching English flowed into how I taught mathematics, just as did ideas from science and vice versa. Our explorations crossed disciplinary boundaries in more ways than one. Observing birds and building paper airplanes could open windows into understanding air and flight. These same bird-viewing episodes could supplement and enhance our reading of biographies and fieldnotes of the Indian "bird man" Salim Ali. Importantly, we could represent data collected from our observations in many ways, such as on a bar graph, in a poster, or through a collage.

Learning to see, hear, and relate took center stage. Learning of content, though important, was significantly deemphasized. And learning of skills was done in a focused manner. As part of these efforts, we separated the teaching of writing conventions from creative writing. And when we were teaching word spellings, we focused on patterns and attempted to arouse curiosity. Ideas from partner work with spellings spilled over into the activities we designed for children to learn number bonds in math. However, if, at that point, I had been asked about the "hows" and the "whys" of what I did, I would not have been able to articulate them.

At that point, the only explicit strategy I knew was K-W-L for helping teachers realize what students already **know** about a topic as well as what they still **want** to know and how they would prefer to **learn** it. As my experience with the K-W-L strategy grew over time, this became a powerful tool that I used across different subject areas. It is noteworthy that even as I was nurturing creativity in children, my self-perception continued to be that I was "not a creative person." I admittedly was uneasy in dealing with this conundrum. Personal awareness as well as personal change in terms of changing mindset is difficult.

It was at this juncture that I went to Indiana University (IU) on a Fulbright scholarship. While there was a range of insights that I gained from the program, a significant one relates to my learning about instructional strategies for developing thinking skills and nurturing collaboration among students. Some of what I had been doing in my classroom in the non-traditional school made sense in a way that I had not thought of before. I discovered that there were names for some of the things I had been doing—falling under the broad umbrella of teaching and learning strategies. In fact, K-W-L turned out to be only the tip of a gigantic iceberg!

The conceptualization of "Education 1.0" and its contrast with "Education 3.0" in our discussions at IU helped me articulate the way I had been taught as a student and how I approached teaching differently as a teacher. Education 1.0 assumes a passive learner whose mind is to be filled with knowledge (typically from textbooks) and learning implies the student's ability to reproduce that knowledge. In an Education 3.0 world, students are empowered, autonomous, and active, having the freedom to inquire about the world around them and pursue their passions. Instead of being subjected to a preexisting and preset curriculum with minimal, if any, chance for creative expression, Education 3.0 students are encouraged to creatively, critically, and collaboratively construct their own learning.

In addition to these discussions, we experienced firsthand some active learning strategies that are detailed later in this chapter. Most surprisingly, through a range of these and other activities that we engaged in, I finally realized that there were elements of creativity within me. Such a realization helped me change my script from "I am not a creative person" to "I am a creative teacher, and I can teach for and with creativity." It was as if I had been magically transported to a treasure vault full of ideas to engage and motivate countless learners. I was now equipped to build their (and my own) critical and creative thinking. I had spent decades in this world, but only now could I see the rich store of pedagogical opportunities that lay in the pathways all around me.

What did I see? Jigsaw, round robin, SCAMPER, circle of consequences, six thinking hats, minute paper, and muddy point paper. Wait, there's more: exit ticket, two truths and one lie, back to the board brainstorming, question asking, summarizing, gallery walks, quotes, analogies, and so forth. I could go on and on about the explosion of strategies around me.

These instructional strategies scaffold creative teaching and learning by structuring open-ended learning environments and address several pedagogical principles. I will recap a few key ones here. The previous strategies encourage the sharing of multiple perspectives, enable students with diverse abilities and interests to participate and, most importantly, empower the teacher to move toward creating spaces for open-ended explorations and away from imparting content. Eagerly drinking in all these ideas, I began merging and morphing the strategies in wholly new ways and returned to India eager to share my insights with other teachers.

At this point, I joined a teacher training institute as a faculty member and was asked to teach a module on classroom management to a mixed group of adults—a few were veteran teachers returning to school to be recertified, some were college graduates looking for a career in teaching, and a lot of them were professionals from other fields who wanted a career change. There was a richness of experience in the classroom. With a wide array of active learning strategies at my fingertips, I decided to introduce the module entirely through a combination of these various strategies. Individual and group brainstorming, problem-posing activities, think-pair-share, round robin activities, circle of viewpoints, and structured role-play activities were among the ones that I included. I was so excited to try them all!

Trainee teachers had to come up with "problematic" or "disruptive" scenarios in the classroom. Then, through group work, they had to write out and enact the script for it. In one group, the scenario involved a teacher who enters the classroom and finds doodles on the board. Frustrated, she immediately blames a particular "child" who she views as disruptive, while the actual doodler is a different student.

Laying the groundwork for these scenarios through a circle of viewpoints and other strategies helped all the trainee teachers see for themselves how extensively stereotyping and creativity-killing episodes happen in the classroom. The fact that the trainees were coming to these understandings by themselves was even more empowering and moving for them—they could see how their creativity and critical thinking had been brought to the fore in the collaborative activities that they engaged in; it was not information given to them by a lecturer or taken from a book, as they had been used to throughout their schooling.

"Why did the teacher never stop to notice the creativity in the doodle and applaud that?" wondered one teacher trainee, while another remarked that she had felt deep empathy for the student, as well as for the teacher. The module made the trainees realize how at various times during their own schooling, that they had been discouraged, ignored, or felt unmotivated. Simply put, they learned just how their creativity had been stymied, over and over and over again. That episodes of learning could take place in a group with minimal teacher intervention was eye opening for them. And they wanted more such learning. However, most of India, similar to most mainstream schooling practices worldwide (with a few exceptions), focuses on an individualistic model of learning. Team-based and peer-learning models are a rarity.

During the end of the module reflections, trainee teachers shared how high their level of engagement had been throughout. It also made them realize that terms like "classroom management" become important only when the learning is not engaging enough, and children act out due to boredom or lack of motivation. Most of them are full-time teachers now, and I continue to learn from them as many of them share what they are doing in their own classrooms. One of them organized an online math camp during the pandemic, whereas another created a set of puzzles. As I hear from them, I remember my school days and see how far we have moved away from rote learning to learning for joy.

Certain structures can thwart creativity, while certain others can foster it. Instructional strategies, properly used, can both scaffold learners' creativity and enable teachers to teach with creativity. They foreground motivation and engagement, and in collaborative settings, can even create such magic that teacher candidates exclaim, "Why weren't we taught like this [in our own schooling]?" That is the very question that I had in my mind when I first encountered myriad alternative instructional strategies at IU. I have come to realize that with its focus on assessments, grades, and learning outcomes, schools leave little room for creativity.

Working with teachers in India and seeing them successfully use active learning strategies in their classrooms, I can envision a small step toward Education 3.0 that will grow into a movement. And I intend to keep taking those small steps forward in the coming decades. Perhaps, in the not-so-distant future, how learners experience learning will be entirely creative and rote learning will be archived as an artifact of the distant past.

Reflection Questions

1. How might children experience the classroom differently in Education 1.0 versus Education 3.0? Think about and perhaps discuss with others what you have seen or envision for the future.
2. The author lists some advantages of using active learning strategies. What are some other advantages that you can think of, as well as disadvantages? Select any three specific strategies as examples and reflectively write about you

might use them in a couple of different contexts. Then perhaps discuss your initial ideas with others for feedback.

3. What is the author's argument about classroom management? Do you agree or disagree with this perspective? Are there any alternative approaches that you prefer?

4. Can something that has not been taught be assessed? Why or why not?

5. What kind of assessment strategies could be used to foster creativity? What kinds of assessment approaches hinder or block forms of creative expression?

30

HOOKING STUDENTS INTO SCIENCE WITH ENGAGING ACTIVITIES

Sutapa Mukund

Sutapa Mukund is currently a national assessment facilitator in New Zealand. Her role involves facilitating and administering the secondary school assessments of New Zealand's National Certificates of Educational Achievement in senior secondary schools. In 2015, Sutapa represented New Zealand on a Fulbright Distinguished Teaching Award in the United States. She has also been the recipient of the Royal Society Award and the Science Teacher Leadership Award in New Zealand. Her teaching career has spanned over three decades across India, Oman, and New Zealand, of which 21 years were spent teaching science in Auckland. Sutapa enjoys travelling and fine arts as much as she enjoys science. She is a storyteller. This is clearly reflected in this chapter, where she narrates a story from her recent teaching experiences. She can be contacted at sumukund@gmail.com.

DOI: 10.4324/9781003213840-36

Introduction

Being a teacher was never my first option. I wanted to be a chef. The result of achieving straight As and high academic grades in science all through my BSc and MSc was my inherent fault. These grades wouldn't let my Indian parents allow me to follow my culinary skills in the kitchen and become a chef. Instead, I got packed off to a teacher training college and became a secondary school biology and science teacher. I always thought teachers were the most boring people on earth: the same syllabus, same content, day after day. And yet, here I was one of them! Welcome to my world.

After I joined my first school, I realised within weeks that teaching was akin to a high-profile sales job. We all know that a top salesman who rakes in the highest commissions does so by ensuring customer buy-in. The sales pitch is very important if you are to be successful in selling your goods. So I decided that my sales pitch had to be extraordinary. This is probably the only tip I have given to the several trainee teachers who have been under my supervision, and it is the success story of my science teaching at various schools across the globe over the last three decades.

This chapter specifically looks at an example of problem-based learning (PBL1) and project-based learning (PBL2) that I carried out for a unit of science in a junior science class (ages-13–14 years) in New Zealand. The topic used in this context was a biology topic on plants. I should note that plant biology is not commonly a popular topic for students at the age of 14 years when they would rather be burning magnesium on a flame or electroplating a key in copper sulphate solution than learning about photosynthesis, seeds, flowers, and pollination!

The student seating plan in my science classroom is organised in such a way that students sit in groups of eight around clustered tables. I normally do not spend too much time writing on the board. My class is used to the fact that their teacher has bad handwriting (or so she says). As a result, one or the other students often walks across to the board to summarise a point that we have studied. In this way, the students are involved and empowered. Death by PowerPoint or excessive use of technology devices is limited in my classroom. I prefer movement. I prefer chatter, as in discussions. I like to see and hear my students interact.

The lesson to this PBL1 and PBL2 unit commenced with a colourful worksheet with iconic images of Singapore, Mumbai, New York, and Hong Kong sans the city names. Students had to identify the city, the city's currency, currency conversion to New Zealand dollars, estimate the population of the city, estimate the geographical area of the city, and then estimate the average housing space for a small four-member family living in these cities. They could use devices and the library to complete this task. As a part of their follow-up homework over the weekend, students had to talk to a person from a realty company, such as a real estate agent, over the phone. Alternatively, they could look up the housing advertisements and find out the average housing price of a three-bedroom house in central Auckland, Papatoetoe (a southern Auckland suburb on this rise where our school was located some 60 kilometres from central Auckland).

Students loved the discussion around the various housing prices. More importantly, they were particularly interested in the available spaces and areas that average income people could afford in Auckland compared with the big cities like Hong Kong. They were surprised to learn that most other cities did not have gardens and yards as is customary in most New Zealand homes unless the owners were super rich! The question that remained topmost on the minds of students over the two-period classes was why we are learning economics and geography in a science class.

When asked what they would be able to afford in terms of buying their own house in the volatile hothouse of the rising Auckland housing market 20 years from their present age, the look of despondence was quite evident. Students mostly argued that they wouldn't be able to buy a house with a yard or garden in Auckland's ever rising and expensive housing market. They would either rent or share the house with their parents. This was their introduction to the world of vertical living in modern times.

The students were then provided with a new task. They were asked to design futuristic houses in small spaces where people like themselves would reside in 20 years within a specific dimensional housing complex. Even with the constraints of space, the challenge was to ensure that the housing complex could grow plants. Discussions among the student groups produced various ideas like communal spaces to enhance greenery, community gardens to grow seasonal vegetables, and various ideas on how residents could grow herbs and vegetables within tiny living spaces through vertical gardens and hydroponics. These designs were initially discussed as a group, and then the group had to produce their own model design for the housing complex using either computer-generated graphics or posters for a submission proposal to the "pretend" Auckland city council for approval.

My job during these lessons was somewhat straightforward and relatively easy though it required understanding of where and when to nudge and offer guidance and suggestions. Discussions were so animated that it almost felt like I was amidst builders and future architects who literally had amazing ideas to bring to the table. Even the quietest students in the class became popular overnight for either their skills on the computer or using their mathematical skills to design floor space and dimensions for individual apartments as well as for a gym, a swimming pool, parking, gardens, a children's play area, and walking spaces.

The next stage in the project was to pitch the class the idea of how we could complete a prototype of a similar communal garden within our own school campus. In their designs, the students had already included tyre gardens, bottle gardens, vertical gardens, hanging gardens, and hydroponics units in their design. So it was left for my science technician, Heather Hart (an amazing science person), and myself to source old tyres and potted plants. Heather contacted the local tyre shop and organised various sizes of tyres. She also got us several pots of free paint and seeds of flowering plants from the local Bunnings Warehouse. The local nursery gave us several colourful plants, and some of the students "stole" from their own gardens and added them to our nursery!

Over the next few weeks, we took it upon ourselves to paint and design a colourful and beautiful tyre garden with loads of flowers near the school canteen. We had also managed to contact a local freight company that gave us free wooden pallets that we painted white and erected amidst the colourful tyres to grow our herbs. The tyre garden soon became the "go-to place for selfies." The next mission for the students was to research why they couldn't grow potatoes or other vegetables within the tyres. This research extended to questions such as how we could possibly grow some vegetables within the school campus in the limited time of the school term.

Conducting research about the leaching of chemicals such as polyaromatic hydrocarbons and heavy metals from various brands and types of tyres became a hot topic in class. We then moved to discuss the chemistry angle of harm caused in a food chain and understood how biology and chemistry were all interconnected. This conversation further leads us to the topic of photosynthesis and the role of light, water, and carbon dioxide in the growth of plants.

Learning was fun. Learning was sharing knowledge, as each student often brought in new information every day. Learning was easy, as students were teaching each other. But most importantly, learning was *meaningful*, as each component of knowledge had some relevance or importance to the students' lives. My Pacifica (i.e., includes the islands close to New Zealand such as Samoa, Fiji, Niue, Tonga) students had reminiscences about their holidays in Samoa and related how their grandparents grew crops and lived off the land, while my Maori students talked about ancestral and traditional farming in their communities. We slowly moved to the cultural aspect of food from this topic and even had a shared ethnic lunch.

With the luck of an alumni scholarship grant from the Fulbright programme in the United States, the crowning glory to this project was to be able to install a glasshouse and set up a complete hydroponics unit at our school. This, of course, was a bonus! Not a regular expenditure that a school would spend on various other PBL1 and PBL2 initiatives that I had undertaken. Students were involved in building and putting together the various units of this hydroponics set-up, followed by adding special nutrients to the distilled water used by the plants. Lettuce, radish, and spinach were our first crops!

With the project almost complete, as discussed next, I had one important final task for my students. In fact, this task, which was associated with a small prize of a gift voucher, resulted in a couple of unique and unexpected responses. First, I was reprimanded by a parent who said that all that her daughter did was come home and sit on the computer that whole week. This parent added that her daughter was wasting all her time playing with images, and as a science teacher, I shouldn't be giving them such frivolous homework! Second, the student who seldom spoke in class and never did his homework completely hijacked my entire lesson one day as he demonstrated to a rapt audience, including myself, the use of a drone to take pictures.

This last segment of work included using several photographs from the entire project to portray a single static image showcasing what they had learned in an innovative way. As fate might have it, the student whose parent reprimanded me was the winner. She had crafted a static image showing herself minimised (almost like the movie *Honey, I Shrunk the Kids*) walking through a shaded futuristic forest of giant bean plants. The significance of this innovative image, according to her, was the "*future of food.*" Her prediction was that biotechnology and genetics research in the future would increase nutrition and the size of the bean seed.

Our ten-week learning episode concluded with the students taking over the staff presentation on a Friday morning and presenting their entire problem-based learning project (PBL1 and PBL2) to a large room of 110 adult staff members. Snippets of this project were also shared during the following year at Indiana University (IU) in the United States as part of my participation in a Fulbright programme for teachers around the world. During my semester-long stay at IU, I continued to reflect on as well as refine and reshape all the wondrous PBL ideas I had dancing in my head to make learning more relevant and meaningful for my students. I hope that you also find ways to facilitate rich, meaningful learning experiences for your students using the PBL methods that work with your content and learners.

Reflection Questions

1. How can you use digital technology in meaningful and innovative ways in your courses and classrooms?
2. How can you change minilessons into problems when you embark on teaching a topic?
3. What activities can you incorporate to allow diverse learners to participate with equity in the classroom?
4. How can you engage your students meaningfully using various science (or other content areas) activities? How can you engage your students like the students were in this chapter? How can you build a learning environment with surprisingly committed students as in this chapter?
5. How can you design your science lessons (or any content area lesson) and overall learning environment to create opportunities that yield greater student interaction and engagement?

31

PEDAGOGICAL INNOVATIONS FROM FINLAND

Using Positive Phenomena for Powerful Learning

Tarja Mykrä

DOI: 10.4324/9781003213840-37

Tarja Mykrä currently works as a freelancer in the field of education. Previously, she was director of development in Mercuria Business College, Finland. She also has been a vocational teacher and a specialist in coaching, mentoring, student-centered teaching methods, vocational education, and work-based learning. Tarja has several publications in her specialist areas. She spent fall 2015 as a Fulbright scholar at Indiana University Bloomington in the United States. She was also selected to the Fulbright Leaders for Global School program in fall 2019. She can be reached at tarjamykra@gmail.com.

Positive Phenomena Tie Complex Learning Together

Your students have a learning goal: they need to learn how to sell products on the market. How do you, as their teacher, help them to reach their goal? Will you give them lessons about marketing, product information, and selling? How about inventory control, customer service, and business ethics? Might you consider giving them assignments concerning budgeting or product placement? How do you support them with these assignments? Do you encourage them to find more information about how to sell products from the internet? You might also ask your students to interview sales professionals, who market many types of products, such as fashion, cosmetics, electronics, dog accessories, and ICT devices, to name a few. How do you ensure that your students have the skills and knowledge to sell products in the real world?

I am sure as a teacher you have used many teaching methods just mentioned. I am also certain that you have experienced the pros and cons of each of these methods. Why wouldn't you use all these methods and more? But have you ever considered the phenomenon-based approach?

An Example of Using Positive Phenomena in a Successful Way

Phenomenon-based learning has been used in Finnish Mercuria Business College for years. In fact, from the hundreds of instructional approaches that are promoted in the education and training literature, phenomenon-based learning has been a consistently high-end success among students. As one student asked, "Why couldn't school always be like this?" Every year a five-day Christmas Market is planned, organized, and evaluated with a group of students who want to learn about selling in a more practical way.

In phenomenon-based learning, students have an active role and a lot of freedom. Responsibility for their own learning is allocated to them in a strong way. The role of a teacher or teacher team is to support learning by coaching and facilitation. It is crucial to allow students to plan, implement the plans with their peers, make mistakes, plan again, fail, and maybe try again and again. Unlike much of education, failure is accepted as part of the learning process. Over the years, phenomenon-based learning has proved to be a unique way of learning, where students are highly motivated. It actually turns out that they learn much more than in a traditional classroom: in addition to subject areas, they learn cooperation, communication, teamwork, responsibility, and problem-solving, to name a few vital 21st-century skills.

What does it require from a teacher to teach by using phenomenon-based learning? I provide some tips and advice for you to get started next.

Cooperate Within Your School

It is always helpful if your principal supports pedagogical experiments. Given that, I suggest you arrange a meeting with him or her first. Think also about how you might form teams of teachers and how you could encourage them to teach using a phenomenon-based approach as a team. You likely will also need help from your school administration to adjust schedules with the teacher team, both for planning and for the actual learning process. In addition, you might need more classrooms, alternative spaces for learning, and other materials and resources. Clearly, this phase might require extensive amounts of time and many intense discussions.

Plan in Advance With Other Teachers

Phenomenon-based learning requires cooperation with other teachers. It means that the preparation must be done well in advance; it is not possible to plan everything in a short burst of gusto the night before you initiate such an activity. Working in a teacher team is different from working as an individual teacher, and it might take some time to learn to work as a team—but believe me, it is worth it!

In the process, you learn an amazing amount from your colleagues and gain a deep respect for the foresight, determination, and skills that they each bring. In Mercuria Business College, teachers who have this experience of working as a team say that they would never go back to traditional teaching. In a teacher team, one plus one is more than two, and each individual teacher gets support from the team. It is also rewarding to reflect on the teaching process and the results together.

Collaborate With Your Students

The starting point for phenomenon-based learning is student-centered orientation. Teachers cooperate with students, and they make a concerted effort to avoid intervening too much in the learning process. Social competence, empathy, and the ability to understand another position are more vital than teacher expertise for a particular subject area.

Create a Safe Atmosphere to Learn

It is the responsibility of a teacher or teacher team to create a safe learning environment where the participants feel a sense of belongingness and psychological comfort. In a safe learning environment, the atmosphere is relaxed, and the students feel free to ponder on their options and try out different ways of learning without the fear of failure. When this happens, the learning can be really fun! In this environment, mistakes, setbacks, and failures are accepted and even encouraged. In fact, sometimes the failure is the most fruitful learning experience. Reflecting on failures with the student team and their teacher can enhance and, at times, even transform the resulting learning.

Coach Your Students

Coaching is a method where the focus is on helping your students discover their potentials and move forward to the goal. As a coach, you help your students to expand and apply their skills, knowledge, and abilities to the case at hand. In general, a coach does not give straight advice to students, but with the use of open and powerful questions, he or she acts in ways similar to Socrates did over two millennia ago with the hope to empower students to find the answers themselves. If your students are used to getting advice from a teacher, they might be confused in this new situation, where a teacher deliberately avoids giving them answers— or might not even have answers! When you as a teacher are in a role of a coach, you often are exposed to situations when you don't know, and because you don't know, you are more cautious when lending advice to your students. All you can do is to encourage them to find answers with your support.

Be Positive!

Positive psychology and positive pedagogy are cornerstones for phenomenon-based learning. In Finland, positive psychology is widely used in elementary schools, and it is expected to produce both learning and high welfare for both students and teachers. The meaning of school is not only to increase the level of knowledge, but also to help students to grow to be good citizens who are aware of their strengths and talents as well as the importance of pursuing their passions.

This pursuit of passions and interests is a prerequisite for a rapidly changing future working life. We in Finland really believe in such authentic and real-world pedagogical methods; in fact, the recently renewed high school core curriculum in Finland includes a minimum one six-week course based on phenomena.

I will now pose a final question: what does it mean for a teacher to be positive? There are attributes that are connected to a profession of a teacher: being kind and tactful, giving feedback and recognition, and—the most important— supporting the hopes, dreams, and aspirations of students. Keep in mind that they can do just that with phenomenon-based learning.

Reflection Questions

1. Have you ever experienced phenomenon-based learning? If so, what was the activity and what happened? Why do you think teachers in Finland find it powerful?
2. What would be the phenomena and topics you would like to teach and why?
3. How would you teach using a phenomenon-based learning approach? Is there anything innovative that you would try to do? Would there be any cautions or hesitancy on your part?
4. How would you encourage your colleagues to work with phenomenon-based teaching? And when should you start to talk about your idea with school management and colleagues?
5. How will you find a suitable mentor for phenomenon-based learning?

32

ACTIVE LEARNING THROUGH USING *ACTIVELY LEARN*

Fiona Jeffries

Fiona Jeffries is an English teacher and specialist classroom teacher at Paraparaumu College, New Zealand. She was awarded a Fulbright Distinguished Award in Teaching scholarship in 2014 at Indiana University in the United States. During her Fulbright experience, Fiona investigated the ways digital tools were being used to support literacy development in classes in U.S. schools. Upon her return to New Zealand, she continued to explore how digital tools could support reading development, particularly for high school students. Subsequently, she

DOI: 10.4324/9781003213840-38

embarked on a Doctor of Education degree through Curtin University, Western Australia, in 2016. Her research investigated the digital platform *Actively Learn* and the ways it supports reading comprehension. She can be reached at fiona.jeffries@pc.school.nz.

Introduction

What is so important that it cannot be left to chance? Reading. Reading with fluency, reading with understanding, reading with a thinking brain, and just more reading. Yet, in the digital age, our reading has too often become shallow. We flit from article to article and sometimes never fully complete the reading of a single text.

Technology presents us with a double-edged sword. We have myriad access points to a vast array of print and text. Words perpetually surround us in a variety of social media platforms we constantly open and close. And yet, the browsing style of reading that occurs when working in a digital format compounds the problem for struggling teenagers who need to learn to read deeply to aid their comprehension. The type of reading they interact with most frequently is fast-paced, quick flicking between screens and posts, resulting in minimal depth. Skimming, scanning, and scrolling quickly through text does nothing to develop vital and lasting skills of deep comprehension.

One problem we were having at my high school was that some students had low reading comprehension ability, and this problem persisted over several years. The academically able students were flourishing; however, the low achievers were not making the necessary progress to advance.

A puzzle of practice weighed upon me as I returned to New Zealand, having completed a Fulbright scholarship in the United States, wherein I investigated ways digital tools can be used to support literacy development. Rather than accepting the status quo that some students struggle to read without much depth of thinking, I wondered if there was a way digital tools could be used to enhance their deep reading skills.

Instead of my study being completed, an opportunity arose to stretch myself further. And so, with such questions, concerns, and observations, my doctoral journey began. This would have seemed an impossible aspiration just one year prior; however, having the benefit of the Fulbright experience under my belt, and through meeting and interacting with many doctoral students at Indiana University, I began to wonder if maybe this was my next step as well. Instead of waiting for answers to my questions to magically appear, I decided that teachers at the chalkface could explore their own questions.

After investigating what digital tools were available to support reading comprehension development, my colleagues and I came upon the *Actively Learn* platform. Based in Portland, Oregon, this platform claimed to promote deep reading and thinking skills.

The platform provided several functions, including (1) opportunities for teachers to chunk texts into smaller segments, (2) a means for students to change the way a text looked through altering the style and size of the font, (3) a vocabulary support tool, and (4) a text-to-speech tool. It also had the opportunity for students to reflect on what they had read and monitor understanding, whilst reading. The variability in terms of assistive tools and the focus placed on thinking during the reading process, soon led to me working with a group of like-minded teachers and trialing the *Actively Learn* platform as a reading comprehension resource.

Although the content in the catalogue of articles was mainly U.S.-centric, the platform had a high-interest section with topical issues from around the world. To use content targeted explicitly to New Zealand issues, the teachers in my school used the three free uploads per month.

So how did our students react to this platform? Were there any characteristics that stood out as being useful and supporting their reading development?

As a result of this study, I identified three key affordances arising from using the *Actively Learn* platform. Firstly, it assisted students to be agentic by providing spaces for them to problem-solve and practice their thinking skills while reading. Secondly, it enabled students to connect with others, their teachers, or other texts and sources of information, which supported their knowledge building. Finally, it provided opportunities for direct involvement of teachers with individual students, enabling them to give targeted advice concerning comprehension reading skills and strategies.

A model of supported reading comprehension in a digital space emerged from this study and synthesised the three intersecting affordances of (1) agency and autonomy, (2) connectedness, and (3) the teacher's role. As described in the next sections, the model provides teachers with a tool for evaluating the efficacies of new digital platforms designed to scaffold comprehension development.

Agency and Autonomy

One key characteristic of *Actively Learn* I found was that students liked a text being divided into chunks with open-ended questions being placed at junctures within the text, decided by the teacher. Students told me that having the opportunity to think at the very moment they were engaged in reading allowed them to develop their thinking about what was being read. Thinking and engaging with the ideas within a text leads to a depth of analysis that might not occur in a situation where a student could get away with either the tactic of skimming their assigned readings or passive listening to the ideas and opinions of other students.

The interspersed questions had an impact on comprehension and metacognition by helping students take control of their thinking. Developing a learner agency and autonomy theme, students reported that they had to think and show their thinking; in effect, they had to own their contributions.

When discussing the types of questions inserted into the chunks of text, I found a strong sense that students enjoyed having the chance to think on the spot. As one student stated, "I liked the questions that make me think about what I've read because there's no point reading if I don't know what I've read." Another variation of this idea was stated by another student as follows: "I like expressing my opinion, and it's good to write it down and think about what you think."

Being able to see only one part of the text at a time, and focus on that part, was seen by many as a positive aspect that kept them reading. Students told me that they had to "really read all the text" and "make sure they understood it" because they had to answer a question before moving on to the next segment of the text. As one student stated, "It makes us do more thinking. I find it easier because they've sectioned it off, so you have to focus on a certain paragraph and not everything else. It lets you direct your focus more onto that paragraph."

Simple retrieval of facts from within a text leads to shallow processing. What we really want from students is their thinking, their ideas, and their courage to have an opinion and state it.

Students also revealed to me that the "definition" tool in *Actively Learn* allowed them to solve their lack of understanding of a word immediately in the moment of reading. For some, this involved right-clicking, highlighting, and simply reading the definition; for others, this also entailed having the word spoken to them to hear how the word sounded.

> *"When I came across a word and could see the definition then and there I thought, 'Oh, that makes a lot more sense now.' It puts a sentence together if you know what a word means rather than just having a random word and thinking, I don't know what that means."*

Almost half of the students in my study stated that at some stage, they had used the listening tool. However, using the text-to-speech tool was largely a selective and irregular occurrence, rather than listening to a text in its entirety.

A further aspect of autonomy and personalisation I discovered that students enjoyed when using the *Actively Learn* platform was the ability to change the visual elements of the texts. For some students, it was helpful to change the "look" of the text. Some of these students wanted to change the way the text looked for ease of reading, whereas others made changes solely for personal preference. The modifications involved changing the font, or the size of the font, changing the background colour, and changing the spacing settings. The "dyslexic settings" made it easier for some due to having the text more widely spaced out, while other tool features made visual changes to make the text visually appealing and easier to read.

Connecting

Another characteristic that students found useful in helping with their reading comprehension was the note-making tool. Students could right-click, highlight text, and "take a note." Through making this note public, others in the class could see it and join in as part of a discussion thread. This system provided an opportunity for students to interact with each other's comments, discuss ideas that arose from the text, and see another point of view.

> *"Notes are cool to have other people's opinions about what you're writing and if they agree or change it a little bit. It causes everyone to have their own say. It's cool."*

An additional aspect that students told me they found helpful was seeing other students' answers. This added a depth of understanding to their reading and helped them see what other students were thinking. The responses of other students are immediately accessible once a student has completed their answer. Many students told me that they checked the answers of some other students when they had completed their responses. For instance, one person claimed, "It lets me see where other people are coming from. You get to see what other points of view people have. It's helpful because if you can see other people's opinions, you take in a different perspective."

Connecting beyond themselves to a support system through seeing other students' answers when reading a text was a valuable means of building the understanding of ideas for almost half of my study group. It allowed them to privately check whether they understood the text by comparing their ideas with those of others. It also helped them expand their understanding by processing the ideas in the text through the words of a peer. This platform feature supports the idea that literacy is a social activity, having opportunities to interact, rather than working in an isolated format.

Teacher's Role

The final theme to emerge from the data was a slight surprise to me. Despite using a digital tool, input and involvement from the teachers was something that many students wanted and saw as an essential part of the process. From tailoring the texts through providing choices that engaged their classes, to creating appropriate chunks and interspersing these with questions, to interacting with students at the time they were working, teacher input was pivotal. There was a sense of accountability, knowing the teacher was checking the work straight away and that the teacher was able to respond to a revision request almost immediately. A digital tool supports what the teacher is teaching and does not take the place of a high-quality teacher.

A final and wonderful bonus of using this digital platform was "hearing" from the quiet students; the ones who all too often fly under the radar because they are hesitant to offer an opinion to the class. This platform gave them a chance to have a "voice," and for others to see what they were thinking.

Something I discovered through this study was that reading comprehension is often assessed using multiple-choice tests. However, my research showed that students want to have a voice when answering questions about a text and not be required to simply select the correct answer. Seeing the depth of thinking in students' answers has given me such a buzz. I was thrilled to read the perceptive thoughts of teenagers. The focus, the insight, the determination, and the personal answers revealed their reactions to a person, a sport, an animal, or an activity.

I loved the way students could connect their reading to their own experiences. I loved the quiet, focused working zone. And I loved the way they wanted my reactions. "Hey, Miss, have you read my last answer?" a young man called out as he left the class when the bell had rung. Not yet, but I will shortly. I wouldn't miss it for the world.

Reflection Questions

1. In what ways have you noticed yourself reading differently when in a digital environment compared with a paper-based one?
2. What are some tools that you have seen or heard about that assist students in understanding what they are reading? Have you used any of them? If so, what were the results?
3. How can students support each other's learning when developing reading comprehension skills?
4. From your perspective, what is the best way to assess reading comprehension?

33

ACTIVATING THE ACTIVE LEARNING CLASSROOM

Making the Connection From Local to Global

Jhenyi Wu

DOI: 10.4324/9781003213840-39

Jhenyi Wu is a primary school teacher and a bilingual counseling teacher of the Bureau of Education, currently working in Tainan, Taiwan. She is also a lecturer in National University of Tainan and a member of the NGO Institution in the Society of Wildness in Taiwan. Her life goal and mission is to provide realistic and authentic scenarios for students to connect the world from the local environments to global issues and then take actions to improve society. She may be contacted at jhenyi@gmail.com.

Introduction

I am a believer in active and engaging learning, such as through role play, project and problem-based learning, and authentic data analyses. If you were to stop by my class, you might come on a day when students are standing to represent a number of different biology species in Taiwan, from amphibians to mammals to birds to insects to gymnosperm plants. The following week, you might notice students working on their phones in the park and imagining themselves as squirrels to promote a policy related to "building an eco-friendly park for the government." If you attend some of my classes this year, you will probably see these students analyzing the results of ocean trashes to support plastic-free action. It is exciting to observe their level of engagement and energy. Their extensive pride and happy emotions are vital ingredients for my pedagogical successes and are the motivation I need to keep dreaming up activities that build on such successes.

These types of amazing sceneries are now found in the undergraduate general education courses that I have been teaching since returning from my Fulbright program in the United States in 2016. As part of the lockdown, we cannot have face-to-face international connections. Yet we still want to do something significant through the "Environment and Ecology" and "Science Communication" classroom to make the world green and natural. As part of these greener environment efforts, we continue to try to connect with the younger generation.

I have worked for nine years as a part-time lecturer at the University of Tainan, Taiwan. The university is among the most respected in Taiwan. This elevated reputation comes in part from being one of the oldest colleges or universities in southern Taiwan. Previously, the University of Tainan was a normal college established principally for primary teacher training. It was transformed in 2006 into a general university by creating diverse and trans-discipline departments, such as the College of Science and Engineering and the College of Management.

What Does the Undergraduate Really Want?
A Dream? Or a Job?

Today in Taiwan, the high density of universities and colleges makes higher education much more competitive than it was a decade or two ago. In 2020, there were 160 universities in Taiwan, which research studies have indicated are more than enough for this relatively small island nation consisting of 13,826 square miles (35,808 square kilometers). Recently, a decreasing birth rate in Taiwan has resulted in lower student enrollment rates in higher education than just a decade before.

In one of my typical higher education classes in Taiwan, two thirds of students have a part-time job, and one tenth of students have their own businesses or You-Tube personal channels. This young and entrepreneurial generation of students has enhanced digital and technical skills to quickly seek, find, and learn information using the internet. At the same time, the role of the teacher and the role of the student at universities in Taiwan have been rapidly transformed during the past decade. As a result, fostering students' motivation has become increasingly challenging. Learning how to engage students in the class and connecting them to the wider world through active learning becomes a huge priority.

Transformation Started From Myself, as a Teacher

I was elected as a Fulbright teacher at Indiana University (IU) in 2016. Classes I took at IU in the fall semester forced me to jump out of the circle of the so-called education frame. I was learning not only instructional strategies but also a new philosophy of education called Education 3.0. From this perspective, as an educator in the 21st century, a teacher is not a top-down position leader or a judge in the court, but, instead, is a tour guide or concierge who facilitates and guides students to be empowered to actively learn on their own where and when possible.

There It Is, the R2D2 Model

When I returned to Taiwan, I revised many of my teaching activities to align with the Read, Reflect, Display, and Do (R2D2) model (Bonk & Zhang, 2008) that I learned at IU. I started thinking about what the students really want in the future and if most of the courses they had taken in the past have provided them with the skills and abilities that they will need to successfully function in society. Are they equipped with the necessary skills and information to survive?

I used the R2D2 model to ask my undergraduate students in my "Ecology and Environment" class at the General Education Center in National University of Tainan to collect their daily necessities and check the content of all the chemical substances in them. Then they will begin to grasp how hazardous they are and become more aware of the need for proper safety treatments in the production process and in terms of health exposure and risk. After being guided by various scientific viewpoints, these students began to grasp how to handle possible polluted and dangerous material. For example, toluene is generally used in the solvent of oil-paint, PCE (i.e., tetrachloroethylene) arises as an issue in dry-wash, and there are myriad problems related to plastic and dioxins. Soon topics like bonding became an important local environmental issue where everyone in the class discovered that doing some action is not a slogan for the world but a motto for themselves for the rest of their lives.

Next, by giving these students options to choose their actions, some started to plan an eco-friendly trip and hold a public hearing among students by using the six thinking hats strategy to understand different thoughts and perspectives from varying roles in society. Some chose to make posters related to their environmental policies that they could use to promote them with the general public. Some decided to do a park survey in their communities and promote the policy of building an eco-friendly biodiversity park.

Encouraging Students to build a LOHAS Life?

In the final weeks of these courses, there was some discussion about the Paris Agreement and various global environmental concerns. This discussion forced my students to reflect on the changing government policies and concerns and what still needs to be done as well as the timeline needed to save the earth from a global catastrophe. After analyzing and understanding the environmental situation, or calamity as many say, from which the world is suffering, I held an international meeting with students from six countries (to my amazement, we had guest students from Russia, Paris, Japan, America, and Switzerland). Can you imagine the excitement felt in my classroom? These students were simultaneously discussing gun control issues in America and the forest fires in Russia. In effect, students around the world were active in pressing social and environmental issues important to their own lives.

In the future, each student will need to compete for a job. Hopefully, they will also actively fight for the long-term health of the environment where they live. I believe they will actively fight for their LOHAS (Lifestyles of Health and Sustainability) life from their local communities, which in turn will help the world. We have inherited only one planet. We must get students actively engaged in issues related to it at both local and global levels.

A K-12 Pedagogical Idea in Environmental Education

I have been an elementary school teacher in Taiwan for 15 years and have worked in academic affairs for six years. Educational reform efforts in 2019 in Taiwan produced a new national curriculum. Given the authentic and active learning focus of these reforms, creating learner-centered, real-life scenarios and literacy-based classrooms becomes crucial for primary teachers like me. For instance, in one activity in my class, I used two different colored beans (i.e., symbolizing the energy ratio) to let students count and calculate the ratio of two types of energy use (i.e., green energy and brown energy), and then I guided them as they attempted to find problems related to energy consumption in Taiwan.

After comparing Taiwan's energy data with other countries, the essential question delivered to students was how to make the classroom cooler and more comfortable (in Taiwan, there is no air conditioning in the classroom even though it often reaches up to 35 °C). After reading support materials, students' mission was to display their findings and attempt to solve the pressing energy problem in Taiwan. In the final part of this energy topic, they needed to build their own model and implement their findings with a scientific method (i.e., prediction, assumption, experiment, prove, and conclusion). At the beginning of the class, most students thought that green energy was mainly used in Taiwan, not brown energy. But they were wrong. Taiwan relies mostly on nonrenewable energy. After discovering their misconceptions, they started to take some actions by setting up "future green class rules."

This particular project-based learning lesson was a huge success and has been shared in many educational workshops in Taiwan. Each time, other teachers have reacted to it quite favorably. Perhaps you might find it of value too. If you do, let me know. I look forward to hearing from you.

Reflection Questions

1. Do you know any endemic species in your country that have been endangered? What types of pedagogical activities could you engage your students in to encourage them to analyze relevant governmental policies?
2. Think about an activity to inspire students to become responsible citizens and increase their civic consciousness. Explain that activity to one or two other people and listen to their ideas. Did you discover any similarities? And did you share some key differences? If so, what are they?
3. Brainstorm an environmental issue and set up your students as members of a diverse task force to address the issue. What do they need to deal with it, and what will they say?
4. Perhaps use different thinking hats or roles such as a politician, businessperson, researcher, NGO member, protester, student, and teacher and hold a public hearing in your class. What was the result?
5. Do you have any ideas for how students might be able to connect (i.e., talk, share, listen) with students and classes in other countries about a topic you are addressing in the classroom? Is there any platform (e.g., ePals, iEARN, Eco-School, the Asia Society, TakingITGlobal, World Savvy) or forum you have heard of to coordinate such interaction? Have you thought about knocking on the door of someone who might be able to help? Is there an office of global or international affairs in your organization or institution? You might feel surprised that you have so many resources at your fingertips.

SECTION 7

Global Education

The seventh section of this book centers on global education. Given the continued development of the internet and related technology over the past few decades, the world community has become increasingly familiar with global forms of collaboration. With mounting cultural divides, it is critical for students to collaborate and engage in rich dialogue with people around the world and begin to respect and appreciate diverse cultures. The five stories in Section 7 from Taiwan, Finland, Mexico, Uzbekistan, and Yemen describe how the authors implemented different programs or initiatives for global education by leveraging both synchronous and asynchronous learning technology.

Chapter 34 describes language learning through cross-cultural projects and exchanges. In this chapter, Minsyuan (Sandy) Tsai, an English teacher in Taiwan, shares stories of cross-cultural projects, both online and face-to-face, which have been carried out with other international teachers from Japan and the United States. As Sandy argues, when it comes to teaching a language, culture is a crucial component that should not be neglected. Teaching a language is not just about mastering grammar or sentence structure but about understanding the culture and the people, whether or not the students understand how to utilize the language accurately and effectively in assorted cultural contexts. Broadening students' world vision as well as strengthening their knowledge about different cultures is critical to teaching a second language. Suffice to say, knowing how to break down barriers between students from different learning backgrounds and cultures is of particular importance today.

Chapter 35 documents a unique exchange project in Europe. Learning to understand the world from another culture's point of view and getting along with different people are crucial in today's world. When we actually meet people and build personal relationships across borders, such cross-cultural understanding

DOI: 10.4324/9781003213840-40

can occur more readily. Student exchange projects can be powerful since they enable students to learn about different cultures in real-life situations. In this chapter, Taru Pohtola, an English and German teacher from Finland, shares a cross-cultural exchange project organized between her school in Finland and a German school.

Explore Chapter 36 and you will learn about a journey of professional and personal change of an English language teacher in Mexico after being granted a Fulbright Distinguished Award in Teaching. Diana Zamudio traveled to the United States with an inquiry project that evolved into research on globally networked learning environments. Her exciting journey of transformative teaching started at Indiana University and had a ripple effect in Mexico and France. Diana continues to ponder ways to form bridges between schools and cultures in this globally networked world as a means of promoting intercultural competence and motivating and engaging learners in pedagogically robust and meaningful ways.

In Chapter 37, Umida Khikmatillaeva tells a story about professional development training from a distance for foreign language teachers in Uzbekistan with limited technology access and use before the COVID-19 pandemic. Her chapter details how the ten motivational principles of the TEC-VARIETY framework (Bonk & Khoo, 2014) were effectively implemented and successfully functioned in this setting. Umida's story highlights the importance of needs analyses prior to new supporting technology access and associated training programs. She also points to several opportunities and potential barriers in implementing her teacher training program from a distance.

In Chapter 38, you will join Amani Gashan in her reflective journey coming from Yemen, a historically rich but isolated country. You will learn how the lack of resources in Yemen as well as the emotional pain and sense of isolation can be turned into effective motivators for creative solutions. This chapter presents an example of how available technology tools can be used to overcome physical and mental barriers and bring students from distant continents together to discuss various topics and develop projects of interest. The chapter offers a practical model to bring mutual understanding among people from differing cultural backgrounds and ultimately lead to greater worldwide appreciation of those differences.

As noted earlier, all five chapters in Section 7 share experiences and perspectives regarding global education. We hope that the stories in this section provide replicable, implementable, and sustainable models and examples of cross-cultural exchange as well as keen insights regarding language, culture, and global education.

34

DISTANT HORIZON, CLOSE FRIENDSHIP: LEARNING THROUGH CROSS-CULTURAL PROJECTS AND EXCHANGES

Minsyuan (Sandy) Tsai

DOI: 10.4324/9781003213840-41

Minsyuan (Sandy) Tsai holds an MA degree in foreign languages and literature. She has been teaching English in Kaohsiung Industrial High School in Taiwan for 16 years. From 2010 to 2015, she was in charge of administrative work associated with the school's international exchange programs and student activities. In August 2015, Sandy embarked on the 2015–2016 Fulbright Distinguished Awards in Teaching (DAT) Program and successfully completed the program in December 2015. Since returning from the Fulbright DAT program, she has been conducting workshops with Taiwan Fulbright ETAs (English teaching assistants) and local English teachers in different cities. She remains involved in many local and international projects; for example, the Free Shop, Couchsurfers in Class, Writing for Rights, and the "Pen Pal" project. She may be contacted at sandy626@hotmail.com.

Introduction

I grew up in a rural area in Taiwan where resources were quite limited at the time. As such, the opportunity to find foreigners or peers to practice English was difficult. My memories of learning English in my high school periods included heavy doses of grammar and vocabulary memorization. It was not until I participated in a four-day English immersion camp held at my high school that I had my very first opportunity to witness how my teachers and other students who were fluent in English actually converse with the foreign teachers.

In this camp, I acquired wonderful knowledge about other cultures through the games and activities that the foreign teachers organized. Perhaps most notably, I experienced my first culture shock from seeing how the Western teachers ate with a fork and knife. I was also surprised by how they communicated with each other; for example, they greeted each other with a kiss on the cheek, and they said their goodbyes with big hugs.

As part of this culture shock, my first face-to-face interaction with a foreign teacher ended in a sense of awkwardness and frustration. I remember distinctly how nervous I was when a tall American teacher approached me and asked, "Where do you live in Tainan?" Instead of responding to him directly, I stuttered. Then, a realization struck me, "Wow, I can't speak English even though I performed top of my class on my English exams!" This immersion camp helped me re-evaluate my approaches to learning English. Friends that I made in this camp were also helpful in instructing me to study English from different perspectives.

Instead of just memorizing vocabulary and grammar, I realized that listening, speaking, reading, and writing are equally important when acquiring a new language skill. In comparison to the previous few years of monotonous learning in the typical classroom setting, I benefited far more from this four-day intensive English camp.

Years later, I became an English teacher, and I finally had the opportunity to put my dream of bringing the world to my students into practice. iEARN

(International Education and Resource Network) and ePals were the first two online platforms that I used to engage my students with different types of international projects, through which they learned how to collaborate with students from different countries. Projects and activities like the Teddy Bear Project and the Holiday Cards Exchange broadened my students' world vision as well as increasing their cultural literacy.

In 2011, I gained an opportunity to be in an administrative position to help my school organize different exchange programs, both domestically and internationally. In this position, I organized both inbound and outbound trips for Kaohsiung Industrial High School students and teachers. Countries that we hosted or cooperated with included Japan, Korea, Australia, the United States, France, Mexico, and Brazil, to name just a few. In addition, taking part in the Asian Student Exchange Program held annually in Kaohsiung connected my students and me to the outer world, where we developed more valuable international friendships.

Among all the projects and exchange programs mentioned earlier, I would like to specifically highlight the Teddy Bear Project and the Holiday Cards Exchange Project from iEARN, as well as the PEACE (Pacific Education and Cultural Exchange) program from ePals. These three projects played huge roles in transforming both my students and me into people with enhanced global vision and higher cultural awareness.

iEARN: Teddy Bear Project

The Teddy Bear Project was the first online global collaborative project that I participated in after registering on iEARN. After I registered, the facilitator paired my class with a partner class at the Hitachi 2nd High School in Japan. We sent out two teddy bears to each other, and after receiving them in the mail, students took them to visit their city and, in effect, introduced their city to the other school through their teddy bears' eyes. Additionally, students kept diaries from the perspective of the teddy bears and posted them on a blog. Students benefited enormously from this eight-month project. Not only did they experience different cultures through virtual interaction, but they also improved their English proficiency by keeping online English journals. Occasionally, they video chatted with their overseas friends in their second language. As might be expected, this practical application made their English language acquisition a more fun and engaging process.

At the end of the project, students made presentations on what they had learned from the project. Additionally, they displayed posters in the hallway for other teachers and students to appreciate and understand more about Japanese culture and school life.

Many of my students profited markedly from this project, as seen in their increased motivation to acquire their targeted language. Some devoted themselves more to learning foreign languages. There were also students who decided to go overseas for further study. Throughout the process, I witnessed how my students transformed themselves from local to global citizens through constant collaboration with overseas students. They learned how to try to better understand cultural differences, which in turn fostered their knowledge and appreciation of globalization. This was truly a magical moment in my teaching, as this was something they could never learn from textbooks.

In retrospect, iEARN had offered both my students and me an unforgettable experience and lifelong memories to cherish. The Teddy Bear Project helped to strengthen my professional development as well.

I have learned numerous innovative techniques for implementing and coordinating a global collaborative project online. Not only has my spoken English proficiency improved but also participating in these projects strengthened my leadership skills. Most importantly, like my students, I also had developed a strong and genuine friendship with the Japanese teacher, Ted Nakano, who had inspired me immensely in implementing the online collaborations. An interesting outcome of that international project with that one of my students even developed a close relationship with one of the female Japanese students, and their relationship lasted for years. Now, that former student speaks fluent Japanese and is working and residing in Japan.

iEARN: Holiday Card Exchange Project

An Australian teacher first facilitated the Holiday Card Exchange Project, which involves teachers and students preparing an envelope with holiday cards to send to the other participants between October and December. After registering, I was matched with a group of teachers from Slovenia, Belarus, the United States, Russia, and Brazil.

First, teachers interacted in the iEARN chat forum to become better acquainted. Next, I proceeded to group my students based on their level of interest in the assigned countries. Each group discussed the format of their holiday cards, either agreeing on handmade or ready-made cards. We then made cards and wrote greetings together in the English classes. Students posted their cards on the forum to share with students from other countries.

My students and I sent out our packages of cards to the countries we were matched with before Christmas. We also received packages of cards from our partner schools around the same time. My students were excited about opening the envelopes and reading the cards. The different styles of cards from various countries piqued their interest and excitement in cross-cultural learning. In fact, I am certain that this virtual cultural exchange rewarded all the classes who participated.

After sharing our cards in class, we also decorated a Christmas tree in the hallway with the cards, so that other students and teachers in the school could share in our joy of exchanging holiday cards with schools from overseas. As the iEARN Holiday Card Exchange Project required less time and work, more and more teachers in my school participated. Within one year, the number of classes participating in the project had increased from two to 12.

ePals: PEACE (Pacific Education and Cultural Exchange) Program

PEACE was an international cultural exchange program with an aim to promote greater cultural awareness among students from both Taiwan and the United States. By participating in this program, we hoped to encourage the participants to exchange ideas and perspectives on contemporary issues, global events, and cultural differences and similarities. We anticipated that the participants of this program would increase their cross-cultural understanding and communication through a series of events and activities in the Tri-State area of the United States (i.e., New York, New Jersey, and Connecticut).

When I expressed my interest in collaborating with a teacher in the United States on an authentic cultural exchange program, which meant visiting each other's schools to experience school life and culture, a facilitator on the ePals forum introduced me to a teacher in New Jersey named Bob. He and I spent a year communicating and organizing all the project details through emails and Skype. In June 2011, I visited Bob's school myself prior to the official visit in 2012.

Everything seemed to be working out perfectly until a series of unfortunate incidents occurred. First, the Ministry of Education Taiwan did not approve the proposal. Second, the school in the United States had a new principal who needed to be educated on our project. Fortunately for us and our students, he ultimately approved it. To make matters more complex, Hurricane Sandy devastated the area in late October 2012. How could something with the name Sandy do this to me?

My collaborative partner in New Jersey and I both felt quite frustrated; however, we were not defeated. We worked together and eventually overcame every single difficulty and obstacle put in front of us. After more than a year of contemplation and planning, we finally made this cultural exchange program happen in November 2012.

The highlights of this exchange program included a homestay experience, observing American school life firsthand, and many other types of cultural events. The host families were all quite hospitable and caring. They treated my students like their children, including preparing meals for them, showing them around the town, and accompanying them to different cultural events. After 17 days, the relationship between my students and their host families grew closer. The bonding became so strong that it was hard to bid farewell on the last day. For my students, their host families in the United States had become their second family. Simply put, it was the host families who made this exchange program so successful, and we couldn't thank them enough. Their willingness to host and interact with my students made this exchange even more meaningful.

To witness my students from Taiwan engaging in learning among American students in an American school was a wonderful experience. With their learning partners, my students experienced the routine of American school life by attending different classes, including math, physics, chemistry, arts, and numerous other subjects. The interaction between American students and Taiwanese students was so natural that they didn't seem to have any language barriers at all. It was interesting to see how my students interacted with their Western peers by means of body language and new technology, such as cell phones or through electronic dictionaries. Seeing my students adapt themselves to American school life so easily and successfully made me feel that all my hard work paid off.

On the morning of our departure, one of the American students proclaimed to me, "Sandy, this is amazing! You should do this again!" Upon hearing this, I had misty eyes, but I held back my tears. However, a handwritten note given directly to me from Mrs. Labella, one of the host mothers, caused the tears to roll down my cheeks; it read: "You are indeed quite a remarkable teacher! You teach from the heart, and your heart is big. Your hugs are big." This was by far the most encouraging compliment that I have ever received from a parent.

I was truly thankful for everyone who helped me to make this exchange possible, especially my American partner teacher, Bob. If it were not for his arrangement, support, and concern, this exchange program wouldn't have happened. We have become incredibly good friends since then. Though Bob lives so far away in New Jersey, we share updates on Facebook all the time.

After this program, I also realized how much international exchange programs help Taiwanese students foster their confidence in their language skills and cultural awareness. Through a series of virtual and in-person interactions with overseas students, I noticed that my students' individual agency skills increased. They were more confident in applying what they learned from the textbook to real-life communication without the fear of making mistakes. And with that, those tears of joy that I mentioned earlier turned into buckets of smiles from which to draw upon when I am challenged or when planned activities don't proceed exactly as planned.

Conclusion

By participating in the online global collaborative projects and the exchange programs, many of my students gained valuable friendships with their international peers. They not only kept in touch on social media, but they also paid mutual visits to each other from time to time. Many of them were inspired to pursue further studies on foreign soil. For teachers, carrying out online global collaborative projects in conjunction with undertaking a real cultural exchange program requires passion, creativity, effort, and perseverance.

During these projects and programs, I've learned what ideas and activities I could apply to my classroom instruction. I have been fortunate to take a plethora of valuable lessons forward into my professional teaching career. Both my future classroom management skills as well as my classroom instructional strategies were tremendously enhanced from these collaborative projects. Last, but not least, through participation in these cross-cultural projects and exchange programs, I have made countless wonderful friends from all over the world. Despite the fact that we live far apart, we have an unbreakable and heartfelt bond that means we will always care for and support one another.

Thank you to all the wonderful people who shared in these international projects and program stories and took me into their hearts. The memories we made together and the rich collaborations have formed a legacy of learning through fellowship that will endure throughout the decades to come as I explore other cross-cultural projects and exchanges.

Reflection Questions

1. Have you ever been part of an exchange program or multicultural experience? If so, what was it like?
2. If you work in a multicultural environment in which your students aren't interested in doing online collaborative projects with students from other countries, how will you encourage them to participate in such a project? Now answer the same question assuming that you worked in a highly homogenous environment lacking in much diversity. Please share two or three possible methods that you might utilize in each situation.
3. If in the future you have an opportunity to organize an exchange program for one country, which country will you pick and why?
4. What are the appropriate criteria for screening and selecting students for your projects or exchange programs? Explain your reasoning.

35

LEARNING THROUGH STUDENT EXCHANGE PROJECTS

Taru Pohtola

DOI: 10.4324/9781003213840-42

Taru Pohtola is an English and German teacher working at an upper secondary school in Finland. Besides teaching foreign languages, Taru has been actively involved in many international projects over the years working, for example, with German and Tanzanian schools. Taru is a Fulbright Distinguished Awards in Teaching Program alumna, having spent the autumn of 2015 at Indiana University in Bloomington.

Introduction

Foreign countries, languages, and cultures have fascinated me ever since I was a young girl. I still remember the excitement of actually moving abroad for the first time as a young exchange student studying for my master's degree to become a language teacher. An academic year spent in Germany was a huge time of growth for me. This exchange year meant facing many new challenges but more importantly overcoming them.

Managing in different new situations in a foreign country granted me self-confidence and courage. In addition, living in different cultural settings and making friends with locals as well as students from all over the world opened my eyes to different cultures. My desire to explore the world hasn't stopped. When starting to work as a language teacher, I knew that I wanted to somehow enable and encourage my students to acquire similar experiences.

Martinlaakso Upper Secondary School, where I now work as an English and German teacher in Vantaa, Finland, had been cooperating with a partner school in Potsdam, a city near Berlin, Germany, for quite a few years before I joined the staff. When I started planning my first trip there with my students, it took some extra effort to find and contact the correct people, however, as some of the staff at both schools had changed or retired. After many emails and hopeful attempts, I was delighted when we finally got confirmed dates set for the first joint project.

I have had the privilege to arrange student exchange projects between our schools almost annually ever since. Together with a few colleagues at the German school, a colleague of mine and I have organized projects for our students that consist of a week's trip to Germany and a week's visit to Finland. As a key part of this exchange, we form pairs of German and Finnish students, and they get to stay with each other's families as part of these visits. It is important to note that we have a full program planned for the entire stay with different activities, both at school and in the surroundings. During their stay, the students also get to spend time with their host families learning about their everyday lives.

I have to admit that at first my only goal in the project was giving the students opportunities to practice the German language in authentic surroundings. I could not hope or expect anything more from a short project like this. However, I was blown away by the effects even a short project could eventually have. Each day our students shared myriad insights that they had made about Germany and its culture. They built new strong international friendships, which they were excited about. They gained courage and self-confidence in everyday encounters with a foreign language in new surroundings. Some even set new future goals by saying that they will visit their new friends again or that they want to try living abroad in the future. Encouraging students to step out of their comfort zones seemed to have very powerful and positive effects on young people's lives.

When the students sign in for the exchange project, they often do not realize what to expect. Some are very interested in which sights and tourist attractions they will get to visit and wonder if they could stay at a hotel instead of with an unfamiliar family. It is easy to picture the exchange as a tourist trip because that is what they are familiar with. Typically, they must first encounter what it is like when contacting and interacting with their international partners before they begin to understand what the exchange is really about. At the airport, everyone is excited but also quite nervous while waiting to board the plane and embarking on this adventure. During the first few days in Germany, many of our students experience a bit of culture shock when the realization of actually being in a new place surrounded by a different language and customs hits. Despite our similar European cultures, there are certain cultural differences as well.

Very soon, however, this nervousness normally changes back into positive excitement. Since the week is extremely intense and full of activities both at school and outside school, it helps the students bond in a special way. Soon they start to find more and more similarities despite assorted cultural and linguistic differences. Normally the visit ends with students exchanging hugs and even quite a few tears at the airport for having to say goodbye to their new German friends. The exchange project continues after a few months when the German students arrive in Finland for a week's visit. Also sharing one's own culture at home is always very eye-opening since those involved are forced to look at every cultural encounter and event from another's perspective. Students are made to pay attention to things that they normally just take for granted.

International real-life experiences can be very powerful, even if they are somewhat brief experiences or very simple everyday encounters. Stepping out of one's comfort zone, learning to understand the world from another culture's point of view, and getting along with various people is crucial in today's world. When we actually meet people and build personal relationships across borders, this becomes easier.

Reflection Questions

1. What are the primary skills you would like your students to develop the most during cross-cultural exchanges and in general? How have these skill expectations changed since you started teaching, if at all? Are you successful in teaching these skills? If not, why not?

2. Have you created opportunities for your students to learn in real-life situations outside the typical classroom? If yes, give some examples. If not, brainstorm three to five ways that might be possible.

3. Are there people from other disciplines or programs wherein you could collaborate? What do you envision as your ideal international collaboration situation or program?

36

FROM MOMENT TO MOMENTUM

Technology-Expanded Classrooms From Mexico to France and Back

Diana Zamudio

Diana Zamudio is interested in global education, curriculum development, and educational technology. As an award-winning Fulbright teacher, she is an advocate for global citizenship and mutual understanding among nations. She has recently been granted the Erasmus Mundus Joint Master Degree Partner Country Scholarship Award 2021–2023 to pursue the International Master in Adult Education for Social Change, starting first semester at the University of Glasgow. She can be reached at dianazamudio16@gmail.com.

DOI: 10.4324/9781003213840-43

Introduction

Washington, DC. August 11, 2016. My Fulbright Orientation Workshop calendar entry stated: All international teachers will fly together to Indiana University (IU) in Bloomington, Indiana, accompanied by Jacob Butler of IU. This was the moment that set it all in motion. I arrived at IU to develop an inquiry project with a broad general question: how to motivate and engage Mexican students in an English as a foreign language class?

At that time, I used to work for the Ministry of Education in a small city by the Gulf of Mexico as an elementary school teacher. After attending IU classes, having Friday seminars at School of Education, spending days at Wells Library, visiting schools in Monroe County, attending conferences, discussing with IU faculty advisors, inquiring about my research topic, and co-living at Evermann apartments with 20 outstanding educators from all around the world, I felt empowered to go back home and make a difference.

One particularly mind-opening presentation, "Through the World of Experts: Cases of Expanded Classrooms Using Conferencing Technology," held on a Friday seminar, struck a chord with me. Ideas in that talk guided and provided me with multiple examples of activities to create a professional development course on globally networked learning environments to share with my school district. I was psyched. I felt further excited when hearing the director of the Fulbright Distinguished Awards in Teaching Program, Holly Emert, discuss our inquiry project presentation event at IU Memorial Union: "This is not the end, but the beginning of an exciting journey of professional and personal change." I was inspired, motivated, and driven to make a positive impact back home.

Little did I know that I was about to face a twisted fate. One day prior to my departure from Bloomington, I received a shocking notification. When I arrived in Mexico, I went straight from the airport to my partner's funeral. Life for me in Mexico as I knew before the Fulbright experience, was now gone. I was shattered. I found myself battling bereavement and a reverse culture shock for what seemed to be endless months. My IU memories filled me with contentment somehow. I held on to these tight.

One month later, I was offered an English language teaching position at Universidad Autónoma de Nuevo León (UANL). I accepted the position without much thinking in the hope of finding some comfort and moved to Monterrey, Mexico. I needed a life purpose to survive, so I decided to take it one day at a time and to focus on what I loved the most: teaching.

Months later, yearning for relief from the grief, I applied to the Spanish Language Assistant Program in France. The Fulbright experience provided me with the access to observe the best educational practices in the United States, but I was still curious and eager to explore educational practices around the globe. Such observations could provide me with guidance on how to face the multiple challenges in Mexican state education concerning the use of technology.

Placed at Académie de Lille in France, I was given the opportunity to observe the similarities in education systems regarding resistance to the use of technology as an instructional tool, as well as the importance of incorporating intercultural competence in the curriculum. In an effort to promote mutual understanding among nations, a former colleague and I developed globally networked learning environments between ITESM High School in Altamira, Mexico, and Lycée Robespierre in Arras, France. Amazingly, 4,954 messages were exchanged between students and teachers in these schools via Slack. Ten channels were created for our students to have the opportunity to deepen their knowledge about both cultures. In addition, videoconferencing sessions were held regularly. Students were also assigned a pen pal and were encouraged to use their mobiles to share text messages, voice notes, photos, and videos about their communities.

As time went by, Spanish language teachers at Lycée Robespierre became more open to the use of technology to expand classrooms. They became so engaged in the project and were highly motivated to take it beyond Slack and FaceTime. With their full support, the principal of Lycée Robespierre extended a letter to ITESM High School, inviting the class to travel to France by the end of the spring semester to get to know their pen pals, the school community, and the city of Arras. Lycée Robespierre offered family housing as well as the organization of cultural activities and funding for visiting the main tourist sites in the city of Arras. It was a breakthrough for both institutions. My contract ended shortly after this announcement, and I had to return to Mexico after sending the invitation to ITESM.

It was so rewarding to have shared such a globally inspiring virtual learning environment with both institutions. One particular feedback comment of a French student struck me the most: "*I liked the project because it allowed us to enrich our personal identity and to improve our Spanish language skills.*" Just as he mentioned, at the end of the Spanish Language Assistant Program, my personal identity was enriched as well. Unfortunately, due to the differences in the school year calendar of both institutions, it was impossible for ITESM to accept the offer. The online exchange between the schools continued. In July 2018, however, the French government banned the use of mobile phones in schools, which led to a major drawback in the continuity of the exchange.

I returned to my English teaching position in Mexico at UANL, eager to promote the use of technology to enhance foreign language learning and expand physical classroom boundaries. I fully realized that in today's digital era, the world is our classroom. As such, I continued sharing my Fulbright project in multiple conferences, inviting professors to collaborate in the redesign of Mexican language learning environments. I also had the privilege of collaborating with some of my fellow Fulbrighters who have shared their expertise with our community through technology expanded classrooms.

In need of updating my Fulbright inquiry project, I enrolled in the master's degree program in Applied Linguistics at UANL. Along with linguists and experts in the field, we are developing an action-research project on globally networked learning environments. As I discovered with the writing of one of my IU professors on the close link between education and technology evolution, there is much exciting research in the roads that lie ahead.

It is amazing how much educational environments have changed in the past four years. Not so long ago, there was still huge resistance to the use of technology in state educational institutions in Mexico, as well as in France. This resistance was due to many factors, such as a lack of resources, limited access to the internet, digital illiteracy, and not enough opportunities for teachers' professional development. Life in a pandemic has revolutionized education worldwide. Today, educational institutions worldwide, whether state funded or for-profit, strictly require videoconferencing tools and virtual learning environments to ensure the continuity of learning. But just because such systems are in place does not mean that they are being used in a pedagogically robust and meaningful way.

The incorporation of technology in a foreign language class is no longer science fiction in Mexican institutions. Nevertheless, teachers' professional development is still imperative. My goal is to be able to conduct professional development courses to invite educators to redesign their current language learning environments. By developing globally networked learning environments, educators will promote intercultural competence, experiential learning, and 21st-century skills in foreign language education through technology and virtual exchange.

By sharing my story, I could reflect on this five-year journey. The most important lesson I have learned is the art of deconstructing and reconstructing knowledge. It applies to both professional and personal contexts. Our world is in permanent change, and we, as transformational agents, need to adapt, survive, and overcome the challenges we constantly face.

Suggestions

1. There will always be some sort of resistance to innovation. Be persistent and think long term.
2. When choosing the best classroom technology, teachers' knowledge of the technology itself is one of the most important factors to consider.
3. Find ways to utilize technology as a tool. Students and teachers are the principal elements in the learning process, but technology can support and, at times, transform it.
4. In redesigning learning environments, technology, flexibility, and collaboration are key components of the process
5. For teachers, versatility is a crucial asset to develop.

Reflection Questions

1. What are the advantages of technology-expanded classrooms? How would you design one?

2. What challenges concerning the use of technology do you currently face in your school, nation, or region of the world? In what ways might you help to address these challenges?

3. In what ways have international exchange and collaboration experiences enriched your personal identity or that of your friends and colleagues?

4. Reflect on the key links in this chapter among education, technology, and society.

5. How have the educational environments you have been in evolved over the past few years? What changes do you see on the horizon of the next few years?

37

EMPOWERING TEACHERS WITH TECHNOLOGY AND PEDAGOGY

Distance Teacher Training in Uzbekistan

Umida Khikmatillaeva

Umida Khikmatillaeva is a doctoral student at the Instructional Systems Technology Department and works for the Center for Language Excellence at Indiana

DOI: 10.4324/9781003213840-44

University. She has been an online content developer for more than 20 years. Umida is interested in using technology in language education, intercultural communication, and online teaching. She can be reached at umidahikmat@ gmail.com.

Introduction

This story will highlight my experiences with conducting professional development training for foreign language educators in a limited technology context from a distance. With the change of leadership and a cultural shift after the first president of Uzbekistan's death in 2016, there was a need for innovative educational opportunities in Uzbekistan. Many educational institutions started looking for new ways of implementing innovative technologies and instructional strategies for teaching and learning.

In the fall of 2017, two leaders from the Institute of Oriental Studies in Tashkent in Uzbekistan contacted me about offering workshops at the institution for foreign language instructors. They asked me to organize a professional development workshop for language educators. Such a call for action was inspiring and provided an excellent opportunity to apply my knowledge gained from experiences in higher education institutions in the United States in service to higher education in Uzbekistan. However, I was pursuing my doctorate in education at Indiana University and at the same time working at the university's Center for Language Excellence. The only way I could help was by organizing training from a distance. I agreed to volunteer and provided semester-long training for world language educators.

Planning Stage

When two leaders contacted me, I was just back from Uzbekistan, where I faced internet issues and was skeptical about the possibility of teaching from a distance. At the same time, I became inspired by the opportunity to train teachers and serve my country. I was ready to share my experiences with the faculty. I asked the institution to support me in conducting a needs analysis to determine the participants' needs and interests, English language proficiency, technology skills, and other challenges.

As I expected, there would be significant demand for internet services and technical support. After many email exchanges and discussions of professional development options with the administration, we decided that the best way to implement the training would be an online, blended format. I agreed to facilitate learning from a distance in collaboration with the local faculty who would work with me and deliver the training. We chose this format because of the time differences, limited technology, accessibility issues, and mobility needs.

Time differences. There is a ten-hour difference between Tashkent and Bloomington, Indiana. Therefore, it was essential to select a fixed time for delivering training that would not conflict with the language instructors' active teaching and my work-study schedule.

Limited technology. Limited technology is seen "as a poor use of technology and as a handicapping instruction," or the real gap "between effective and ineffective use of technology" (Egbert, 2010, p. 1). At the setting in Uzbekistan, I observed the following types of limits and constraints:

- Limited access to technology: administrative objections, conflicting lab schedules, and firewalls;
- Limited connection: electricity, slow and unstable connections, and narrow bandwidth;
- Limited funding: old hardware or no hardware, old software, internet connections, technical support, professional development, space, furniture, and so forth (Egbert & Yang, 2004);
- Limited access to resources: lack of culturally relevant, language-specific materials; digital literacy; native language content; community support; and existing biased perceptions and linguistic imperialism;
- Limited instructional strategies for digital media use.

Teacher trainees were skeptical of the possibility of online training and thought that the institution was organizing professional development training only to fulfill their promise to the government. They believed that this process was just a "checkmark" since the initiative resulted from a top-down administrative approach and was not genuinely motivated by a desire for a change. However, the limited technology available at the site in Uzbekistan can be as effective as the use of "unlimited" technology if approached creatively and critically through program design (Egbert & Yang, 2004, p. 281). Stated another way, the prevailing conditions can lead you to think critically and solve problems creatively.

Accessibility issues. When I asked the administration about the learning management system, they mentioned Moodle; however, the institute used Moodle only through the university intranet. Selecting a platform for this project was challenging because Moodle was not practical for them, and Canvas was not accessible due to bandwidth issues. They wanted something more straightforward to implement and compatible with their internet speed. We decided to go with Google Classroom because it is free and allows embedding many other Google features. It is possible to change Google settings to Uzbek, and we hoped that might be helpful. However, the course readings remained in English.

Mobility needs. All the instructors were teaching at least ten to 15 hours a week. Several teacher trainees were about to travel to conferences and wanted to participate in the training program. Therefore, it was convenient for them to have online access to the materials.

Curriculum Design and Development

After considering all factors and examining all issues, I designed the "Innovative approaches to the use of technology in education" curriculum. Classes met once every two weeks to discuss the weekly readings and instructional strategies for 16 weeks from January through May 2018. The assessment included participation in online discussions led by me and bi-weekly face-to-face meetings led by local participants, projects, and resources (i.e., syllabus, assessment, and interactive materials design), and a final presentation. Teachers were assigned to present in teams once during the workshop.

Each team member was responsible for reading articles in English, meeting me online, asking questions regarding the papers and presentations, and preparing the bi-weekly group presentations. The topics included the following:

- Future of learning;
- Syllabus design and assessment strategies;
- Communicative strategies in language learning and teaching;
- Technology in the language classroom;
- Motivational strategies for language learning and teaching;
- Open educational resources for language learning and teaching.

Program Implementation

I remember the training kickoff day as if it was yesterday. After the testing phase, we kicked off the program with a live session via Zoom. The Institute's president also attended the kickoff meeting. In response to my comments regarding the internet issues experienced by teacher trainees and the Innovation Center's role in training and professional development, he promised that the Innovation Center would be redesigned, equipped with new computers, and updated with robust internet bandwidth. I nearly jumped in the sky when I heard this. The Uzbek teachers, some perhaps close to crying, could not believe that this was happening. It was clear to me that the institutional support was inspiring to them. Now there would be support staff to help them with technical issues with the Google Classroom.

The participants were sitting in a big room with their mobile devices and could not believe the online training taking place was real. They asked me, "How come you directly asked the president for the internet services and the computers?" These questions signified that there were major power issues, and this context would be different.

I greeted teachers on a big monitor via Zoom. Before the kickoff day, I trained the information technology staff of the Oriental Institute's Innovation Center to introduce Google Classroom and other Google Apps (e.g., Google Docs, Google Slides, Google Forms, and Google Sites) to the teacher trainees in Uzbek. In effect, it was Google, Google, and more Google. And, in the process, I created loads of Google guides for using the Google classroom. I guess you could say we were Googlified. Everyone in the room created a Google account and joined the Google classroom.

To inspire the teachers, we started the first week by reading Marc Prensky's (2001) "Digital natives, digital immigrants" and introducing Curt Bonk's (2009) book, "The World Is Open." The result was tremendous: they were impressed by the number of article citations and fascinated by the possibilities of technology. These teachers discovered the new learning demands of Generation Z. I used role-play activities for the Uzbek teachers to introduce themselves and as means to showcase as many instructional strategies as possible. All of them introduced themselves in the Google Classroom discussions in addition to having introductions with pictures on Google Slides. Again, we were Google dominated.

The various teams started sharing their PPTs with me, and I provided feedback to them to make sure they understood English readings or added some interactive components. For instance, the teachers had to get an entrance visa to the program by answering questions about their classes. The next time they entered, they created memes to showcase students' feelings after the exams and how assessments can motivate students. Another activity asked them to evaluate their rubrics. Other interactive activities involved creating and crafting videos, infographics, posters, mind maps, and online games. Since the teacher trainees were all language educators, their presentations were highly influenced by their context and personal experiences. For instance, Japanese instructors brought the PechaKucha 20×20 talk format to the class, and some teacher trainees felt more comfortable presenting in Russian. Overall, the experience with the program implementation was positive and inspiring.

Lessons Learned

This was my first experience conducting training online for Uzbekistan. Ongoing needs analysis is crucial when imposing projects for the first time to determine what is going well and what is not working. The Telegram app is especially popular in Uzbekistan, and it was wonderful to ask questions and exchange information instantly. Teachers stated they had found the answers to their endless questions such as how much are evolving techniques and technology affecting the human mind? How different are the students of today's technological age from them? And finally, is it enough to use new devices in educating this new generation during the online training course?

Implications

I will now go through the TEC-VARIETY framework (Bonk & Khoo, 2014) and describe how it was implemented and worked in this setting. The ten motivational principles of the framework are as follows:

1. Tone/Climate: psychological safety, comfort, sense of belonging;
2. Encouragement: feedback, responsiveness, praise, supports;

3. **C**uriosity: surprise, intrigue, unknowns;
4. **V**ariety: novelty, fun, fantasy;
5. **A**utonomy: choice, control, flexibility, opportunities;
6. **R**elevance: meaningful, authentic, interesting;
7. **I**nteractivity: collaborative, team based, community;
8. **E**ngagement: effort, involvement, investment;
9. **T**ension: challenge, dissonance, controversy;
10. **Y**ielding Products: goal driven, purposeful vision, ownership.

Tone/Climate. The curriculum had straightforward statements regarding the tone of discussions, copyright issues, and plagiarism as they are common issues in any setting. You could feel that the tone of discussions was deferential in class discussions, which was vital in facilitating the training. Open communication with the administration and trust is essential when collaborating with the partner institution.

I previously worked in this institution and was aware of the teachers' needs and interests. In addition, while teaching from a distance, I had former colleagues who provided day-to-day situational information that I could not otherwise imagine. For instance, once I learned that the classroom was freezing, and the teachers did not want to come to the meeting since they had tremendous administrative and other volunteer work that they had to do for different organizations since they are foreign language speakers.

Encouragement. The support provided by the administration highly influenced teachers' interest in the training. Designing a space, getting access to the internet, and receiving immediate feedback all were making instant results.

While Google Classroom's free version can embed many features of Google Drive, it has some notable flaws and issues. Thus, getting local leaders' support was influential.

Curiosity, Variety, and Autonomy. Teachers became motivated in creating interactive activities and, lately, were involved in an e-portfolio project. Many tools were new to them, and they had a variety of options to work on projects and showcase them.

Relevance. The training was directly applicable to their teaching, and that made them interested in creating more materials. A few teachers dropped the course because they anticipated learning the English language in the class. Some dropped due to language barriers. For instance, one Russian heritage language speaker instructor did not understand Uzbek. Note that the ideal size for facilitating activities was about ten learners at a time.

Interactivity and Engagement. Teachers started sharing the information about the course with others and telling them that it is actually working, not phony. They confessed that the empowerment came from materials that they have read and from the group presentations. Online discussions allowed them to get to know one another. The Telegram channel was an informal place to share reflections, their other professional activities, conference announcements, and bringing humor to the class.

Tension.

> *Digital Divide and Literacy Issues.* I also learned from teachers how to teach within the limited technology environment. Teachers offered the following solutions:

- Always have Plan A and Plan B (electricity, bandwidth issues);
- Have energy and Wi-Fi solutions (carry extra chargers, USB drives);
- Carry materials in different formats (PowerPoint, printed handouts);
- Use multiple devices at a time (laptop, mini projector).

> *Accessibility and Advocacy Issues.* Changing language settings in Google was very helpful. Sometimes I struggled with using some technical terminology in Uzbek. To solve the issue, we created a discussion thread where teachers offered translations for terms.
>
> Not all the instructors had access to mobile devices and personal or office computers. However, they showed silent resistance by asking "how are we going to work online if we don't have a good connection?" At the beginning of training (also known as the "needs analysis stage"), the instructors expressed a need for better internet services. Many of them shared pictures or their strategies on how to use technology in a limited accessibility environment and their backup plans. After some negotiations and clarifications of technology use needs for professional development and future teaching purposes, the institution provided a separate space, bought 12 computers, and supplied robust internet bandwidth for our training.
>
> *Privacy and Confidentiality Concerns.* Some teachers were afraid to participate in discussions and write about their challenges during the program planning phase. We had to reassure them that the needs analysis results will not be shared with the administration and is confidential.

Yielding Products. The training program ended with a big festival at the institution: all teams presented at the festival and showcased their e-portfolio projects. Media representatives came to highlight the event at the National TV station and a local newspaper. All teacher trainees were issued participation certificates. In addition, those who finished all the projects received small monetary awards.

Conclusion

This experiential training highlights successes and potential barriers in the implementation of a teacher training program from a distance in Central Asia. Teacher reflections showed increased motivation and transformational practices in syllabus design, new approaches to instructional strategies, and new learning technologies.

Accessibility and language barriers are challenging when implementing the program. Digital divide, power structures, and language issues caused an added layer of stress. Therefore, it is essential to address such issues in future training.

Reflection Questions

1. In your professional life, have you ever contemplated on the types of intersections between technology and creativity practices? If so, what did this entail?
2. What types of creative solutions might you offer to motivate people in a limited technology environment?
3. How can you increase the self-confidence of educators facing social and cultural issues during a program implementation? What strategies would you offer for such situations?

38

WE CAN STILL BE GLOBAL CITIZENS

Virtual Exchange Program to Connect Yemeni EFL Youth With AFL American Counterparts

Amani Gashan

Amani Gashan is a doctoral candidate in literacy, culture, and language education at Indiana University, with two minors, one in instructional systems technology and the other in Middle Eastern languages and cultures. She has a

DOI: 10.4324/9781003213840-45

master's degree in teaching English to speakers of other languages from King Saud University. Amani's research interests focus on applying technology into classrooms, exploring the integration of innovative technologies in enhancing language learning, acquiring languages, and preserving heritage languages. She has received several academic awards, such as the King Saud University Award of Scientific Excellence. She has several publications in international journals and has presented at national and international conferences. She can be reached at amangashan@hotmail.com.

Layers of Quarantine

I remember an afternoon back in 2007 during an English language class when I had a hard time explaining the lesson titled "Happy Halloween!" and specifically the phrase, "Trick or Treat." It was my first year teaching at Naser School in Sana, the capital city of Yemen. Ten years later, I realized that language cannot be taught in isolation from its culture. Knowing the linguistic elements of a language does not make you a perfect teacher. You need to learn and practice the language within its cultural context. I was able to better utilize the English language when I engaged with the language culture in the United States as a graduate student at Indiana University (IU). Finally, I was able to interact with people and witness cultural events such as Halloween, the Fourth of July, Christmas, and the New Year.

In Yemen, young people have limited opportunities to interact with other citizens of the world. Yemen, a country of very old history and civilization, has been suffering in isolation during the past decade. It has been under several layers of quarantine created not only by the COVID-19 pandemic but also by travel ban restrictions and an ongoing horrible war. Airports, seaports, and borders are closed for complex political reasons causing much personal anguish and frustration. Due to the war, several schools have been bombed or occupied by families who lost their homes or shelter. In places that still have schools, they are deprived of their financial budget, and teachers do not get paid. Many families have decided to prioritize life basics over education as students find it difficult to commute to schools after the gas prices have recently rocketed. To make matters worse, the travel restrictions denied hundreds of ambitious Yemeni students to join scholarships and study abroad.

Such circumstances have created a complicated situation of ignorance and misunderstanding of other cultures. Worse still, Yemen is deprived of being a member of the globalized world, although this situation is not limited to Yemenis, as I later discovered.

The World Is Open

As indicated earlier, in 2017, I joined Indiana University (IU) in the United States. As I am one of the few Yemeni female graduate students at IU, I typically have to include information about where I come from whenever people ask me about my country of origin. On several occasions, I would say I am from Yemen and recognize that the other individual had further questions and looked confused about where Yemen is. They may even say, "Well, is it in Africa?"

They are excused, though. They do not meet as many people from Yemen as they do people from places like Saudi Arabia, our next-door neighbor. However, you will find some people who have heard about Yemen from the news if only because Yemen was one of the countries whose citizens were banned from entering the United States during the previous presidential administration. This has created even more questions about my country and extended curiosity about the banned citizens!

Life in the United States has exposed me to several possibilities for educational change and perhaps even transformation that can be characterized as the "World Is Open," a term I heard frequently in some of my classes at IU. I soon was telling myself, "Yemen should not be an exception;" it should provide open avenues for learning too. When at IU, I learned about terms such as "global citizen," "social justice," and "diverse people and places." I thought about these ideas from the standpoint of my country.

"Funds of knowledge" is another inspiring term that explains that native speakers of other languages attend classes with something to contribute to the culture. Similarly, we can imagine a global class that has students from Yemen and the United States who can contribute equally to the learning process; perhaps eventually extending such global connections to class participants from many other places on the planet.

My work with the Arabic Language Flagship Program in the United States showed me that people in the new world are interested in learning about Yemen and Yemenis. They want to learn the Yemeni Arabic dialect and about the rich Yemeni culture. I was able to feed this hunger with lectures about Yemeni culture and slides covering the location of Yemen, clothes and food of Yemenis, their songs, folklore, dancing, and some history. My students are astonished to learn that the coffee they drink every day is Yemeni! They look surprised when I tell them that Mocha is the name of the seaport in Yemen where Yemenis export their high-quality coffee beans. I also saw expressions of astonishment and amazement whenever I spoke about life in Socotra Island in Yemen, which is described as the most alien-looking place on earth. However, my words on these interesting places and cultural norms in Yemen were definitely not enough to fully grasp the differences in cultures. In other words, bridges of mutual communication need to be built between members of the communities.

Added COVID-19 to all the previous facts, and we have been forced to move our Arabic training program to an online portal via Zoom. I still could meet my students online to talk about the dialect and the culture of Yemen. However, I asked myself, why don't I connect my Arabic language students in the United States with their peers learning the English language in Yemen? They can be in one class to teach each other, to learn from each other's culture, and to find answers to their questions. I have been inspired to think of a way to bring Yemeni youth together with their peers in the United States around a shared goal.

The Birth of an Idea

I have developed a cross-cultural pedagogical idea with two Yemeni graduate students in the United States, Ebrahim Bamanger and Omer Bin Someida from the Hadramout Foundation-Human Development. We decided to launch an initiative that opens windows and doors for Yemeni and American students to each other's languages and cultures. To increase the impact, the starting program will have 90 Yemeni students from three governorates located in different parts of Yemen: from Aden in the south, from Sana'a in the North, and from Hadramout in the East. These students will engage with peers from three schools in three different states in the United States. The Yemeni students will be English language learners who will be connected with Arabic language learners in the United States.

It will be the first opportunity for both groups of students to engage with natives of their target languages and cultures. In fact, this event will likely be the first time that "Arabic as a foreign language" learners in the United States have the chance to converse with Yemeni partners and experience the Arabic dialects of three major governorates.

The program is now planning the curriculum and evaluating personnel to run the project. When it commences, there will be cultural topics to discuss as well as questions to answer about each other's cultures with a goal to develop mutual understanding among the participants as they practice English or Arabic language. It is my belief that our young Yemeni students have a rich culture to exchange with others by freeing up their minds and exploring the world through the eyes of those from other communities and cultures. They can identify cultural limits to go beyond and further educational goals to achieve.

Lessons Learned

At different points in humanity's history, the invention of trains, planes, and automobiles were each deemed to be the answer to the separation of humans in remote areas of the world. Today, tools like Zoom, Slack, WhatsApp, WeChat, and Google Meet are the heralded transporters that bring people closer in the midst of the continuous cascade of quite serious obstacles and challenges such as the current pandemic, the travel ban, and the war in Yemen.

With Zoom and Google Meet, teachers can still have classes and meet students virtually. Students can join from remote areas in diverse continents. There are now features that allow class participation, small-group discussions, and whiteboard annotation. For tools to plan the class and asynchronous conversation, students and instructors can use WhatsApp and Slack. These applications are universal and convenient to use and, at present, require no complicated registration.

No doubt, COVID-19 has been catastrophic at all levels. However, it has inspired much of humanity to start to think differently, to adapt to the new situation, and get ready to move forward. My husband and I used to take pride that we live in a small village back in Yemen without much technology access. Today, we want to be part of those who invest in technology to take pride in hosting people in a small networked village.

At present, this initiative hinges on grant approval that will be used to create a partnership between the Arabic Flagship in Indiana University and Hadhramout Foundation-Human Development in Yemen. If funded and we can lay the groundwork for greater cross-cultural understanding between our cultures, it will be the project of a lifetime. This project will provide the seeds which can potentially germinate into further projects that include more students from the diverse array of countries in the Middle East as well as additional students from the United States and other countries. Such global participates might engage in highly productive projects that enhance cultural awareness and establish internationally collaborative projects across educational sectors.

Reflection Questions

1. Hardship, adversity, and failure can be genuine motivators of success. Can you share an example of a needs-driven success story?
2. With the proliferation of free and open educational resources and courses, today's world is often characterized as an open world. Can you imagine a future world from which you stand, and look back to today and say, "The world is open?" What does that world look like ten, 20, or 50 years from now?
3. If you were a student or a teacher participating in an exchange program, what group of individuals would you like to share your class with? What questions would you like to ask them?
4. Do you think cultural awareness is a necessity here in the 21st century? What cultures would you like to explore and learn about and why?

SECTION 8

Overcoming Challenges

The last section of this book is focused on strategies for overcoming significant instructional challenges, including those that occur in highly tense or dangerous situations that many teachers encounter during their educational practices at some point in their lives. The challenges mentioned in this section might be somewhat familiar or totally new to you. Hopefully, as you read the collection of stories in Section 8, and throughout this book, the anecdotes will provide some insights and nuggets of wisdom for you to address the teaching and learning challenges that you are encountering right now or might face in the future.

As an example, in Chapter 39, Rhuperdia Crowe-Clay, a special education teacher in the Indianapolis Public School system, describes how she overcame assorted personal and professional challenges at the start of the pandemic. Already reeling from a cancer diagnosis and the possibility of leaving the classroom for an extended leave of absence, Rhuperdia soon finds renewed hope for the future of classroom instruction when the COVID-19 outbreak forces classroom teachers to shift from the traditional lecture format to a digital platform.

Chapter 40 takes us to two countries in the Global South, Bhutan and Papua New Guinea (PNG), where Khendum Gyabak worked with teachers to improve their teaching and instructional design skills. In the developing world, education in rural schools is often characterized by the lack of access to adequate teaching and learning resources. Other problematic issues include novice teachers challenged with teaching large class sizes and students with limited support from their homes. Due to such constraints, learning in these environments is inequitable.

In this chapter, Khendum draws from stories of exemplary teachers with whom she has worked in Bhutan and PNG. A common thread of these stories

DOI: 10.4324/9781003213840-46

is appreciating the teacher agency of working within the myriad educational constraints and challenges. Another thread relates to the deliberate application of empathy and creative thinking to scaffold understanding and foster meaningful learning for rural students.

In Chapter 41, Natalia Ramirez-Casalvolone, an English as a Foreign Language (EFL) teacher educator at Universidad de Costa Rica, and PhD candidate at Indiana University, brings us a quite touching story and dose of reality related to the education of teenage youth in Costa Rica. Natalia's narrative involves Jacky and the artifact she chooses to bring to an informal EFL classroom. Through this one simple activity of artifact sharing and storytelling, educators can begin to see and hear about students' daily lives and struggles. It is our job as teachers to unpack these personal stories and probe deeper, and bring out ideas, experiences, and emotions that are not so evident. A successful teaching and learning process can more readily occur when students are recognized for their life trajectories and experiences.

Chapter 42 is an amazing account of the various experiences of Simon Pierre Munyaneza during his early stages as a teacher in Rwanda. Simon discusses how different changes in his country conditioned his determination toward certain educational goals. His reflections on the postwar context of Rwanda sheds light on the role of schools at the center of community development. It is extremely important to give testimony to how motivation and collaboration became a survival toolkit for teachers and students in vastly under-resourced Rwandan schools. By reading and reflecting on this chapter, you will have a better glimpse of how teachers, parents, and students in Rwanda worked together to keep the education wheels turning, notwithstanding the extreme challenges of a war-torn country as it attempts to rebuild.

Finally, in Chapter 43, Ebrahim Bamanger introduces you to similar life-changing experiences in education in Yemen. Interestingly, he discusses how technology can work even in a devastated community that suffers from war and an outdated school system to help create hope for a better education. When reading his chapter, you will learn how innovative uses of augmented reality (AR) can work in language classrooms as an approach to bring in a richer and more engaging curriculum that is filled with media, activities, and self-assessment tools. You will also join Ebrahim in a reflective process of developing an AR-based language curriculum guided by his own childhood memories.

All these chapters in Section 8 share serious challenges teachers had to overcome in their school environments and educational practices that may have seemed insurmountable at the time. Importantly, as shown in each story, they each found the creative strategies and resources to cope with the roadblocks, obstacles, and dilemmas in front of them. And they all persisted with the dedication and commitment to building better structures and supports for the educational needs in their respective communities and countries.

At this point, we should say that we hope that this compilation of stories helps you to cope with the various challenges that you are facing or will face in your own educational settings. In reality, we really want you to do more than cope; the aim is to help educators rise above pressing barriers to create innovative pedagogical activities and technology integration ideas that will have a lasting cultural impact. Yes, impact!

39

CANCER, COVID-19, AND THE CULTURAL IMPACT OF TECHNOLOGY IN THE CLASSROOM

Rhuperdia Crowe-Clay

Rhuperdia Crowe-Clay is not your typical special education teacher. Born in rural Mississippi and diagnosed with physical and cognitive disabilities, Rhuperdia overcame a dismal prognosis that she is now using to shape who she is as an

DOI: 10.4324/9781003213840-47

educator. Rhuperdia loves seeking knowledge. She holds a BS in early childhood education, an undergraduate minor in psychology, and a master's degree in special education. Rhuperdia exudes empathy, consistency, effective communication, and steadfast advocacy. She wishes to be known as an avid supporter in the fight to eradicate negative stigmas associated with special education, especially within minority communities. She can be contacted at rhuperdiaclay@gmail.com.

Introduction

March 12, 2020, was the last day that I was physically in a classroom. In the blink of an eye, the mode in which I would teach dramatically changed. Thankfully, using technology to reach and teach was not a new concept for me but one that I needed to revisit to employ it with maximum fidelity for the foreseeable future.

I was introduced to effective uses for technology in the classroom during the fall of 2016 when I took a course at Indiana University—Purdue University Indianapolis (IUPUI). Since that time, technology was used intermittently in my classes as a tool to support the development of thinking skills, motivation, and collaboration. However, because it was not a school-wide initiative or bolstered by a district-level mandate, technological usage within the school setting was not fluid. As a special education teacher for the largest school district in the state, I am reluctant to admit that digital technology was underutilized by staff and students in my school district. Such technology was generally limited to being used as an option for brain breaks, independent reading, and game playing.

The First Crisis

All this was soon about to change. By January 2020, I began to realize the instrumental need for effective digital platforms that could help drive interactive and engaging learning. More specifically, on January 8, 2020, I was diagnosed with breast cancer. I received the news via a phone call while at school. I admittedly thought of the impact this diagnosis would have not only on my family and me, but also on my students. I realized that many students and families depended on my advocacy and support of their needs. The emotional toll of this news did not set in right away; that would happen in the months to come.

Within days of the diagnosis, I shared it with the administration and informed them I wanted to remain an integral part of daily instruction. After that, I immediately began planning what that involvement could possibly look like. Of course, I understood that I would have to shift from the traditional lecture platform and embrace a hybrid version—I would remain in person when plausible and possibly participate online when necessary; however, the idea was met with many roadblocks.

Perhaps the biggest barrier was that what I was asking to do was an uncommon practice within this district. In effect, the only real options I had were to take a full leave of absence or continue working as much as I could using sick days if and when treatments left me feeling ill or without the requisite stamina needed to teach. I began to feel disheartened; fortunately, my faith sustained me, as I held out hope that something would pan out that would allow me to continue doing what I am so passionate about—teaching. Admittedly, I had some truly emotionally difficult days.

Though filled with hope and faith, I wondered how I could continue doing what I loved and take care of my own mental and physical needs while attempting to be a partner in the environment. Class Dojo, YouTube, Zoom, and various district purchased learning apps were well known, but underutilized tools at my disposal. By February 2020, many of these resources were being used to communicate with students and families but were not yet employed as the primary manner of communication and instruction. Why not? Well, systemic learning structures in place during in-person learning and teacher lecturing involved completing assignments via pencil and paper with some technology sprinkled here and there.

The Second Crisis

However, on March 12, 2020, as students and staff prepared for our annual spring break and I prepared to take an unwanted but much needed formal leave of absence, everything changed. On that date, we were informed that due to an uptick in a highly contagious virus called coronavirus, aka COVID-19, our spring break would begin early, and we were to stay tuned for further instruction.

By early April, it was evident that we would not be returning to in-person learning anytime soon. This, for me, was both welcomed and concerning news. I welcomed the opportunity to teach from home because I was well into chemotherapy treatments for breast cancer. Given my situation, I had prepared to take a leave of absence though I felt like I was abandoning my students. I was concerned because I was not certain how learning would take place, how well students and families would adjust to the proposed learning models and if, given my physical health, I would be up for the challenge.

We began with an asynchronous learning approach, a form of education, instruction, and learning that does not occur in the same place or at the same time. Students were provided computers, Wi-Fi hotspots, and learning packets. For the teacher's role, we were to upload pre-recorded instructions and plans onto a digital platform to be shared with the students weekly. For special education teachers, this presented significant challenges, as many of the students for whom we provided services required differentiated instruction. As a result, we could not record one-size-fits-all instructional videos. Again, teachers were learning alongside students.

I drew from my developmental training and quickly referenced materials from the "Instructional Strategies for Thinking, Collaboration, and Motivation" course

I took in 2016. This wondrous course was taught via videoconferencing between Indiana University in Bloomington and IUPUI, where I took the class. As advocated in that course, a recurring theme in my classroom was the right for my students to ask questions, make mistakes, and be uncertain. In effect, I attempted to craft a comfortable atmosphere that fostered inquiry, experimentation, and creative expression where learners can learn from failure and try again and again.

Flipping Backward and Forward

A huge and most welcome advantage of posting online video lecture content allowed me to record lessons on my "good days," and to adjust instruction in a more intentioned manner. I was able to review the video quality before uploading, modify the verbiage and instructions as needed, and include cues and prompts to account for each student's varying needs.

At the same time, these videos kept my students abreast of my ongoing cancer journey as they could see the physical changes I was going though, most notably the weight gain from steroids and the hair loss from chemo. Students, for their part, could pause the recordings, accelerate through points if they did not need the details, and then listen to and follow along with instruction at their pace without the stressors that come with time constraints. They would record messages and share quite touching well wishes, questions, and their various concerns.

The virtual classroom gave way to innovative teaching strategies inclusive of culturally sustaining pedagogy and universal design for learning. When the pandemic struck, we had to move away from rote learning tactics that have been all too common for centuries, as well as some of the more effective active teaching and learning approaches that have emerged during the past few decades for face-to-face instruction. During the pandemic, learning using innovative pedagogical strategies inclusive of technology and student interest was suddenly skyrocketing in importance. And many schools and teachers began employing active teaching tools and resources such as Microsoft Teams, Google Jamboard, Zoom, and a host of other online tools to foster critical thinking skills, flexibility, and adaptability.

Students were encouraged to focus on the objectives of lessons, while at the same time, the output was relevant to their personal skills and abilities. They could engage in discussions both verbally and in writing simultaneously using video/audio interactions or discussion boards, which allowed varying modes of communication. With such tools and resources, all members of the classroom had opportunities to be more intentional in their learning pursuits, and teachers now had unique and evolving ways to be more inclusive.

With the learning technologies at my disposal, I could plan student discussion boards among the entire class or divide them into small groups for social interaction. I could also create paired and independent assignments around my chemotherapy schedule. Furthermore, I could even collaborate with other instructors so they could cover their topics during times that I was not available and with little to no disruption to student learning. Success was imminent! However, not all students were eager to engage, as this was new and different from the structure to which they were accustomed. But, by the third week, many of the reluctant students engaged with the content in various ways; the most engagement was observed during large-group activities when students could respond using different media to represent a finished product.

Effective implementation required collaboration by all participants, including parents, students, and staff. Such collaborations were well thought out and structured based on the cultures and experiences represented within the class setting. For our class, success and effectiveness were measured by quality, not quantity, and recognizing education is not a one-size-fits-all model.

As time progressed, the Centers for Disease Control and Prevention (CDC) continued to share guidance on best practices as well as issue mandates on gatherings during the pandemic to prevent the spread of this disease. To reinforce that information from the CDC, the school district also shared best practices and guidelines for teaching during the pandemic.

Transitioning to the Present

For the 2020–2021 school year, it was decided that we would remain in the virtual class setting, but learning would occur in real time. This decision made me reflect back in time. Looking back, I believe for the first time in educational history, a major shift in education happened that would not have occurred as rapidly had we not been in a global pandemic. The pandemic fostered an educational transformation across educational institutions and organizations as well as a personal shift for me in my educational delivery methods, pedagogical strategies and activities, and overall identity as a teacher.

In this time, I transitioned from the teacher role into a specialist role. While I knew I would miss my daily interactions with students, I needed a position that would account for my ongoing absences without penalizing or disrupting the learning environment of the students. In the role as the special education specialist, I was expected to use my acquired knowledge to coach other teachers in my field. At one of the first professional learning community meetings I held online during the pandemic, I shared a pdf copy of the free e-book, *Adding Some TEC-VARIETY*, by Bonk and Khoo (2014), with fellow teachers. The skills I learned while taking the course that used that book back in 2016 were invaluable to me. I knew the information was timeless and perfect for a time such as this.

I truly believe education has forever changed in the wake of COVID-19. For me, the intersectionality of COVID-19 and cancer helped me to still be mindful and, most importantly, be an intentional instructor and collaborator. They each presented an opportunity to leave the traditional confines of the classroom and increase the use of technological tools and resources.

As we left those confines, I witnessed heightened parental and student engagement. I should point out that for many of these students this was the first real opportunity to increase their computer-based skills and knowledge, resulting in increased participation and motivation. I am proud to have learned alongside my students, becoming more familiar with various highly useful and engaging software tools and innovative instructional methods. With such growing knowledge and experience, I could begin to embrace technology as a crucial element in the ongoing evolution of education.

Concluding Thoughts on the Future

Online options will be a continuing part of the classroom culture post-pandemic. Consequently, school districts are partnering with educational technology companies to increase access to technology to make it more available and relevant to all learners. The mindset of the collective education majority also has shifted. With the advent of blended learning options and viability, long gone are the "make-up days" due to severe weather. Lesson plans in the 21st century now embrace asynchronous learning plans as well as synchronous events using platforms such as Zoom. Suffice to say, online learning is a highly viable option in the event of an unplanned teacher absence, whether due to winter storms, hurricanes, cancer or, heaven forbid, another global pandemic.

Reflection Questions

1. When considering equitable opportunities for your learners, in what ways is access to technology a consideration? What are possible solutions when access is a barrier to learning? How have you dealt with access issues in the past?
2. How can educators be better prepared to teach, train, or learn something new? Does such content or lesson preparation require intrinsic or extrinsic motivation or both? Perhaps explain with an example.
3. Given the glaring disparities in classroom environments and instruction that the pandemic exposed, how can such knowledge be better utilized in the future? Stated another way, what can be done about the inequities, disparities, and inconsistencies in K–12 learning environments?
4. What roles do various stakeholders play in revisioning, reframing, and reforming school systems and curriculum practices? Provide examples, stories, or illustrations.
5. What opportunities, if any, are given to your students to use technology academically and creatively in the classroom? If none currently exist, should teachers be required to create such opportunities? Why or why not?

40

EQUITABLE LEARNING IN INEQUITABLE CLASSROOMS

Cases of Teacher Design Thinking in Rural Schools in Bhutan and Papua New Guinea

Khendum Gyabak

Khendum Gyabak has a PhD from Indiana University and works as an education consultant for the University of Minnesota. She designs online education, innovates hybrid and in-person instructional programs, and has collaborated on curriculum design with educators and community leaders in a variety of teaching and learning contexts at both international and national levels. Her research intersects design service, design thinking, critical pedagogy, teacher agency, and creativity in low-resourced rural classrooms in the developing world. She can be reached at khendum@umn.edu.

DOI: 10.4324/9781003213840-48

Background

Rural education in the developing world, by default, is an inequitable learning environment. There are more novice teachers than experienced teachers, poorly maintained classrooms with large class sizes, a lack of access to a fully functioning library and science laboratory facilities, and limited tools and resources for teachers to develop scaffolds to aid student learning. While the learning conditions do promote a culture of apathy among teachers, not all teachers resort to rote and drill methods. Instead, teachers learn to make do. They constantly and shrewdly think on their feet. As part of such efforts, they skillfully navigate the myriad bounded constraints in education to adapt their instruction by working with what they have, rather than relying on invasive interventions, which have typically led to poor outcomes in these disenfranchised communities.

The cases foregrounded are informed from my time observing and working with teachers in community schools in Bhutan and Papua New Guinea. These collective stories of teachers making do demonstrate the intersection of teacher agency, empathy, and creative thinking. They document efforts by these community heroes to foster learning by engaging students with meaningful scaffolds created and curated with resources found in their local environment.

Designing Health Lessons in Papua New Guinea

In 2015, I was invited to design an elementary health curriculum by the Ministry of Education in Papua New Guinea (PNG). The grant that sponsored my stay in the country was building toilets, crafting hand-washing sinks, and installing water tanks and filters in schools around the community in the Eastern Highlands provinces of PNG. Sanitation and hygiene are poorly understood among the people in these areas, leading to a rise in infectious and waterborne diseases among tribal communities in the rural parts of the country.

Schools in these communities can play a fundamental role in influencing the health habits of the students and, by extension, their parents and communities. Teacher roles in community schools are largely reduced to the simplistic practice of delivering content from the textbook and teacher resource manual mandated and distributed by the PNG Department of Education. Teachers in these schools have reported facing numerous challenges in carrying out activities outlined in these textbooks. For example, community schools lack basic teaching tools such as chalk, while materials such as poster paper, crayons, and pencils typically run out in the middle of the school year. Most resources required to carry out the activities are not readily available in the villages, leaving teachers with the gut-wrenching decision of having to skip most instructional activities that require materials.

Moreover, teachers have limited knowledge and professional training as teachers. In fact, most join schools as community teachers after passing grades 6 and 7. Without extensive educational experience and training, they cannot confidently adjust and adapt their instruction for individual student needs and the ever-present instructional dilemmas and challenges that arise. In the end, this situation causes them to resort to rote and drill memorization of facts and knowledge, thereby leaving less room for critical thinking and deeper forms of learning.

For students to effectively adapt the use of hand-washing sinks and modern toilets in the schools, teachers in the Eastern Highlands of PNG need to gauge student understanding of abstract concepts like germs. To purposefully change the health habits of the children and the community around them, I found that teachers would be more effective if they embedded strategies and tools such as active learning and problem-based learning.

Teachers from nearby community schools were invited to participate in a two-week design workshop that I facilitated with the intention of using that space to ideate and write the elementary health curriculum. This was their first time with curriculum writing and the topic of clean water and hygiene. For the first week, I facilitated activities to engage teachers in reflecting on their teaching practice. To scaffold these development efforts, I introduced ideas and theories related to how learners effectively and more powerfully learn as well as the value of active and engaging learning. I also brought in guest speakers like community health workers to explain the effects and impact of sanitation and good hygiene.

The teachers agreed to write a teacher's resource manual, which included text, images, and activities that related to their environment (see sample activity in Figure 40.1). Importantly, all activities developed in the book can be carried out in exceedingly low-resourced learning settings.

Classroom Activity: Clean Water Discovery
Learning Goal: To increase student understanding of the concept of clean water

Learning Objectives	• Identify the sources of clean water • Compare and contrast the difference between clean and dirty water
Materials Needed	• Three small, clear empty bottles (recycled juice containers)
Teacher Note	• Take students to the closest water source and collect water in one of the containers. * *If your school does not yet have a water tank, bring with you a bottle of clear, boiled water from home.* • Take students to the next closest water source (river/creek/drain) and collect water in another container. • Fill the third bottle with water divided from both sources. • Ask students which water looks best for drinking and introduce the concept that even if water looks clear, the water can still be contaminated with germs that make us sick. The safest way to access clean water is by boiling the water.

FIGURE 40.1 Sample Activity From a Teacher's Resource Manual

While some teachers worked on constructing learning objectives and out-comes for topics on sanitation and hygiene, teachers such as Nana volunteered their services as the resident artist to sketch all the images for the book. For one quite fun and memorable classroom activity, Anna and Ruth wrote a hand-washing song in their native language, Tok Pisin.

Fostering Equitable Learning in Rural Bhutan

Education in government schools is free for all children in Bhutan, yet resources are inequitably distributed along the urban and rural lines. Rural schools lack libraries and other study spaces, restrict students to small class spaces, and too often have come to expect inadequate teaching supplies. Most teachers in these schools tend to be novice teachers transferred to teach in a rural district before being sent back to an urban town after completing their mandatory duty to serve in rural schools.

When in Bhutan, even in highly constrained learning spaces like rural class-rooms, you do encounter that caring, curious, and creative teacher. The stories shared next come from my own studies of teacher creativity among teachers in a school for special needs children in the western region of the country. The school primarily serves students who face speech and hearing difficulties. To address their needs, the staff (i.e., teachers and administrators) learn and use an in-house developed sign language. Resources to aid learning are in limited supply. As a result, teachers are often left to their own creative devices to design learning aids or sometimes resolve a particular issue that has arisen.

To illustrate this point, Dolma is one of those innovative teacher leaders in Paros. I should point out that when I observed teachers in that school, I referred to them as the Name Giver of Children. In Dolma's class, while they were making their class roster, they found that most of their students did not have assigned names from their villages and most of them were referred to as "tsagey" or "tsagem," which carries the literal meaning of "stupid boy" and "stupid girl." This is a term of endearment referring to a little child in the western region of Bhutan, but it is not meant that way in the case of these children who are born with hearing impairments, unfortunately.

Dolma carried out an activity with their students where they named them-selves and created their own signs for their names. Empathy guides the lesson designs of teachers like Dolma. Their action gives students a sense of identity and belonging that, not surprisingly, increased their levels of engagement and performance. Dolma refers to their class as being one big family. We know from decades of educational studies on motivation and learning that students who feel a sense of connectedness and belonging to their learning environment improve their ability to learn.

Bearing witness to the material reality of their classrooms, teachers develop an appreciative understanding of adapting and being flexible with their instruction.

An example of this adaptive flexibility is when Zangmo, a fourth-grade teacher, had to overcome the challenge of not having enough classroom supplies to demonstrate the concept of measurement to their students. They knew most students' parents are not able to afford to spend money on supplies; even instruments like a ruler are not readily available in the village. Instead, Zangmo created an activity where students were instructed to go to the forest to collect some wood, and then these students created rulers to understand the concept of measurement.

These fixes or adaptive moves made by these rural teachers may seem simplistic, yet they carry high value in terms of impact. Students in rural classrooms are able to engage in higher order thinking skills. For example, teachers like Zangmo or Passang, a science teacher, would constantly invite friends of theirs in the village to come to their classes as guest speakers. Passang would have students create their own weighing balance made from recycled soda canisters to scaffold understanding of abstract concepts of measurement.

As is apparent from the previous examples, teachers play a significant role in making learning meaningful for students in rural areas in PNG, Bhutan, and around the world. The agency to *make do* is perhaps more pronounced in rural schools and most typically in developing countries because teachers are among the few people found in the educational community. In addition, they are oftentimes looked up to as community leaders. You can be such an educational and community leader!

Reflection Questions

1. What approaches can teacher preparation programs make in preparing preservice teachers with the competencies of adaptive thinking and flexibility? How do these competencies position teachers to be better adept at reflection, reasoning, navigating, and structuring their lesson designs? How are they also especially useful skill sets for teachers encountering highly constrained teaching and learning contexts?
2. A significant process of developing adaptive thinking comes from a teacher's prior knowledge and experiences. What scaffolds can be developed to aid preservice teachers in the articulation and development of contextual knowledge?
3. Constraints push teachers to act in designer-like ways. Can constraints be studied as a tool for problem-solving and creative thinking? If so, in what ways?
4. Stories in this chapter took place in Bhutan and Papua New Guinea. Do you have dreams of supporting learning around the globe? If so, where would you want to be and why? What personal and educational constraints might you face there?

41

THE STORY BEHIND JACKY'S CELL PHONE

Bring the Invisible Forward

Natalia Ramirez-Casalvolone

Natalia Ramirez–Casalvolone is an English as a Foreign Language (EFL) teacher educator at Universidad de Costa Rica. She taught EFL in night high schools in Costa Rica for over 16 years. Currently, she is a PhD candidate at Indiana University Bloomington and is conducting research involving adult education for women, informal education, funds of knowledge, and feminism pedagogy. She can be reached at nataliarc@hotmail.com.

DOI: 10.4324/9781003213840-49

Research in the Classroom

I am currently working on my dissertation. I am conducting an ethnographic study to identify the resources that 20 Costa Rican women attending night high school bring into the classroom when they participate in the process of informally learning English as a Foreign Language. The participants of my research are from low-income backgrounds. Most of them are single mothers who work during the day picking coffee, cleaning houses, selling fruit, or working jobs in factories. During the evening, they attend Night High School.

Jacky's story is not the only representative of these women's lives, but also the described activity illustrates how educators can incorporate different techniques to learn about students' lives and the skills they use daily to be successful learners and strive for their learning goals.

A trained ethnographer looks around, notices small details, and observes what and how people use artifacts in their culture. Researchers make such observations to access important information and understandings about the group they are studying (Stone & Chiseri-Strater, 2012). Teachers similarly learn about their students' interests, values, priorities, hobbies, and preferences. Learning about one's students can help create a rich and engaging learning environment that can have a positive and motivating effect on their learning process and perhaps eventually evolve into a caring learning community.

Artifacts carry with them stories that give access to data that cannot be obtained through inquiry or other means like observations, interviews, or analyses (Rowsell, 2011). Artifacts can be used as an "optic to get an insider, emic gaze of individuals, their communities and their lived histories" (Rowsell, 2011, p. 332). The study of artifacts produces contextualization of different environments in terms of space and time, but they can also replicate people's reality and where they live (Rowsell, 2011). When students are allowed to share artifacts that are important to them because they represent them in a specific way, they feel important and confident that they are being valued and included. Stated another way, there is a sense of belonging.

Bringing Artifacts

Inspired by these ideas, in the summer of 2019, I asked my students to bring to class an important artifact for them. My instructions were that the object should be valuable, not necessarily in a material sense. More importantly, it should be representative of their feelings, emotions, and connections with key people or moments in their lives. A second instruction was that they should come ready to explain to the class why they had chosen that specific artifact to share.

It was not a major surprise that most of my students brought their cell phones as their artifacts. As a mother of a teenager, I am more than aware of adolescents' apparent "infatuation" with their mobile devices; however, I was surprised about the stories that some students shared about their phones.

Cell phones are in the hands of billions of people today. The reasons for getting a cell phone vary; some people own them for the camera or to listen to music. Other people have them for social purposes such as to have quick access to social media, to instantaneously chat with friends, or to stay in touch with family. Still others carry them due to job requirements that mandate that they be accessible at all times. Clearly, the motives for acquiring a cell phone range from highly valuable reasons to superficial ones.

Coming from a developing country such as Costa Rica, which too often is exceedingly influenced by the American marketing and consumerist culture, I have seen how many Costa Ricans ask for loans or go into payment plans to get the latest and most expensive smartphone. Many times, they have purchased phones that are worth more than what they actually can afford. I have always worked with students from low economic backgrounds; nevertheless, many of them carry phones that are high-end luxury items compared with the ones I carry around.

My artifact activity was a huge success. Students were excited and happy to share many objects like necklaces, printed pictures, jewelry, and pieces of clothing. One of these stories was Jacky's. When it was her turn, she took the phone and held it tight against her chest. She was in love; albeit, with her phone. When I saw her do this, I thought she was exaggerating and overreacting about the significance of her phone. I was honestly expecting the typical story about how her phone allowed her to talk to friends, listen to music, take pictures, and use social media. However, her explanation was not as anticipated.

Jacky explained that her mom worked a lot and that it was hard for her to buy nice things like this. An exception was made for her 15th birthday. Turning 15 is a very special date for young women from Costa Rica; on par with a Sweet 16 birthday in America. Jacky's mother gave her a new phone that she had bought at Gollo; a store that sells overpriced technology but with customized payment plans. Jacky continued:

> Every month, I go with her to pay for it. This phone reminds me that my mother works hard for me and my siblings. Still, two years later, she is paying for this phone that I really like, so I try to use it for important things; mostly, I use it to learn things on the internet. My mom wants me to be a doctor, so I read a lot about things I am interested in, and I try to use it to learn English too. I think I use my phone differently because I know when my mom bought it, she trusted I would give it a good use, so I try to honor that.

> (paraphrased from Spanish)

Behind this story, I learned about Jacky. I was able to understand her economic situation and how priorities in life are different for everyone. It is likely one way for Jacky's mother to show her daughter love was by buying her the phone. For her, Jacky deserved such sacrifice. She justified the expense with her interest in

Jacky's education. Furthermore, a phone is much cheaper and more versatile than a computer. Thus, it makes sense for these people to look for this option. Most importantly, Jacky felt her mother's love.

In another moment in time, I would have found such fondness for a phone irrelevant and superficial. Through my interviews of young women trying to improve their lives through night high school in Costa Rica, I have come to the realization that every person is in their own world. Through this one simple activity of artifact sharing and storytelling, you begin to see and hear about their daily lives and struggles. It is our job as teachers to unpack these personal stories and probe deeper, and bring out ideas, experiences, and emotions that are not so evident.

Reflection Questions

1. What are some of the cultural values that your students, friends, or children place on artifacts they use daily? How can you employ them in your teaching or training?
2. How can teachers incorporate classroom activities that highlight students' interests and experiences? Give an example or two.
3. How do artifacts and the different values students give to them offer teachers information about their students that they can incorporate into the classroom?
4. How can teachers apply different inquiry methods in their classroom to learn about their students and give value to the experiences and knowledge that they bring to the table, even before participating in formal schooling? Do you have any examples?

42

THE STORY OF KEEPING EDUCATION WHEELS TURNING

Motivation and Collaboration When Teaching in a Postwar Context

Simon Pierre Munyaneza

Simon Pierre Munyaneza is a doctoral candidate in literacy culture and language education in the School of Education at Indiana University Bloomington. He is pursuing a minor in instructional systems technology as well as a minor in African studies. A native of Rwanda, his areas of interest extend from literacy and culture, social linguistics, discourse analysis, and language education to

DOI: 10.4324/9781003213840-50

instructional design and technology in the context of Africa. He can be reached at munysim015@gmail.com.

Introduction

Rwanda, a country in East Central Africa, has a history emotionally charged by eventful ups and downs. Education, like the country, has followed the course of history from the pre-colonial, colonial, and post-colonial periods. The dynamics of educational reforms have been instrumental in forming language policy in Rwanda. This chapter is neither an overview of the entire history of education in Rwanda nor a compilation of events that marked different reforms in the education system. However, it is a brief account of my own experience as an educator in Rwanda and the manner of different changes that combined to strengthen my determination toward certain key educational goals.

A School in the Middle of a Community

I was not born in a school but in a region near the border of Rwanda and Uganda in the late 1970s. At that time, my parents had already started to put their children in school. They would often talk about how they missed out on furthering their education. Considering the importance given to the schools in the neighborhood, the entire village seemed to share the same education ideal.

A teacher was a role model for all of us: besides the elders, the teacher was considered the wisest and most skilled person in the community. Every family had a connection with our primary school, which would make easier any follow-up or inquiry into how a child was doing in their studies. I could not possibly know when growing up that such widespread community respect for education and for educators would be pivotal in forming my career interests and in gravitating me toward the field of education. As with most people, my early experiences teaching in a secondary school in Rwanda played a substantive role in my future career plans.

Starting my first teaching job during very difficult times of a postwar country, I was able to work together with teachers, parents, and students to pave the ground for the education of a community in a reconstruction phase. In effect, teaching in a previously war-torn country gave me a purpose and a passion that perhaps few ever find. Simply put, my life now had rich meaning.

A Teacher in Need Is a Teacher Indeed

Every time that I was graduating from one cycle of education to another, the knowledge institutions would keep me as a teacher. One important story that I continue to play in my mind today occurred in 1999, the first year of my professional career after completing my secondary studies. At that time, in postwar

Rwanda, there were pronounced educational challenges due to the scarcity of teachers. Many intellectuals had lost their lives during nearly a decade of a country-wide crisis (1990–1999), whereas others were still in exile and or were simply unable to show up for teaching. I give great credit to those unsung heroes, both teachers and parents, who ingeniously came up with the idea of going from house to house looking for kids in need of schooling and then helping them get needed educational services.

There was a huge motivational campaign at the time toward the benefits of education. Don't ask me about the library, the books, my notebooks, and so forth. They were not there. For reading materials, we had to go with other teachers on a scavenger hunt to collect books that survived the war. Here and there we could find books, especially for languages and sciences.

In many cases, with the help of former students, we could find class notes and textbooks, which schools had to put together in the light of a national curriculum. That was not a work of one person; it was a concerted effort of the entire community. We had to collaborate with available students, parents, school leaders, and so forth to put the Rwandan education system on its tracks. In effect, we were rebuilding our educational system with the scraps of resources that were not destroyed, hidden, or hauled away.

Survival Kit: Motivation and Collaboration

"*Intoki ebyiri ni ukunabana.*" That is a Kinyarwanda proverb meaning that "to wash your hands, you need two hands." It reflects how individual efforts are not sufficient, especially when members of the team have the same or similar goals. Stated another way, the motivational energy in a class would be elevated if we work together and collaborate; more hands involved means more minds involved. Facilitating students to have different groups in which they conduct their class projects and then share in larger groups allows myriad opportunities for encouragement, feedback, and support.

My first day of teaching was not easy, even though I was so curious about what it would be like and what the students and I would do. Most of my students were older than I, and, according to the local culture, elders were considered to have more authority than young people. Many of my students were men and women who had dropped out during the war and who wanted to catch up with their secondary education.

How could anyone not find this inspiring and motivational? Once again, I could see a real sense of life purpose and meaning in my chosen occupation. Naturally, a conversation with these students was most vital because it opened opportunities to know each other and collaborate for mutual educational benefits.

That is how I discovered that their immense knowledge from real-life experiences and their recent and extended history of tribulations could, in many cases, supplement, augment and, at times, even replace the standard class recipes. To be honest, I made it clear to them that we are not students and teachers but collaborators in a mutual and never-ending quest to learn. With that promise and overriding perspective, we decided to work together to prepare for the national exams, which are one of the greatest motivating factors in Rwandan society as they are a gateway to future job opportunities and potential university studies.

These collaborations with my students were both in academic and para-academic activities. In class, it was routine for me as well as my students to bring topics for discussion and then place students into groups before a plenary type of presentation. In para-academics, I could engage in different nontraditional activities with my students, such as playing football, farming on the school farm, and going on a community walk or hike, especially on the way to great public ceremonies.

Final Thoughts and Reflections

Even today, more than two decades from my start, the experience of the postwar Rwanda teaching remains indelibly engraved in my mind. These memories and prior experiences have acted as a huge impetus toward my educational and career goals. After my bachelor's and master's degree studies, I continued to work as a teacher in different secondary schools and as a lecturer in various colleges and universities in Rwanda. All these prior teaching experiences have helped me firmly grasp what makes education the key to a successful community.

After more than 20 years as an educator, I have come to realize that I have worked with more than 1,500 students, each of whom has hopefully received some input and feedback from me for the betterment of their lives. These people are now in different areas of professional life: banks, colleges, public administration, entrepreneurship, business, health services, to name a few. I look across the spectrum and feel thankful that the work of a teacher is not done in vain. If you are planning to become a teacher, welcome to one of the most rewarding, challenging, and exciting fields that I know.

Reflection Questions

1. Given the context of this story and chapter, how prepared do you think you are to teach now? What types of additional training might you need?
2. As a community or country reconstructs its entire educational system, what role can innovative teaching and creative instructional strategies play in such efforts?
3. In what ways might motivation and collaboration help construct an adequate survival kit in post-conflict teaching? What would you put in that kit?

4. What are some other instructional methods and ideas that could be applied when teaching in cities, countries, or regions of the world where such types of tragedies have struck?
5. How similar or different is the admiration displayed to a teacher in the Rwandan community to that seen in your community?

43

AUGMENTING CURRICULUM IN A WAR-TORN COUNTRY

Augmented Reality in Online Teaching

Ebrahim Bamanger

Ebrahim Bamanger is a doctoral candidate at Indiana University in literacy, culture and language education with a minor in instructional systems technology and a second minor in Middle Eastern languages and cultures. He is also a

DOI: 10.4324/9781003213840-51

doctoral candidate in curriculum and instruction at King Saud University. Ebrahim has been teaching foreign languages and literacy for eight years in national and global contexts. His research interests focus on exploring the integration of innovative technologies in enhancing language learning and methods of teaching second languages and literacy across diverse cultures. In his spare time, Ebrahim enjoys playing soccer, hiking, and swimming. He can be reached at ebra1982@ hotmail.com.

In a Town Called Tarim

As a child, I wanted to learn a new language in a country with no language but Arabic. Being able to speak some words in English gave me a sort of power to lead other kids of my age to speak to the few tourists who came to see the ancient mud-made buildings in my small town of Tarim, in the southeast of Yemen.

In 1997, I was a student in the high school of that small town. I still remember when the English language teacher came into the class with a huge cassette player; a quite fancy technology at that time. We all listened carefully to that gigantic device on the table in front of the class. Typically, students raced to their identified classes on the first day of school to occupy chairs in the front rows, and they'd continue to own them for the rest of the year, leaving them on the last day of school. Those who "possessed" the front rows were privileged to be the closest to the old technology device and could hear clearly from the cassette player! We envied them. Sometimes, the teacher allowed us to bring our chairs closer to listen better.

Unfortunately, the teacher rarely brought that technology device to the class. Listening to the cassette player, I still remember a speaker with a British accent as he speaks within a conversation, "*How do you do?*" and another individual responds, saying the same, "*How do you do?*" It was an advantage to listen to a native speaker and learn how English words are pronounced. This advantage was very apparent to everyone because we were taught by Yemeni teachers who had never been out of the country or come in contact with English speakers.

The school was the only source of instruction at that time; a role that now is challenged by myriad other educational agents and resources. I remember how, as a youngster, I used to silently repeat the newly learned words because I was afraid I would forget how they are pronounced. I would keep saying them during my long walk back home from school, to suddenly realize that I had forgotten some!

Ten years later, in 2007, I graduated from the School of Education at a Hadhramout University for Science and Technology in Yemen with a bachelor's degree in language teaching. Remarkably, I taught for one year in that same high school. I was soon surprised to discover that ten years was not enough time to change the curriculum. I was forced to teach using the same textbooks that I studied as a student! At that time, cell phone technology had begun to spread in Yemen and, in fact, entered every household. Nonetheless, it was not part of our curriculum. This sudden mobile technology infiltration occurred in Yemen despite the fact that it had been a place of national and regional conflicts that have kept the country suffering from a lack of basic needs, not to mention being seriously impaired by the lack of penetration of other technological advances.

Currently, Yemen is torn into regions that are governed by different warring factions in the north and the south, with no national government able to effectively function across this land I call home. To put it differently, even as government members work most of the time from outside the country, it is a war-centered government that barely helps with food distribution and has little, if any, capacity for curriculum development. Worse still, there are no intentions to develop a curriculum! Unfortunately, education is the last thing the government can think about at this time.

One interesting dilemma for curriculum development is a question about the role of the school. Some insist that schools should prepare students to address current problems in the community, whereas others argue that curriculum should prepare learners for the future and enable them to predict future needs. Unfortunately, the Yemeni curriculum will achieve neither of these goals because the textbooks bear no relation with the present nor the future.

Today, after more than a quarter century, our students still use the same curriculum and the same textbooks! Those books, from the pre-cell phone era, have not been adapted to mobile learning, artificial intelligence, data science, blockchain, or 5G technology. They are simply aged as *pre-cell phone era!* They do not reflect the dynamic nature of the language; even the vocabulary is not relevant. If you miss the old days, you can just turn the pages of those textbooks.

Technology as a Cheap but Fancy Solution

I was lucky enough to pursue my doctoral studies in the United States at Indiana University Bloomington. After a journey through the field of curriculum and instruction and a minor in instructional systems technology, I have learned about and been inspired by an assortment of comprehensive technology applications in the field. I have learned that technology can provide cheap but still fancy solutions to our life problems, as proved in the era of COVID-19. My ideas related to developing a better curriculum in Yemen were prompted by my exploration of one of the most advanced technologies today, augmented reality (AR).

Because AR technology can overcome the limits of time and space, I believe that developing an AR-based curriculum can be an appropriate solution for the current curriculum problems in Yemen. I have also considered the financial benefit of reducing the expense of reprinting new books. AR is also a flexible way to study remotely during the pandemic.

After analyzing this situation, I decided to implement this technology to provide an attractive and practical curriculum while bringing life to the textbooks by letting English words speak loudly to students and having abstract notions expressed as pictures and 3D objects. As explained next, this is just a starting point.

How It Works

Deciding on and then developing an English language curriculum for ninth graders was the first step. The second step is to try it out. Fortunately, my own town was selected as the pilot sample in the study. The curriculum has been evaluated, needs analysis has been conducted, and objectives have been identified to address the gaps and to set areas of enhancement. At this particular age, students tend to be attached to technology, and almost all have their own smartphones. The goal is to deliver a new layer of the curriculum virtually to the previous textbooks via AR technology. Using a free AR application, students can easily download it into their cell phones and follow the developed curriculum.

To develop authentic content, some students at Indiana University who are native speakers of English did not hesitate to help record videos and conversations to develop learning activities. Life has always taught me that one is not alone, and, once again, this rings true. People will always care about each other. When you have a plan to help, just let others know, and they will join you to provide the needed support.

The old textbooks were scanned to select images to work as triggers in the AR application. These triggers were attached to the new content, learning tasks, and multimodal activities. To access the materials and activities, students can use their cell phone cameras to scan each page and new activities, materials, multimedia, and assignments pop up into their reality. They can interact with the new curriculum at any time and from anywhere at their fingertips. In effect, it is a curriculum that looks like the modern time they live in. Students can listen to native speakers, interact with the content, engage in attractive activities, and fulfill inquiry-based tasks.

Being on a different continent is no longer an obstacle, thanks to technology. During Zoom meetings about the project, language teachers expressed a mixture of feelings. They were doubtful, reluctant, and curious. I totally understand the reluctance to try new things and their attachment to the old system. With some encouragement and motivation to take the lead, my old school, Tarim High School, was the first one to try the AR project. I am so proud!

We implemented various types of formative assessments of the AR initiative. Importantly, students at Tarim High School expressed higher motivation levels compared with their motivation toward the age-old curriculum. As a post-experiment interview with a sample of the participants, Ahmed explained his high ratings of the program, highlighting the attractive presentation of the content. According to Ahmed,

> *This program contains several forms of activities that stimulated my curiosity. It was interesting to interact with the media and listen to or watch people as they speak and tell what happened with them in the story rather than just read all the time. I just was able to feel included and feel what the characters felt.*

Ali, another student at Tarim High, liked the interactive nature of the activities and the various forms of the assignments:

> *Typically when I submit an assignment, I get the feedback from the teacher within three days. In contrast, I liked that the program allows me to do several exercises at any time and get immediate feedback. I sometimes, go back to the same exercise and try it in a different form as there are several forms of the exercise that I can practice. For instance, I can practice the new vocabulary items doing matching, multiple-choice, spelling exercises, among others, and it is all on my cell phone.*

A third student, Salim, was impressed by the communicative nature of the activities. Salim stated, "The activities in this program helped me understand how I can use the language in real life. I was able to see individuals utilize the newly learned phrases to achieve their goals."

I was excited by such positive student anecdotes. I was also delighted since I was able to trace students' active participation and use of the AR-based curriculum and was able to see how engaged they were in the AR-based activities. They can go back to their cell phones to check the proper pronunciation; a feature I wish I had been able to use when I was their age!

Lessons Learned

I still remember that day before traveling abroad for graduate studies, my friends and colleagues told me that the community would be waiting for my return to pay it forward and help to build a better education system. Today, it is increasingly obvious that being away from home does not mean one cannot help. With technology tools for global collaboration and interaction, it does not mean I will not be able to be there to teach!

Education can provide the right tools to pay forward to the community. It introduces you to the power of knowledge that can work even in the absence of financial assets to solve problems created by a lack of resources. There are still many miles to go in developing a curriculum for all school grades. My project remains a work in progress. At present, the plan is to collaborate with more colleagues and expand the program to develop a curriculum for other grades and maybe other disciplines. Who wants to join me?

Reflection Questions

1. Describe some of the ways that you have learned as a child that are vastly changed or transformed today. What are you missing? What new things are you thankful for and why?
2. In some cultures, they argue that each time period or era has its successful tools. Can you think of an earlier generation of technology that was influential in your life but no longer is? How has that technology shaped your learning experiences and life?
3. If an AR-based curriculum were implemented at your school, what activities would you want to try first and why?
4. Reflect on your field of study; how can you utilize the AR technology in your courses? What are the potential AR-based activities that can be effective?
5. Reflect on a time when you were part of an initiative that was created or designed to bring needed change to an educational activity, course, or program initiative. What impact did that initiative have on you and others around you?

44

AFTER MAKING IMPACT

Meina Zhu and Curtis J. Bonk

DOI: 10.4324/9781003213840-52

Meina Zhu is Assistant Professor of Learning Design and Technology in the College of Education at Wayne State University. She received her PhD degree in instructional systems technology at Indiana University Bloomington and her master's degree in educational technology at Beijing Normal University. Her research interests include online education, massive open online courses, self-directed learning, STEM education, and learning analytics. Meina has published her work in such places as the *International Review of Research in Open and Distributed Learning*, *British Journal of Education Technology*, *Internet and Higher Education*, *Canadian Journal of Learning and Technology*, *Online Learning*, and *Distance Education*. She has taught courses in instructional design, emerging technologies, instructional strategies, Web design, and the history, issues, and trends in instructional technology. Meina can be reached at meinazhuiu@gmail.com or meinazhu@wayne.edu.

Curtis J. Bonk is Professor in the Instructional Systems Technology Department in the School of Education and Adjunct in the School of Informatics at Indiana University (IU). His academic interests are in online learning, massive open online courses (MOOCs), open education, collaborative technology, informal learning, emerging learning technologies, self-directed learning, and blended learning. He has authored many widely used technology books, including *The World Is Open*, *Empowering Online Learning*, *The Handbook of Blended Learning*, *Electronic Collaborators*, *Adding Some TEC-VARIETY*, which is free as an e-book (http://tec-variety.com/), and *MOOCs and Open Education Around the World* as well as *MOOCs and Open Education in the Global South* (www.moocsbook.com/). He has published more than 130 journal articles as well as 65 book chapters and 20 books. In 2020, Curt was awarded the IU President's Award for Excellence in Teaching and Learning Technology, while in 2021, he received the David H. Jonassen Excellence in Research Award from AECT. Curt can be contacted at cjbonk@indiana.edu. His homepage is http://curtbonk.com/.

Coming to a Close

After reading the various chapters in this book, you should have gained a basic understanding of how substantive and sustainable learning impact has been made by dozens of educators around the world with their creative ideas and dedication. Perhaps you found one or more anecdotes with which you resonated and took the liberty of writing to the author for more details or to share your own experiences. Or maybe you decided to locate and read additional resources on topics that caught your interest. And there is also the possibility that you took the bold step and tested out one or more strategies in your own teaching or training episodes. If so, we hope that these experiments met with some success, however tentative and limited they might be. You can always tweak these activities next time and build from the initial results and then expand your collegial networks.

While the stories in *Transformative Teaching Around the World: Stories of Cultural Impact, Technology Integration, and Innovative Pedagogy* are primarily at the K-12 level, the lessons learned have wide-ranging applicability across educational sectors and disciplines. If we were successful, one or more of the anecdotes in this book has begun to influence your own teaching philosophy, which may eventually have a deep and lasting impact on your teaching practices as well as the advice you lend to colleagues and the mentoring you give to newcomers, advisees, and those you supervise.

Having arrived at the end of the book, it is definitely time to use your imagination and envision the most successful version of yourself implementing these strategies. While you might create a plan or vision of how you will improve or elevate your teaching practices in the near future, after several trials, you may need to rethink the benefits of employing different strategies in your own classroom or educational setting. When an idea sounds particularly appealing, jot it down and then make a mental list of the opportunities that are possible as well as challenges you may face when you try to implement that strategy. Remember, it was only a few pages ago that you read a personal account from a fellow educator of how it worked or was found to be problematic.

As you have read time and again in this book, many education practices have been changed due to free and easy-to-deploy technology and innovative and interactive pedagogies. You, too, can design some amazing pedagogical activities for your home base. Before such design efforts, you should reflect on some critical questions. Of course, in any such reflection as an educator, you should think about who benefits and who does not as well as pondering for whose benefit a particular method is implemented. In the ensuing paragraphs, we lay out a series of such questions for you to assess your readiness to apply the knowledge gained and perhaps carry the ideas forward to now make an impact on students' higher order thinking, motivation, and overall attitudes of success.

Pondering Questions

Among the first things you might ask yourself at the end of such a book is how you can become more innovative in your instructional approaches and methods. Might such innovations result in enhanced learner creativity and critical thinking as displayed in the daring projects attempted and aesthetically stunning projects completed? Over time, the accumulation of physical as well as online exhibit halls and galleries of student creative work is what teachers find most satisfying about their jobs. Now is the time to start funding such student art through innovative task options and stimulating challenges and begin adding to your collections.

Second, a parallel set of questions relate to whether the strategies regarding collaborative learning, critical thinking, and creative thinking mentioned in this book apply to your subject areas and grade or age levels. We hope that at least a few of them directly do and many more of them relate to your subjects, modules, and courses indirectly. If not, how can you stretch them and mix them in ways that are applicable to your instruction and relevant and meaningful to your students? Stretch, pull, tug, yank, and mix away. It will likely be a fun journey and even more fun seeing where you end up.

Given the various chapters of this book involving the movement to online learning during the COVID-19 pandemic, the third area to self-question relates to how emerging learning technology can change or even transform your teaching practices and pedagogical innovations. Just how can you leverage current emerging learning technology to improve education? Of course, you must keep in mind that the technology tools and associated opportunities are constantly changing.

Fourth, no matter your discipline, educational sector, experience level, and targeted audience, you should always reflect on the pros and cons of using different instructional strategies and technologies and then compare that list to the end result. Such generation and regeneration of lists are a constant and a given if you are to find success. As this process occurs repeatedly, your persistent pondering on your instructional approaches will likely cause you to reexamine your teaching and learning philosophies time and again. Focus for a moment on what has changed and why. Can you explain it to others? Just what is your model or framework for exemplary teaching or training practices now? How might this teaching framework or philosophy need to change in the coming decade as new instructional methods, technologies, and government mandates come your way?

Will you be ready for Education 4.0 and beyond? If not, what can you do right now to begin preparing for massive global change in the field of education?

A fifth area of reflection concerns how you expect students will react to your new instructional techniques and creatively brainstormed ideas. Will the light bulbs going on and off in your head result in enough light to show you the way to mild, modest, or perhaps magnificent success? And when student concerns arrive or aspects of the ideas do not work exactly as planned and designed, how will you address them? Be sure to write reflective blog posts, e-newsletter stories, or conference papers about those ideas and changes in approach that work so others can benefit from them.

A final area relates to the reactions from those in charge. Will your organizational or institutional leaders and colleagues support the new strategies that you are going to use? If not, how are you going to persuade or educate them? Will you feel safe or comfortable when taking pedagogical risks that your colleagues are not? Once again, you might consider designing training programs on how of persist in a department or organization that is highly resistant to such pedagogical innovation and risk taking. See Bonk and Khoo (2014) for a chapter in a free e-book (http://tec-variety.com/) that outlines additional ways to support and motivate resistant and reluctant instructors and administrators.

Hopefully, the previous questions and focal points will help you concentrate on the intended goals and possibilities in your upcoming instructional practices. Naturally, there will be a sea of challenges attempting to block your success. A few of the major ones are mapped out next.

Responding to Challenges

After reading the stories of the diverse educators contributing to this book, you likely started to reflect on the myriad obstacles and challenges that the chapter authors face in their teaching practices. Among the key challenges you likely encounter include personalizing learning and addressing student needs when they come from diverse linguistic, ethnic, cultural, religious, and socioeconomic backgrounds. Other challenges pertain to limited access to adequate technology infrastructure and online educational resources, stringent state standards, deficient professional development opportunities, and limited or nonexistent support from colleagues and administrators. Additional issues relate to the difficulties of understanding different instructional strategies and then implementing them in an engaging and effective way when students have extremely diverse backgrounds and wide-ranging expectations.

Besides the challenges mentioned in the chapters, in the future, educators will undoubtedly also face new tests and obstacles such as fast-changing educational technology and enormous and often messy data from automated systems with a stream of learning analytics. As the common educational tools, resources, and systems are redesigned and elevated, we must resist becoming enamored with the latest gadget or feature and, instead, ask how to effectively cultivate students' creative thinking, critical thinking, and collaborative skills. Another associated and persistent difficulty relates to how and when to measure such skills gains.

To address these challenges, you could conduct action research on their teaching practices and share what you have found via webinars, institutes, and mini conferences. You also might craft blog pages and mini books that summarize your teaching experiences and share these resources with others for their insights and suggestions. Of course, most of you will attend professional development activities and training programs to obtain relevant knowledge; you might even enroll in certificate and micro-credential programs. Additionally, many of you will gather resources from different relevant websites within and outside your institutions and organizations. Whatever you do to overcome the challenges you face, you should always reflect on, refresh, and rethink your educational philosophies and perspectives on effective and powerful learning.

Lasting Impact

We challenge you to: (1) read additional resources; (2) find, store, and share supplemental ones; (3) and have dialogues with your colleagues about these pedagogies of transformation. In the back of our minds is the hope that you will add to the tactics and strategies found in this book and do something remarkable that only you could have thought of and designed! We also would be delighted if you combine and extend some of pedagogical ideas mentioned in these chapters and try them out before you ultimately share them with others in your discipline and perhaps across disciplinary borders. When that happens, the chapters in this book will find lasting impact in unanticipated and exciting ways.

As indicated, this concluding chapter refers to what happens after making impact. Of course, this chapter title has double meaning. First, we want you to ponder the wisdom, insights, and ideas you gained from reading one or more chapters of *Transformative Teaching Around the World*. Perhaps in the various chapters you saw some repeated themes or robust learning principles that you can now apply. And perhaps you might create some type of in-service training program or self-directed learning experience for others in your organization or institution based on these active learning principles and themes. We also encourage you to reflect on the many ways that you have made an impact on learners and learning in the past, as well as how you might be even more successful in the future.

You have read how instructional strategies for critical and creative thinking, motivation, cooperative and collaborative learning, and technology integration influenced these 42 educators around the world. As a result of their proactive minds and deep-rooted dedication, the chapters of this book are filled with rich ideas and activities that should continue to evolve and find application for you over the coming years and decades. While each implementation may be modest in terms of the audience in attendance, over time, such audiences build up to gigantic stadiums filled with educators who have ingested the making impact virus for which you need no vaccine. As this occurs, we just might see some initial signs of transformative teaching around the world.

Feel free to write to us with the exciting stories of change and transformation that you are observing. There is no time like now to hold your head up and take note of them. And there is no time like now to be making an impact.

AFTERWORD

The Power of Planning

Anastasia S. Morrone

Anastasia S. Morrone is Dean and Professor in the Indiana University School of Education at Bloomington. She received her PhD degree in educational psychology from the University of Texas at Austin and her bachelor of science degree in

DOI: 10.4324/9781003213840-53

technical communication from the University of Minnesota. She previously served as Associate Vice President for Learning Technologies and Deputy Chief Information Officer in the Office of the Vice President for IT at Indiana University. Her research interests focus on technology-rich, active learning environments that promote student motivation and learning. She can be reached at amorrone@iu.edu.

Introduction

It was late June 2020 and I had spent the previous three months intensely engaged in planning for and then supporting the transition to online learning as part of my longtime university role as Indiana University's (IU) Associate Vice President for Learning Technologies. The pandemic was raging and teachers and students across the world needed to rapidly adjust to new ways of teaching and learning. In retrospect, Indiana University was better prepared than many universities because since the H1N1 threat of 2009, we had maintained our Keepteaching.iu.edu website. That open-access website was filled with innovative resources dedicated to helping faculty move their instruction online in the event of unplanned campus closures. The pandemic, however, put our ability to deploy quality, technology-supported teaching practices under a very real stress test. During the transition, in fact, we all predicted that we would learn a lot about new teaching practices.

I could not, however, have predicted that late in June 2020, I would be invited to serve as the IU Bloomington School of Education Dean, which has been the greatest honor of my professional life. I joined the core-campus School of Education in 1997 as an Assistant Professor of Educational Psychology. At the time of my hiring, Curt Bonk was already fast becoming an internationally known scholar—this at a time when technology in teaching was still in its relative infancy. Fast forward two decades later when I also had the good fortune to work with Meina Zhu in 2018 and 2019 as part of my research team in the Office of the Vice President for IT. So it is a great honor to write the afterword for *Transformative Teaching Around the World: Stories of Cultural Impact, Technology Integration, and Innovative Pedagogy*.

This book is a testament to the commitment to a scholarly approach to teaching, to challenging current practice, and to provoking continuous improvement in the academy. It serves as a bellwether for the dissemination of creative and inspiring ideas from teachers who have taken their innovative spirit around the world. The book considers the global spread of innovative pedagogy in different cultural contexts. It is clear that every author in the book has embraced the power of pedagogical change and has done so with great courage.

Change is always a challenge with associated risks and doubts. Those of us in this space understand that our fellow teacher scholars expect risk taking to be well-grounded in the literature and to provide evidence of the value of innovation. This volume's authors demonstrate over and over again their deep understanding of theories of learning and motivation. Social constructivist practices are at the heart of many of their instructional approaches. The examples of rich metacognitive experiences that promote deeper student learning are inspiring. There are also frequent references to giving students choices, which, as noted, resulted in students who were excited to learn. In their chapters, many of the authors express great joy that their students are now learning in more powerful ways.

I have spent my career looking for ways to advance innovative pedagogy, often through the use of emerging learning technology. Through the Mosaic Active Learning initiative at IU, I was committed to designing learning spaces that promoted active and engaging learning. As might be expected, these innovative spaces had experimental and often amazing technology. However, the focus of the Mosaic project team was never simply about new technologies, but on the power of these technologies to impact instruction. Similarly, many authors of this book describe how they use technology for deeper engagement with the content, both within and outside of traditional classroom spaces. The stories in the book that focus on the pandemic make clear the importance of technology in teaching and learning. Naturally, we have all learned a great deal about teaching and learning from the pandemic; fortunately, these inspiring stories highlight the power of technology to transform teaching in ways that will endure long after the pandemic.

Across these chapters, the authors acknowledge that change can be hard. Many write about the need to understand their students' feelings and to respond with empathy when their students struggle. There is a consistent theme of making sure that students feel a sense of belonging in the classroom. As an educational psychologist, I was struck by the commitment of these teachers to make a difference in their students' lives through pedagogical transformation. The impact of Professor Bonk's course R546, "Instructional Strategies for Thinking, Collaboration, and Motivation," is clearly seen throughout this book.

Nearly all teacher education programs have a foundational course in educational psychology as well as multicultural education, but what is often missing from the assigned textbooks are stories like the ones in this book. The rich detail in the stories brings theories of learning and motivation to life. These stories often also brought tears to my eyes.

This is a book about Making Impact. The impactful teachers in this book engaged in extensive planning and replanning and constant reflection to get to where they are today. COVID-19 was not something educators would typically plan for and yet many of them succeeded because of their open and flexible teaching philosophies. As you look ten to 20 years into future, I challenge you to consider what education will look like and how you can begin to plan for that world for there is indeed much power in planning!

ACKNOWLEDGMENTS

The book is the product of innumerable brilliant minds and caring hearts. First, we would like to thank all the chapter authors worldwide who contributed to *Transformative Teaching Around the World* and shared their vast educational wisdom and wonderful pedagogical practices with us and with the readers of this book. In total, 46 people from 22 countries contributed to the 44 chapters or introductory and closing pieces found in this book. As noted in the preface, all these authors have roots in the Indiana University (IU) School of Education as a current or former graduate student, visiting international scholar, Fulbright scholar, faculty member, or dean.

It truly was a unique experience having so many of these people come back to the School of Education at IU, albeit temporarily and virtually, to contribute to this book. As each of these chapters makes clear, you all are transformative teachers and perpetual learners who are helping change the world in your own unique ways. It has been an honor to work with each of you highly creative souls and a true privilege to call each of you a friend. Thanks for incorporating our many rounds of comments, ideas, and suggestions into your manuscripts as fast as you could. You each generated marvelously informative and fascinating stories.

Second, we send a special thank you to Jacob Butler, who contributed the wonderful opening chapter of Section 1 of this book. More importantly, Jacob coordinated the special Fulbright Distinguished Awards in Teaching (DAT) Program at Indiana University that resulted in more than half of the contributors to this book. The awesome chapter writers who are alumni of this phenomenally successful cultural and professional exchange program represent Botswana, India, Finland, Israel, Mexico, Morocco, Singapore, and New Zealand. In total, there are 24 Fulbright DAT Program alums with chapters in this book along with 17 other chapters written by current and former IU School of Education graduate students or previous international scholars who visited IU and R546 during the past decade. Combined, they make up the 42 main chapter stories found in this book. Notably, all attended the R546 course "Instructional Strategies for Thinking, Collaboration, and Motivation," in which Curtis Bonk was the instructor and Meina Zhu was the teaching assistant on four recent occasions. As shown in the passages of this book, all these gifted educators are operationalizing the R546 content in their own unique ways to make an impact on learners and learning around the globe.

During the book writing process, it dawned on us that we needed input from a couple of the prominent leaders of the IU School of Education. First, we send enormous gratitude to former IU School of Education Dean Gerardo M. González who helped with the book introduction. We are quite thankful Gerardo, an emeritus professor at IU, emerged from his retirement home in Florida to pen a most illuminating foreword to the book. We were also extremely delighted that current School of Education Dean Anastasia S. Morrone could carve out space in her time-bound schedule to contribute a delicious book closing with the thoughts expressed in the afterword. Without the leadership, vision, and support of these two marvelous people, the ingredients for this book would not have emerged.

There are many other people to thank including those who authored books with Bonk related to the R546 class including Ke Zhang who co-wrote *Empowering Online Learning: 100+ Activities for Reading, Reflecting, Displaying, and Doing* and Elaine Khoo who collaborated with Bonk on *Adding Some TEC-VARIETY: 100+ Activities for Motivating and Retaining Learners Online*, which is free as an e-book. We give a shout-out to some of the recent teaching assistants for R546 including Justin Whiting, Dabae Lee, Yeol Ha, Mengyuan Zhao, Minkyoung Kim, Remzi Kizilboga, Ji-Yeon Lee, Umida Khikmatillaeva, Shuya Xu, Anjali Kanitkar, Zixi Li, Merve Basdogan, and many more. IU alumni Chaoran Wang is also thanked for their kind and timely editorial support.

Naturally, we also thank the hundreds of students who have enrolled in different versions of R546 over more than three decades that it has been offered, first at West Virginia University back in 1991 and since then at Indiana University. Notably, since the mid-1990s, this course has often been conducted via videoconferencing to locations throughout the state of Indiana. We hope that all the amazing R546 participants are continuing to use the ideas from that course in both their personal and professional lives to make all sorts of impacts, big and small.

The nubs of this course and, hence, this book, arose in the mid-1980s when Curt Bonk was taking correspondence courses on creativity and gifted education with Robert (Bob) Clasen at the University of Wisconsin (UW) while working as an extremely bored accountant and certified public accountant in Milwaukee. Clasen and his wife, Donna Rae Clasen, hired Bonk shortly after his graduate school arrival at the UW in 1986, where he helped them develop what would become a nationally distributed telecourse on critical thinking entitled, "Teachers Tackle Thinking: Critical Thinking in the Classroom." At the same time, Bonk started reading the book, *Creativity Is Forever*, written by his advisor Gary Davis. Accordingly, critical and creative thinking formed the basis of the first version of the R546 course several years later. Thanks for your ideas and inspiration, Bob, Donna Rae, and Gary.

Like all edited volumes with dozens of global contributors, this project seemed to have an endless appetite that tended to eat up our limited time resources and mental utensils. There were many pieces to track and coordinate along the way. Consequently, we must recognize the wondrous editorial staff and production team at Routledge. They are all first rate. To, once again, have the organizational powers of Olivia Powers as well as the prompt support, unwavering encouragement, and sage advice of our editor, Daniel Schwartz, proved invaluable. Thank you so much, Olivia and Dan!

REFERENCES

Albrecht-Crane, C. (2005). Pedagogy as friendship: Identity and affect in the conservative classroom. *Cultural Studies, 19*(4), 491–514. doi:10.1080/09502380500219548

Amir, N. (2014). Showcasing the creative talents in science of the academically less-inclined students through a values-driven toy story-telling project. In L. C. Lennex & K. F. Nettleton (Eds.), *Cases on instructional technology in gifted and talented Education* (pp. 141–179). Hershey, PA: IGI Global Publishing.

Amir, N. (2021a). Fostering joy and creativity amongst students in a Singapore classroom through fun design-and-make STEM projects. In D. Ktoridou, E. Doukanari, & N. Eteokleous (Eds.), *Fostering meaningful learning experiences through student engagement* (pp. 51–73). Hershey, PA: IGI Global Publishing.

Amir, N. (2021b). Views from parents of at-risk students in Singapore towards the use of fun design-and-make STEM projects to foster creativity and joy of learning. In C. Gaines & K. Hutson (Eds.), *Promoting positive learning experiences in middle school education* (pp. 87–105). Hershey, PA: IGI Global Publishing.

Ang, J. (2021). Teachers, students use design mindset to spark learning and creativity. *The Straits Times.* Singapore. Retrieved from www.straitstimes.com/singapore/parenting-education/teachers-students-use-design-mindset-to-spark-learning-and-creativity

Arantani, L. (2020, November 27). Robots on the rise as Americans experience record job losses amid pandemic. *The Guardian.* Retrieved from www.theguardian.com/technology/2020/nov/27/robots-replacing-jobs-automation-unemployment-us

Bonk, C. J. (2009). *The world is open: How Web technology is revolutionizing education.* San Francisco, CA: Jossey-Bass.

Bonk, C. J. (2016a, November 4). *Education 20/20 meets education 3.0: Visions of our changing learning world!* Keynote presentation at the Education 20/20: Innovative Teaching and Learning at a Distance Conference, the University of Houston, Houston, TX. Retrieved from https://vimeo.com/190339645

Bonk, C. J. (2016b). What is the state of e-learning? Reflections on 30 ways learning is changing. *Journal of Open, Flexible and Distance Learning, 20*(2), 6–20. Retrieved from http://jofdl.nz/index.php/JOFDL/article/viewFile/300/205

Bonk, C. J., & Khoo, E. (2014). *Adding some TEC-VARIETY: 100+ activities for motivating and retaining learners online* (pp. 1–368). Bloomington, IN: OpenWorldBooks. com and Amazon CreateSpace.

Bonk, C. J., & Zhang, K. (2008). *Empowering online learning: 100+ activities for reading, reflecting, displaying, and doing.* San Francisco, CA: John Wiley & Sons.

Catmull, E., & Wallace, A. (2014). *Creativity, Inc.: Overcoming the unseen forces that stand in the way of true inspiration.* New York: Random House.

Cavafy, C. P. (1975, 1992). "The city" from *C.P. Cavafy: Collected poems.* Translated by Edmund Keeley and Philip Sherrard. Translation Copyright © 1975, 1992 by Edmund Keeley and Philip Sherrard. Princeton, NJ: Reproduced with permission of Princeton University Press.

Clasen, D. R., & Bonk, C. J. (Compilers). (1988). *Teachers tackle thinking: Critical thinking in the classroom.* Madison, WI: University of Wisconsin-Extension.

Crewe, B., Warr, J., Bennett, P., & Smith, A. (2014). The emotional geography of prison life. *Theoretical Criminology, 18*(1), 56–74. doi:10.1177/1362480613497778

Davis, G. A. (2004). *Creativity is forever* (5th ed.). Dubuque: Kendall/Hunt.

Egbert, J. (Ed.). (2010). *CALL in limited technology contexts.* CALICO, San Marcos, TX: Texas State University.

Egbert, J., & Yang, Y. F. D. (2004). Mediating the digital divide in CALL classrooms: Promoting effective language tasks in limited technology contexts. *ReCALL, 16*(2), 280–291.

Feuerstein, R., Rand, Y., Hoffman, M. B., & Miller, R. (1980). *Instrumental Enrichment: An intervention program for cognitive modifiability.* Baltimore: University Park Press.

Goffman, E. (1961/2017). *Asylums: Essays on the social situation of mental patients and other inmates* (1st ed., p. 409). https://doi-org.ezproxy.canterbury.ac.nz/10.4324/9781351327763

González, G. M. (2018). *A Cuban refugee's journey to the American dream: The power of education.* Bloomington: Indiana University Press.

Guilford, J. P. (1959). Traits of creativity. In H. H. Anderson (Ed.), *Creativity and its cultivation* (pp. 142–161). New York: Harper & Row.

Harmes, M. K., Hopkins, S., & Farley, H. (2019). Beyond incarcerated identities. *International Journal of Bias, Identity and Diversities in Education, 4*(1), 1–16. doi:10.4018/IJBIDE.2019010101

Howie, D. R. (2019). *Thinking about the teaching of thinking: The Feuerstein approach* (2nd ed.). London: Routledge.

Hughes, D. J., Lee, A., Tian, A. W., Newman, A., & Legood, A. (2018). Leadership, creativity, and innovation: A critical review and practical recommendations. *The Leadership Quarterly, 29*(5), 549–569.

Indiana University. (2016). *Fulbright teacher finds creative ways to convey science.* School of Education, Indiana University. Retrieved from https://education.indiana.edu/news-events/_news/2016/2016-12-05-nazir.html

Isaacson, W. (2014). *The innovators: How a group of hackers, geniuses, and geeks created the digital revolution.* New York: Simon & Schuster.

Keats, D., & Schmidt, J. P. (2007, March). The genesis and emergence of Education 3.0 in higher education and its potential for Africa. *First Monday.* Retrieved from http://firstmonday.org/ojs/index.php/fm/article/view/1625/1540

Kelly, J. (2020, October 27). U.S. Lost over 60 million jobs—now robots, tech and artificial intelligence will take millions more. *Forbes.* Retrieved from www.forbes.com/sites/jackkelly/2020/10/27/us-lost-over-60-million-jobs-now-robots-tech-and-artificial-intelligence-will-take-millions-more/

Kong, W., & Li, Q. H. (2013). Peer feedback in second language writing: Symmetry or asymmetry? The argument between Piaget and Vygotsky. *Foreign Language Education, 34*(4), 50–55.

Li, S. (2000). A measure to improve the teaching of English writing instruction-process based teaching. *Foreign Language World* (1), 19–23.

Llorens, S., Schaufeli, W., Bakker, A., & Salanova, M. (2007). Does a positive gain spiral of resources, efficacy beliefs and engagement exist? *Computers in Human Behavior, 23,* 825–841.

Mulcahy, D. (2012). Affective assemblages: Body matters in the pedagogic practices of contemporary school classrooms. *Pedagogy, Culture & Society, 20*(1), 9–27. http://dx.doi.org/10.1080/14681366.2012.649413

Palmer, P. (2007). *The courage to teach: Exploring the inner landscape of a teacher's life.* San Francisco, CA: Jossey-Bass.

Pawan, F., Daley, S., Kou, X., & Bonk, C. J. (2022). *Motivation and online language teaching and learning.* Washington, DC: TESOL.

Peppler, K. A., & Solomou, M. (2011). Building creativity: Collaborative learning and creativity in social media environments. *On the Horizon, 19*(1), 13–23.

Pew Research Center. (2014, April). *Global religious diversity. Half of the most religiously diverse countries are in the Asia-Pacific region.* Retrieved from www.pewresearch.org/wp-content/uploads/sites/7/2014/04/Religious-Diversity-full-report.pdf

Prensky, M. (2001). Digital natives, digital immigrants part 1. *On the Horizon, 9*(5), 1–6. https://doi.org/10.1108/10748120110424816

Robinson, K., & Aronica, L. (2015). *Creative schools: The grassroots revolution that's transforming education.* New York, NY: Penguin Books.

Rowsell, J. (2011). Carrying my family with me: Artifacts as emic perspectives. *Qualitative Research, 11*(3), 331–346.

Salmon, G. (2019). May the fourth be with you: Creating education 4.0. *Journal of Learning for Development, 6*(2), 95–115. Retrieved from https://jl4d.org/index.php/ejl4d/article/view/352/403

Schoolbag. (2014). *The "RAP" approach to enhance teaching.* Retrieved September 4, 2014, from www.schoolbag.edu.sg/story/the-rap-approach-to-enhance-teaching

Schoolbag. (2015). *Science—It's child's play.* Retrieved from www.schoolbag.edu.sg/story/science-it-s-child-s-play

Semuels, A. (2020, August 6). Millions of Americans have lost jobs in the pandemic—And robots and AI are replacing them faster than ever. *Time.* Retrieved from https://time.com/5876604/machines-jobs-coronavirus/

Smyth, J., McInerney, P., & Fish, T. (2013). Blurring the boundaries: From relational learning towards a critical pedagogy of engagement for disengaged disadvantaged young people. *Pedagogy, Culture & Society, 21*(2), 299–320. http://dx.doi.org/10.1080/14681366.2012.759136

Solomou, M. (2014). *Designing for reflexivity: Exploring elements in intentionally designed trajectories in an online gaming community. Doctoral dissertation.* Bloomington, IN: Indiana University.

Songkram, N., Chootongchai, S., Khlaisang, G., & Prakob, P. (2021). Education 3.0 system to enhance twenty-first century skills for higher education learning in Thailand. *Interactive Learning Environments, 29*(4), 566–582. https://doi.org/10.1080/10494820.2019.1592197

Stansbury, M. (2017, May 17). The rising "Phigital" student: Education must adapt now to accommodate Gen Z—but how? *edCircuit.* Retrieved from www.edcircuit.com/rising-phigital-student/

Stone Sunstein, B., & Chiseri-Strater, E. (2012). *Fieldworking. Reading and writing research.* Boston, MA: Bedford/St. Martin's.

Torrance, E. P. (1979). *The search for satori and creativity.* Buffalo, NY: Creative Education Foundation and Creative Synergetic Associates.

Wagner, T. (2012). *Creating innovators: The making of young people who will change the world.* New York: Scribner.

Watkins, M. (2011). Teachers' tears and the affective geography of the classroom. *Emotion, Space and Society* (4), 137–143. Retrieved from www.elsevier.com/locate/emospa

Wen, Q. F. (2020). Column introduction—Re-interpretation of production-oriented approach. *Foreign Language Education in China* (2), 3–3.

Yorke, M., & Knight, P. (2004). Self-theories: Some implications for teaching and learning in higher education. *Studies in Higher Education, 29*(1), 25–37.

Zembylas, M. (2016). Making sense of the complex entanglement between emotion and pedagogy: Contributions of the *affective* turn. *Cultural Studies of Science Education, 111*, 539–550. doi:10.1007/s11422-014-9623-y

Zhang, J., & Cheng, X. L. (2020). Research on peer feedback in my country in the past decade: Retrospect and prospect. *Journal of Xian International Studies University, 028*(001), 48–55.

Zhang, L., & Sheng, Y. (2011). Research on the effect of online peer feedback strategy training. *Contemporary Foreign Language Studies* (3), 32–36.

Zhang, Z. X., Wu, H. Y., Wang, X. L., & Zhang, J. X. (1995). Major problems in Chinese writing instruction. *Foreign Language Teaching and Research* (4), 43–50.

Zhu, J. L. (2019). Research and enlightenment of academic writing teaching in American universities. *Journal of Xian International Studies University, 027*(004), 56–61.

Zohar, A., & Barzilai, S. (2015). Metacognition and teaching higher order thinking (HOT) in science education: Students' thinking, teachers' knowledge, and instructional practices. In R. Wegerif, L. Li, & J. Kaufman (Eds.), *Routledge international handbook of research on teaching thinking* (pp. 229–242). Oxon, UK: Routledge.

Web Links and Resources

ArtLesson.blog (from Chris Gadbury): https://artlesson.blog/ and https://artlesson.blog/author/chrisgadbury/

Asia Society: https://asiasociety.org/

Couchsurfers in Class: www.volunteersbase.com/asia/taiwan/couchsurfers-in-class-visit-schools-in-taiwan_i1663

Desmos: www.desmos.com/

Eco-Schools: www.ecoschools.global/

ePals: www.epals.com/#/connections

GeoGebra: www.geogebra.org/?lang=en

Google Docs: www.google.com/docs/about/

iEARN: www.iearn.org/

Magic Storybooks: www.magicstorybooks.com/

ManageBac: www.managebac.com/

Out of Eden Learn: https://learn.outofedenwalk.com/

Quest Atlantis: https://en.wikipedia.org/wiki/Quest_Atlantis

Shaping a Better World Through Storytelling (Chris Gadbury, TEDx Hong Kong, 2019): www.ted.com/talks/chris_gadbury_shaping_a_better_world_through_storytelling

TakingITGlobal: www.tigweb.org/
TeachSDG's Ambassadors: www.teachsdgs.org/our-ambassadors.html
World Savvy: www.worldsavvy.org/
World's Largest Lesson: https://worldslargestlesson.globalgoals.org/
Zoom: https://zoom.us/

INDEX

Printed in Great Britain
by Amazon